The Foundations of Female Entrepreneurship

Routledge Studies in Business History

EDITED BY RAY STOKES AND MATTHIAS KIPPING

The Foundations of Female Entrepreneurship

Enterprise, Home and Household in London, c. 1800–1870

Alison C. Kay

Routledge
Taylor & Francis Group
New York   London

First published 2009
by Routledge
711 Third Ave, New York, NY 10017

Simultaneously published in the UK
by Routledge
2 Park Square, Milton Park, Abingdon, Oxon OX14 4RN

Routledge is an imprint of the Taylor & Francis Group, an informa business

First issued in paperback 2011

Typeset in Sabon by IBT Global.

Library of Congress Cataloging in Publication Data
Kay, Alison C., 1973–
    The foundations of female entrepreneurship : enterprise, home, and household in
London, c. 1800–1870 / Alison C. Kay.
        p. cm.—(Routledge international studies in business history)
    Includes bibliographical references and index.
    1. Women-owned business enterprises—England—London—History—19th cen-
tury. 2. Businesswomen—England—London—History—19th century. 3. Self-
employed women—England—London—History—19th century. 4. Women-owned
business enterprises—England—London—History—19th century. 5. Entrepreneurship—England—London—History—19th century. 6. Work and family—Great Britain—History—19th century. I. Title.
    HD6072.6.G7L665 2009
    338'.0408209421—dc22
    2008046368

ISBN: 978-0-415-43174-3 (hbk)
ISBN: 978-0-415-52268-7 (pbk)

Contents

Figures

Tables

Abbreviations

BM	British Museum
BOD	Bodleian Library
FRO	Family Record Office
LGL	Guildhall Library, Corporation of London

Acknowledgements

A note of thanks is overdue to my DPhil supervisor, Professor Jane Humphries (All Souls College, Oxford University) and my external examiner Professor Pat Hudson (Cardiff University), both of whom have continued to offer support and guidance beyond my student days. My husband Matthew Kay, my parents and my friend Glennis McGregor have also stood by me throughout this project. Financial assistance is gratefully acknowledged from the *Economic and Social Research Council* (Studentship R00429934493) and the *Arnold, Bryce and Reid Fund* of the Modern History Faculty, Oxford University. The ideas and analysis presented here have also improved through participation in various conferences. In particular, I would like to thank the organisers and participants of several conference series in particular the *Economic History Society*; the *Business History Conference*; the *World Congress of the International Economic History Society*. Participation in these events was made possible by the financial assistance of Nuffield College, Oxford University in the form of the *Goodhart* and *Williams* bequests, the *Economic History Travel Fund*, and the *A.D. Chandler Fund*. Many scholars have motivated me through the darkness and are too numerous to mention but those that went beyond the call of duty or friendship included Professor Avner Offer, Professor Beveley Lemire, Dr. David Green, Dr. Alastair Owens, Dr. Shinobu Majima, Dr. Georgio Riello, Dr. Michael Schneider and most recently, Dr. Stephen Constantine and my Lancaster colleagues. I am also grateful for thoughtful comments on draft papers provided by Professor John Goldthorpe, Professor Ann Carlos, and Professor Wendy Gamber. Finally, I may never have begun on this pathway in life without the inspiration and example provided by Dr. Nuala Zahedieh and Dr. Stana Nenadic.

Alison C. Kay

Images have been reproduced with the permission of Guildhall Library, Corporation of London and Trustees of The British Museum. Some of the research presented here has previously been published elsewhere. Permission has been granted by The London Journal, Maney Publishing; Ashgate; Business History: Sources and Archives, The Business Archives Council; and Berg.

Introduction

But it is very hard that the middle-class woman, possessing often a fair share of common knowledge and plenty of sense, should be driven downwards to such a lot. Could she not in many more instances join the ranks of *tradeswomen*, making a tolerable profit, and keeping that which is so dear to a woman's heart, a comfortable and respectable roof over her head?

(B. Raynor Parks, *Essays on Women's Work*, 1865).[1]

In 1850 a dressmaker made a very humbling address to her world of fashion that stretched far beyond fancy finery. In putting pen to her thoughts on how the methods of conducting business might be improved, she repeatedly drew on notions of duty, responsibility and honour. She acknowledged to her readers that the general conduct of business and its goals, beyond making a living, were different than hers and stressed that, however important a 'sphere' of her life, she would have to give it up if she could not conduct her business on her own terms. This dressmaker also declared that she was the head of her own household and consequently responsible for the welfare of all its members. Her fortunes were their fortunes, a fate she took very seriously.[2] This passionate outpouring from a woman engaged in a genteel trade is interesting on many levels. It suggests that even in the mid-nineteenth century business could still be regarded as a sphere of duty for middle-class women, rather than domesticity, philanthropy and work as a governess being their only spheres. It also raises the possibility that having engaged in enterprise that the goals and conduct in business of these middle-class women were in some way discernibly different from the perceived dominant form. Making a respectable living was for women like this dressmaker more important than profit maximization at any cost. Finally, this vignette suggests the significance of household headship in the life of a woman in business. These are not insignificant issues. Not only do they suggest a richer picture than the stereotypical widow-proprietor, they offer a powerful corrective to the historical record. Before the late twentieth century women in the British context are rarely recognized as having been active in business after the long eighteenth century. In this light, this book sets out to uncover why business was still a useful and possible avenue for women in the early- to mid-nineteenth century and to examine the types of trades women engaged in. It also seeks to build bridges between business and household in order to reveal a depth of detail and understanding of female entrepreneurial activity.

This study bases itself in Britain's largest Victorian commercial centre. London most likely offered more opportunity for women in business than smaller towns and villages and even other large urban centres if they were dominated by single industry production. It was famously polycentric and consisted of far more than the City, the hub of international trade and finance. At Victoria's accession in 1837, its built-up area reached north to the Regent's Canal and south to Clapham and Camberwell; west to Paddington and east to Limehouse. It was six miles across. However, it was not until 1851 that London became a full census division and had its boundaries defined. By then the population had reached 2,363,641. In 1750, when London housed about 11 per cent of England's total population, its inhabitants had numbered around a quarter of this figure (575,000).[3] Such massive population growth had filled the old core and overflowed into the surrounding districts.[4] Contemporary Horace Walpole noted: 'So prodigiously the population is augmented. I have twice been going to stop my coach in Piccadilly, thinking there was a mob, and it was only nymphs and swains sauntering or trudging.'[5] This population explosion took place largely in the new outer London, the ring of parishes surrounding the City, Westminster and Southwark. From Marylebone to Hackney in the north, from Richmond to Lambeth in the south, this ring contained some 300,000 inhabitants in 1700, over 500,000 in 1800, and nearly 1,900,000 by 1851.[6] This rendered London a diverse canvas of connected local communities, each with its own distinct character, population, and sometimes business cluster. Self-employment and small business opportunities were in abundance. Indeed, small workshop production was a significant feature of the broad landscape of metropolitan London, itself a tapestry of distinct but interdependent economic districts. In mid-nineteenth century London close to 70 per cent of employers had less than five employees and as the Registrar General for the 1851 census noted, 'The most impressive feature of industry is not that the few are so large, but that the many are so small.'[7] So perhaps more than anywhere else in England at this time, it is in her 'infernal wen', that 'human awful wonder of god',[8] that we might reasonably expect to find women in possession of a little enterprise.

Focussing primarily on one location, however large, varied and highly populated, does of course mean that this study has the limitations of any depth study. However this approach permitted a deeper dig for the lone scholar and hopefully compensates in the richness of subsequent detail. Also, unlike for earlier centuries, Victorian London's enterprising women have received little attention from historians of either the metropolitan economy or women in business more generally. This is partly a reflection of the strength of the Victorians' own idealising and consequently the sources available for scrutiny. The Victorian moralizer frequently tells us that virtually all women, consciously or unconsciously, desired only the career of marriage. The alternatives presented are few and, among heroines, either spring from or lead to disaster. If the novels of the period are examined, one finds little or no evidence of women above the working class engaged in work beyond the role of governess until very late in the century.[9] This powerful imagery and prescription misled an earlier historian to conclude erroneously that before the birth of the nineteenth century 'the triumph of the useless woman was complete'.[10]

Yet caution must be exercised in accepting the impact and effectiveness of Victorian prescriptions of appropriate roles and behaviour, particularly for the lower middle class, whose incomes could often not sustain the idealised lifestyle of those further up the class hierarchy. This was a group heavily characterised by an interest in small business and yet the bulk of evidence on their life experience is drawn from accounts that originate elsewhere and not from sources relating directly to their business endeavours, thus divorcing their business enterprise from its context in the concerns and practices of their society. This is not to say that advice books and novels written for the middle class more generally should be disregarded. On the contrary, they tell us a great deal about ideals. Indeed they sometimes provide insight into the perceived nature of women's encounters with entrepreneurship and how this fitted in to the tug-of-war rhetoric over what women should and could do. The research presented here sifts through such moralising to identify an acceptance, if reluctant, of women's presence in business. This is combined with a variety of evidence ranging from trade cards to memoirs, and source linkage between fire insurance records, directories and the census, to reveal London's enterprising women—their ventures, their households and the nature of their entrepreneurship.

This study begins with an overview of three ideas that can both obscure and reveal women's enterprise in the nineteenth century depending on how they are used. Chapter 1 considers the Victorian discussion of suitable work for women of the broad middle class and the ideal and interpretive framework of separate spheres. This is followed in Chapter 2 by an examination of the arguments that the women who did enter into business would by default be widows due to the barriers of coverture, credit and so on. Having established this contextual foundation, a series of chapters then follow which look at specific evidence of women engaged in business in the mid-nineteenth century—namely fire insurance policies, trade directories and trade cards. These reveal that it was not just dressmakers that conceived of business being their sphere of duty. It also permits a comparison between men's and women's businesses and an examination of how women of enterprise communicated with their public. The last chapters of this book then look more closely at the links between their businesses and their households and the utilization of the home as business. Before concluding, Chapter 7 explores how these London women's endeavours can be placed *within* Victorian values as opposed to representing a breakaway or escape. This chapter also seeks to contextualize the findings of this study alongside the broader national and international patterns and understandings of female historical entrepreneurship.

There are several key sources utilised herein. As a complement to the writings of contemporaries, the London Post Office Directory, various trade card collections, and the Sun Fire Office insurance policy registers have provided an empirical foundation. The latter have been building some momentum as a useful source for economic, business and social historians over recent decades. Earle's (1989) work on the female labour market and London middle class in the late-seventeenth to early-eighteenth century acted very much as a springboard for further study.[11] In particular, it has been followed by Schwarz's (1992) study of the London labour force, 1700 to 1850,[12] and Barnet's (1998) extensive data analysis of London firms and their capital, 1775 to 1825.[13] More recently, publications specifically on women have been added to this including Kay's (2002, 2003, 2004, 2006) studies of female self-employment, small business proprietorship and the accommodation businesses in London circa 1750–1880[14] and Phillip's (2006) detailed exploration of the relationship between women, business and the law in the long-eighteenth century.[15] The Sun Fire registers, although hand scribed and un-indexed are an extremely detailed source and have been used in this book on female enterprise in London to not only uncover the ventures of female policyholders but to collect information on men's businesses too; thus enabling some contextualization of women's businesses. In order to add depth to this foundation, extensive record linkage was also undertaken between the Sun Fire records and the census to reveal more about the proprietors' personal circumstances, their households and their fellow residents.

Other recent publications with some focus on women in business in Britain have used alternative sources to produce a rich picture of women's involvement in urban commercial culture and credit networks in particular. For example, Barker's (2007) work on northern industrial towns, Wiskin's (2006) investigation of businesswomen's financial management, and Gordon and Nair's (2000, 2003) study of middle-class women's economic lives in Glasgow.[16] De Bellaigue's (2007) work on schoolkeeping has also drawn out the business aspect of this line of work.[17] These studies have all complemented the earlier work of Hunt (1996), Prior (1985) and Sanderson (1996) on women in trading communities.[18] Women's role in property and investment is also now receiving increasing attention and the accepted interpretation of this as a passive economic activity is increasingly being discussed and questioned. In addition to the work of Owens (2002), Green and Owens (2003), Phillips (2006, Chapter 7), and Freeman, Pearson and Taylor (2006), there is also Rutterford and Maltby's (2006) investigation of women investors and Morris' (2005) study of men, women and the property cycle.[19] These studies on women, business and property are changing the history of women's economic activity and creating a fresh dialogue about the relationship between gender and investment, property and business. The simple model of activity to passivity is being left behind, as not only the complexity of investment is considered, but also the complexity of choice between economic activities.

So, this book is not only a book about gender and business. It is about business proprietorship, specifically by women but with some reference to men. It is a study of enterprise and society: how and why business becomes the revenue raising 'activity' of choice; what is wanted from that endeavour (profit or something else); how these connect to the personal circumstances of the proprietor. It does set out to seek the discernibly different in male and female proprietorship in terms of choice of sector, capitalization and so on, but it also looks for commonalities too. In doing so it aims to contribute to the bringing together of considerations of 'business' and 'women in business' in the historical context. Hopefully this begins to address the gap identified by Van den Heuval who writes that a systematic comparison with the experiences of men in business is still needed in scholarship in this area, without which it is unclear to what extent these differed from those of women.[20] This book endeavours to move in this direction.

As Wiskin put out the call: 'We need to acknowledge, describe and evaluate the female business owner'. Terms such as 'the female labour market', 'women's work', and 'women's employment opportunities' are not inclusive of all women and do not sum up what was involved in being economically active. There were many women who provided for themselves and their families. Their activities need to be examined as businesses, rather than as minor extensions of their domestic lives. Anything less would be to ignore the economic evidence and diminish the achievements of female proprietors.[21] Overall, the evidence collected here moves away from a reductionist, glass-ceiling view of female enterprise and toward a consideration of their activities based around the recognition that there were different types of historical entrepreneurial endeavour for men and women. At its heart is recognition that venture size is only one measure of success or worthiness in business and its history.

1 Separate and Suitable

In the mid-nineteenth century, paid employment detracted from women's standing in middle-class society and work deemed suitable to meet standards of feminine behaviour, that could 'be pursued without endangering their virtue, or corrupting their manners', was not plentiful.[1] Small business presented an alternative pathway to independence and survival. However such enterprises are often hidden from view not only by their nature (often small and carried on from the home) but also by the too eager acceptance of the Victorian rhetoric of domesticity. *Separate spheres*, the term used to refer to the ideal of the public versus private realms of Victorian men and women, has been used by the historians of women's lives as a model to illustrate the capitalist power of men and as a demonstration of 'how far we have come'. However this has resulted in accusations of the model's 'sloppy' metaphorical use, referring interchangeably 'to an ideology *imposed on* women, a culture *created by* women, a set of boundaries *expected to be observed* by women'.[2] In particular, until recently the domestic woman / public man dichotomy was erroneously taken as a description of social reality. This book falls into that camp of scholarship demonstrating that the lives of Victorian women could and did permeate the boundaries of rhetoric.

Although the Victorians themselves do refer to spheres of duty, separate spheres as an interpretive paradigm for understanding women and work largely originates in the work of two early twentieth-century authors: Clark's *Working Life of Women in the Seventeenth Century* (1919) and Pinchbeck's *Women Workers and the Industrial Revolution 1750–1850* (1930).[3] Although they disagreed on the chronology and nature of the impact, both authors depicted a transition in women's labour market participation somewhere between 1600 and 1850. The separation of home and workplace into factory or workshop was key to both Clark and Pinchbeck's analysis of transition. It is likely that Clark and Pinchbeck's models of 'separation' were at least loosely informed by contemporary theories on the subjection of women, particularly that of Friedrich Engels. His book, *The Origin of the Family, Private Property and the State*, argued that the transition to individualistic commercial society drove a wedge between the public world of work and the private household, consigning the sexes to different arenas.[4]

However, Clark and Pinchbeck were writing at a time when the traditional 'industrial revolution' had not yet been called into question. More recently, quantitative analysis has enabled a re-examination of the economic trends, changing the landscape of economic history. Crafts, Mokyr and Wrigley have argued for a picture of continuity rather than discontinuity in the economy's development.[5] This in turn has led those who specialise in women's work to re-draw the economic environment in which their subjects operated. For example, Hill points out that factory work did not become the overriding experience of the many. A great part of the nineteenth century saw small-scale domestic handicraft industry, operating within the home or workshop, persist alongside Pinchbeck's factories.[6] Similarly, much of Clark's analysis rests on the prophesied breakdown of pre-industrial production patterns of domestic and family industry by the monolithic force of capitalism: 'That force which, while producing wealth beyond the dreams of avarice, has hitherto robbed us of so large a part of the joy of creation.'[7]

To Clark, capitalism and its sidekick waged labour erased the egalitarianism of economic endeavour within the family.[8] In the words of Thirsk, she delivers us 'a somewhat idealistic picture of family life under a regime of near self-sufficiency in the seventeenth-century.'[9] The notion that such harmony ever existed in the organisation of the home has increasingly been called into question. Middleton offers stern warnings against such generalisation and oversimplification of economic organisation under the feudal mode of production.[10] Similarly, Simonton has argued that men and women's complementary and mutual dependency of activities does not mean they were equal. Women's status in the workplace was not necessarily determined by their participation in it but by gendered meanings attached to it.[11] The implication of such criticisms is that Clark's 'golden age' was not quite so golden, nor was Pinchbeck's radical economic changes quite so radical. Ultimately, Hudson and Lee have stressed, only a disaggregated, regional and sectoral approach will allow us to view the subtleties of women's economic lives.[12]

In fairness, and sometimes overlooked by historians, Pinchbeck did distinguish women in business as a special category, conceding them a chapter all of their own.[13] She noted the existence of skilled trades left almost entirely in the hands of women—millinery, mantua making, embroidery and the role of the sempstress. However in keeping with her model of industrial capitalism, by the nineteenth century, she argues, these women withdrew into their separate sphere.[14] She concludes:

> It is only necessary to contrast the vigorous life of the eighteenth century business woman, travelling about the country in her own interests, with the sheltered existence of the Victorian woman, to realise how

much the latter had lost in initiative and independence by being pro-
tected from all real contact with life. [15]

Earle's analysis of the church court depositions of 1,436 London women
collected between 1695 and 1725 led him to estimate that one in five of
all working women opted to run businesses at this time.[16] However, he
criticises the 'golden-age to withdrawal' dichotomy. He claims many of the
trends, most notably relegation into what he terms 'feminine trades', can
already be witnessed in the latter half of the seventeenth century.[17] Other
studies have questioned whether the businesswoman disappeared as the
eighteenth century progressed. Wright's examination of occupations in
the Midland town of Ludlow found that an increasing number of female
household heads were involved in trade across the century. Furthermore,
she found that of 148 women bereaved between 1710 and 1749, just under
half carried on their husband's trade and that over the period an increasing
percentage did so.[18] Similarly, Sanderson's study of the Edinburgh trading community also reveals the extensive role of women in business, with
women as young as twenty setting up in trade. She concludes that in the
Scottish urban context there is little evidence to suggest any objection to
single women exerting their economic effort outside the home.[19] Despite
such evidence the notion of a withdrawal from business into domesticity
and idleness has proved enduring in the historiography of the eighteenth
and nineteenth century.

One explanation for the enduring nature of the separate spheres paradigm is the place it has been given in explanations regarding the formation of middle-class identity. It is commonly accepted that the expanding
group positioned between the nobility and commonality, referred to as
the middling sort followed by the middling class, were growing in numbers.[20] They varied in occupation but could predominantly be characterised by their involvement in commerce.[21] Nenadic has suggested that, in
the Scottish context, the commercially preoccupied constituted at least
80 per cent of the total.[22] Consumerism and its predicator wealth contributed to their 'sense of class' and in particular the ability to maintain a
non-working wife.[23] Claims for middle-class recognition as an economic
and political group were thus refracted through a gendered lens. Masculine identity was equated with an emerging concept of 'occupation',
while women remained within a familial frame.[24] Furthermore, it has
been argued, the fear of economic and political disorder as a result of the
counter-revolutionary French wars (1790–1815) encouraged separation
of social categories, exaggerating differences between groups, including
men and women. This re-formulation of gender roles could also still be
accommodated within classical liberal theory. Although Locke rejected
familial authority as the model for political authority, he nonetheless saw
the development of rationality as hand in hand with a split between public
and private / reason versus passion.[25]

Alongside counter-Jacobinism and classical liberal thought, a third influence has been woven into the formation of middle-class identity—religion. Most of the attention here has focused on Evangelicalism. A reform movement working *within* the Church of England, this group held as its central aim the reform of manners and morals—the creation of a new ethic. It was the religious consciousness of England after all, they argued, which determined her political condition. Reform by example, from the aristocracy downward, was the way forward. By the end of the French wars, much of this responsibility had filtered down to rest on the shoulders of the middle class.[26] It is here, Alexander has argued, that the Victorian ideal of womanhood originated. The woman, as wife and mother, was the pivot of the family and consequently the guardian of all Christian and domestic virtues.[27] The domestic abode was seen as a key place where attempts could and should be made to curb sin. In this domain, the woman provided a haven from the corrupting influences men faced daily, a juxtaposition epitomised in Coventry Patmore's poem 'The Angel in the House'.[28]

Thus, although 'work' has had a central place in the writing of eighteenth- and nineteenth-century women's history, this has only included middle-class women in a very limited way. Women's work has primarily been defined as working class waged labour, mainly in factories and domestic handicraft production, or unpaid labour in the domestic environment.[29] Although the 1980s brought innovative research on the role of gender in middle-class formation this did not progress, on the whole, into an investigation of the working lives of middle-class women.[30] As a result, until quite recently women's work in historical scholarship had come to be viewed through the concentric prisms of working class drudgery, middle-class symbolism and theoretical abstraction. Middle-class women were extracted from much of the economic and social reality of their daily lives and partitioned firmly within a separate spheres interpretation of the past, as the dominant ideology's role models for working class women. Increasingly the nature of middle-class female identity has been more fully unpicked to reveal multiple, competing identities.[31] Furthermore, identity has been recognized as more fluid than static, adapting with experience and circumstances—daughter to orphan, spinster to wife, wife to widow, widow to wife, child-free to mother or guardian, religious to irreligious, supported to unsupported.

Probably the most key point to make here in relation to the focus of this book is that the gendering of 'proper' spheres of activity for men and women is not *necessarily* the same as equating the female with the domestic.[32] In any regard, even if it can be assumed that the role of the kept wife was the preferred one, this was not an option for a significant proportion of the female population. Nationally at mid-century, some 1.8 million adult women were unmarried or widowed.[33] Women outnumbered men to a significant degree, especially in London where between the ages of 20 and 40 there were 119 women to every 100 men of this age. Those between 40 and 60 years of age exceeded men by 116 to 100 and those aged between 60 and 80 by 137 to 100.[34] There were simply too many women, especially in the middle and upper classes; at least this was the common complaint of contemporary commentators. These 'redundant' women, wrote W.R. Greg, were 'quite disproportionate and quite abnormal' in numbers and consequently were forced 'to earn their own living, instead of spending and husbanding the earnings of men'.[35] Furthermore, some of those women that did successfully marry could still find themselves left unsupported by the death, desertion, sickness or chronic unemployment of their husbands, often with children to raise and dependent adults to support.[36] Therefore by default or choice, a substantial number of middle-class women turned to the economic marketplace for their survival. Nineteenth-century commentators, such as Elizabeth Wolstenholme, frequently asserted this reality:

> It is assumed in the face of the most patent facts that all women marry and are provided for by their husbands; whilst nothing is more plainly to be seen by those who will open their eyes, than these three things:—1. That a very large minority of women do not marry. 2. That of those who do marry, a very considerable proportion are not supported by their husbands. 3. That upon a very large number of widows (more than one-third of the widows in the country), the burden of self-maintenance and of the maintenance of children is thrown.[37]

Yet despite many such women's need to work, they faced formal and informal restrictions on their participation in the economy as paid employees. In particular, they were limited by the inappropriate or inadequate education of women, particularly of the lower middle class. Wolstenholme warned:

> You who have daughters, wives and sisters, whom you guard tenderly from present evils, take care that you are not preparing for them graver evils when you are no longer able to provide for them . . . If your affection be anything more than that common form of selfishness which considers women as the mere playthings of men, you will look further into the future than you have yet done, and will prepare differently for the days which may come to all, which *will* come to many of your dear ones.[38]

The restricted range of options for generating the rent in a respectable way led some commentators to suggest that the only answer for unsupported women lay in emigration! However, others sought to assist women at home by campaigning for better training, wider choices and by seeking to broaden the definition of suitable work for women.

Harriet Taylor, the eventual wife of J.S. Mill, wrote a particularly passionate plea for the free choice of women in regard to their occupation.[39] She writes: 'The maternity argument deserts its supporters in the case of single women, a large and increasing class of the population.' Nor, she argued, was motherhood the desired 'career' of all women by nature, but rather the only career officially open to them.[40] The solution in her eyes lay in free choice of employment for all:

> Let every occupation be open to all, without favour or discourage-ment to any, and employments will fall into the hands of those men or women who are forced by experience to be most capable of worthily exercising them. There need be no fear that women will take out of the hands of men any occupation which men perform better than they. Each individual will prove his or her capacities, in the only way in which capacities can be proved—by trial; and the world will have the best faculties of all its inhabitants.[41]

Similarly, Arthur Young, barrister and professor of political economy, addressing an audience on the benefits of unrestricted competition, also cajoled his audience to consider free choice of employment for women. The surplus of women would always prevail, he argued, unless the barriers to their employment were broken down, thereby providing the country with a new fund of labour ' . . . instead of passing their lives, as at present they do, in a process as nearly allied as possible to vegetation'.[42]

However, free choice was a concept far removed from the reality of mid-dle-class women's lives. So closely was their social acceptance and stand-ing perceived to be tied to their actions that when thrown on their own resources they engaged in a juggling act between the competing forces of respectability and the need to obtain a livelihood. How were women to navigate this quagmire? According to J.D. Milne, author of the *Industrial and Social Position of Women in the Middle and Lower Ranks*, they had two choices. Either they could endeavour to gain a means of subsistence in a way fitting to their station in life; or, they could leave that status behind and join the ranks below.[43]

Sometimes women really did choose this latter option. A vignette is pro-vided by the memoirs of Mary Ann Ashford. In 1844, motivated by a lack of authentic life stories of working women, Ashford penned her own work-life account: *The Life of a Licensed Victualler's Daughter*. Although born into the lower middle class, the daughter of innkeepers, when orphaned she opted for a career in the lower status employment of domestic service instead of the 'indoor', genteel apprenticeship in millinery for which her relatives offered to pay. Millinery was a more 'suitable' employment for a girl of her class. Although domestic service did offer a certain degree of respectability and security, it was an unsuitable choice in the eyes of many of her relatives and as a consequence she was no longer invited into their society.[44] A middle-class women working was acceptable but the activity she engaged in had to be deemed suitable to her class.

Mary Ann Ashford had made a difficult choice. Unconvinced that choosing 'to Stitch' would provide her with the security she wanted; she sought advice from a family friend. Such apprenticeships were 'all very well for those who have got a home and parents to shelter them, when work is slack' argued Mrs Bond, 'but depend upon it, many clever women find it, at times, a half-starved kind of life in those employments'.[45] Such a negative view was reinforced by her aunt Margaret who declared that being placed out 'genteely' was all very well but ultimately 'gentility without ability, was like pudding without fat', and said she was of Mrs. Bond's opinion. At least in domestic service, Mary Ann would have a roof over her head and food on the table.[46]

When she declined her relations' offer for the funds for an apprenticeship and declared her intention of 'going to service', Ashford met directly with the social consequences outlined by J.D. Milne earlier. Astonished, her relatives sent her to see a cousin of her mothers, whose husband was a clerk of long standing in the Bank. Her folly was pointed out in strong terms: 'She said a great deal about injuring my future prospects, as I could not be introduced into society by her or any of my respectable friends if I was a servant.'[47] Despite this, Mary Ann opted for the relative stability, security and certainty of a career in service over a suitable apprenticeship with uncertain prospects.

As this vignette demonstrates, options were so narrow that for some women being ejected from polite middle-class society was the lesser evil. Other women, in exceptional cases, adopted even more dramatic strategies and removed themselves not necessarily from their class but from their gender and thereby escaped, temporarily, the restriction of finding work suitable for a woman. An examination of *The Times* and *The Weekly Dispatch* reveals stories of women who masqueraded as men so that they could work in the positions of bricklayer, sawyer, button maker, groom, ballad seller and even horse thief.[48] In the early modern era passing oneself off as a man had been a real and viable option for women who had fallen on bad times and were struggling to overcome their difficult circumstances. This tradition existed throughout Europe but was strongest by far in the Netherlands, Germany and England.[49] But while this was not a new phenomenon, in the nineteenth century it took on fresh significance and brought harsher reactions. Civil registration, enforced military service and medical examinations made cross-dressing more difficult for women. Nonetheless, some women did successfully operate as men, at least for a time. One example of such a woman has survived through court records. Sarah Geals of Mile End successfully lived as a man for 12 years.

Sometime in her mid-twenties, Sarah Geals began to call herself William Smith and moved to London, obtaining employment as a clicker in the shoemaking industry—a high status role.[50] Most of Sarah's business for over 10 years had consisted of outwork and some shopwork for James Giles, a wholesale shoe manufacturer on the Hackney Road. During the fatal illness of his wife, James asked Sarah if Caroline, with whom she shared a home, could come to keep house for him. At some point during this arrangement he discovered Sarah's guise and seemingly used it as a tool of manipulation—Caroline married James and Sarah was forced to resume the dress of a woman. The two women agreed to his terms on the condition that James set Sarah up in a retail shoe shop. However after 2 years in business, James decided that the shop was not profitable enough and decided to close it. A few months later Sarah attempted to shoot him and found herself in the Old Bailey, where she was sentenced to 5 years penal servitude.[51] Obviously this is an extreme case but highlights the awkward relationship between gender, class and work at this time.

It was argued that if a woman tried to pursue a man's role, then she must be either a drunkard or an unfortunate creature taken in by unorthodox feminist ideas.[52] Although it was acknowledged that working class women had to discard the idea of feminine dependency on men and could exchange one social role for another, the same could not be said for middle-class women. While the middle classes also praised hard work and the desire for independence, the latter was not considered nearly as important in a woman as the preservation of her femininity.[53] Yet many middle-class women, particularly of the lower ranks, needed to work and femininity and gentility often acted as barriers to a liveable wage. James Giles would later say about Sarah Geals: 'I paid her regular wages, the same as the men working in the same capacity. I had no idea she was not a man.'[54] His comment could be interpreted as suggesting that had he known her true gender, he would have ranked her labour as unskilled and paid her less. Cross-dressing was an extreme reaction to their situation but many women argued that they had done it because it made it easier for them to make a living.[55] As one explained: 'boys could shift better for themselves than girls'.[56] As Wheelwright has argued, the thread which pulls the individual cases together is their desire for male privilege and a longing to escape from their domestic confines.[57] By donning men's clothes, whatever their other motives, women gained access to a wider range of occupations and better pay.

Of course the majority of women did not wish to compromise either their class or their femininity. They were left to navigate the murky waters of work deemed suitable for women. Fortunately, there were concerted efforts to help them, albeit sometimes adding to the layers of prescription. Nonetheless many trade and employment books, such as the popular *Book of Trades, Arts, & Professions Relative to Food, Clothing, Shelter and Ornament*,[58] contained not even a mention of trades for women, even of the most stereotypical variety—not a dressmaker, milliner, or female haberdasher in sight. Other guidance did seek to plug the gap such as Mercy Grogan's, *How Women May Earn a Living*. Motivated by the increasing need of women to identify suitable and remunerative employments, their focus is usually on girls and their parents. Grogan waxes lyrical:

It is hoped it may prove useful to parents who are anxious to arm their daughters for the battle of life with a weapon no one can take from them. . . . A thorough knowledge of some remunerative employment would do more to make them independent of the 'slings and arrows of outrageous fortune' than the possession of any amount of money, especially in these days of bank failures and general depression of trade.[59]

The weapon she armed them with was knowledge of 'suitable' employments. This included: teaching generally and tutoring in music and cookery; artistic activities such as china painting and art needlework; clerk based roles in the Post Office and law copying, telegraphy and bookkeeping; printing; shop assistant work in linen draperies; becoming a school board visitor; the role of superintendent in laundries; concertina making; and hairdressing. In addition, the medical professions of nursing and pharmacy are devoted a chapter of their own. But ultimately, Mercy warned, echoing W.R. Greg: 'Ladies who have never received any special training, and have neither time nor means to procure it, would probably do wisely to emigrate.'[60]

Phillis Browne's *What Girls Can Do: A Book for Mothers and Daughters*, expressed similar intentions to Grogan, although the majority of the book is taken up by advice on *Work for Duty* and *Work for Pleasure*. The rather small final chapter is called *Work for Necessity*. Beyond teaching, which she regarded as the main paid occupation for middle-class women, Browne lists a narrow range of employments, limited to art and fancy needlework, literary arts, lady doctors and nurses, clerks and what she refers to as la petite culture—'the production of minor foods, such as eggs, poultry, honey, butter, vegetables, and fruit'.[61] Nonetheless, although Browne's suggestions were very limited, at least she was making suggestions and there is an acknowledgment running throughout her book that women could make choices:

I by no means presume to decide what is the best and wisest course to choose under given circumstances. That each girl must decide for herself, no one can take the responsibility of doing it for her. It is a matter of experiment for all of us to find out the particular career that is suited for us, and that we suit.[62]

The nineteenth century also saw the emergence of various reforming agencies, often formed by ladies of the upper middle class, who began to define and promote acceptable work options. Motivated by benevolent consideration they sought a 'new sphere for their sex', one in which it would no longer be 'half a disgrace' to become an independent factor in any other post but that of a governess.[63] They also sought to retain 'respectability' for working women.[64] In so doing, they sometimes compounded the already restricted occupational choices of their needy sisters. As Bessie Rayner Parkes wrote, it is 'evident that the conditions of business life can never be identical for men and women', and hence that 'no sane person will tolerate the notion of flinging girls into those very temptations and dangers which we lament and regret for boys'.[65]

Importantly, the establishment of the *English Woman's Journal* (*EWJ*) by Barbara Leigh Smith, Matilda Hays, Jessie Boucherett, Emily Faithfull and others, created a meeting point drawing together those women working for the reform of female employment, education and property rights.[66] Hence when Jessie Boucherett arrived in London in 1859 with the vague intention of 'forming some plan by which to promote the employment of women', she was able to make her way directly to the *EWJ*'s offices, then on Princes Street, Cavendish Square. Within months her plan was a reality. She had inherited the *EWJ* register of women seeking employment and the Society for Promoting the Employment of Women (PEW) had been founded, with Lord Shaftesbury as its first President and Emily Faithfull as its Secretary.[67] The Society chiefly sought to:

> . . . see whether men are never to be found occupying easy, remunerative places, that could be as well or better filled by women; places that originally belonged to them, and that they would have remained in possession of to this day, had not artificial means been used to displace them. We refer to those departments in the great shops, which are devoted to the sale of light articles of female attire. Why should bearded men be employed to sell ribbon, lace, gloves, neck-kerchiefs and the dozen other trifles to be found in a silk-mercer or haberdasher's shop?[68]

It proposed to set up a large school for 'girls and young ladies' in which they could be taught the appropriate skills which would allow them to replace the bearded impostors. Such training, it was argued, would provide girls with the capabilities of becoming clerks, cashiers, and ticket sellers at railway stations. 'Other trades' were to be taught in workshops in connection with the school.[69] In addition, Jessie Boucherett founded a bookkeeping school to train women in this 'new and suitable' field of employment. Similarly, Maria Rye started a law copyist's office.[70]

While some of the options the *EWJ* and Society for PEW tried to harness for women were actually quite limited and traditional, nonetheless their actions in themselves modelled potential avenues for women needing to generate an income. For example, the *EWJ* was operated as a business: 'the necessary money having been collected from various good friends to the cause, in the form of shares in a limited liability company.'[71] Also, it was followed in 1859 by another business when Emily Faithfull began *The Victoria Press*, employing and training female compositors. Within a year, this enterprise regularly printed the *EWJ*, the vast *Transactions of the National Association for the Promotion of Social Science*, the *Law Magazine* and a host of other pamphlets and tracts. In 1863, it began the publication of *The Victoria Magazine*, a monthly organ of the women's movement within which of course its own conception lay.[72] Furthermore, in their meetings and advice columns these women did propagate the notion in an understated way that setting up in business was a suitable work option for unsupported women, especially in printing, hairdressing and 'possibly even watch-making'.[73]

In addition, although the *EWJ* is the best known of the training schools of this nature, it certainly was not alone. The effort was much more widely spread. Matilda Pullan advertised her training school in *The Lady's Newspaper*. It was in her own house that she offered as an establishment for young ladies 'who either are or may be, dependent on their own exertions, and to convert them into clever, well-paid women of business, instead of ill-paid governesses'. Thirty Guineas per year secured a place and after two years of seven hours instruction a day 'women of business' would emerge, she claimed. 'Why should it not be as honourable for a woman in this commercial country to be in trade, as it is for her husband, or father, or brother?', Pullen cajoles the reader.[74] Indeed, she herself is making a business of preparing young women for business.

Hence, it was increasingly acknowledged and accepted that many middle-class women needed to generate an income of their own by some means, however at odds this was with the Victorians' ideal imagery of the woman in the home. The middle class was a broad group within which income varied widely. Whether a woman's family were tradespeople and shopkeepers, those engaged in manufacturing, carrying and servicing trades, or the professions and arts,[75] she could easily find herself in need of an income but desirous not to compromise her respectability. For those women that discarded the other options of losing status, cross-dressing or taking up the more obvious suitable paid employments, establishing a little enterprise of her own was one possible means of supporting herself respectably. Some supporters even went so far as to argue that the self-supporting woman could be regarded with respect by other women, the image of the woman waiting at home in idleness for 'a young man kind enough to come and marry her' having proved so impractical:

> Girls themselves look, I am sure, with respect and even with envy upon those of their companions who are busy, independent, and self-supporting. And they have cause to do so. Next to the pleasure of working to help others, comes the satisfaction of feeling that we work that we may not be a burden to others.[76]

Furthermore, while other 'suitable' work options continued to be promoted for young girls, it was recognised that business not only helped the prospects of the young but also offered ongoing, lifetime advantages. Self-employment and small business proprietorship could give women not only an immediate livelihood but could be used as an old age survival strategy.

Retirement was not an option for many in this period and there was no age ceiling to business, as long as a woman remained physically able. In addition, servants, employees and family members could be used to keep the business functioning and the income coming in. Business could secure continued respectability through continued independence. Such issues were not lost on contemporaries, even J.D. Milne admitted:

> It would be more in accordance with justice and with humanity to enable woman, by her independent exertions, to earn a livelihood sufficient not only for the wants of adult life, but sufficient also to enable her to lay by enough to carry her in peace through the gray days of old age, and, on her death, to lay her head decently under the grass.[77]

Hence, small business became an increasingly viable option as women left their girlhood behind. As women aged they gained more autonomy to choose. Single women of middling status often experienced later life as a period of greater activity and authority. As they aged, these women gained more residential and economic independence. In addition, ever-single women, past what society viewed as marriageable age, could move beyond the recriminations they had faced for never marrying and producing children. Once a woman had reached the end of her child-bearing years, she was no longer regarded as a sexual threat or morally vulnerable. She was free to choose the means by which she could secure immediate comfort and prepare for old age and this included taking up a trade. Moreover, the death of a parent could supply such a woman with the capital and goods she needed to set-up in business. Also too, the death of a spinster aunt could provide similar means.[78]

Therefore, to reveal the enterprising woman of the nineteenth century we have to pick our way through the 'labyrinth of middle-class moralism and mystification'[79] and the experiential reality obscured by the theoretical paradigm or ideal of separate spheres. The adapted version of the latter, with its permeable membrane between the two spheres, remains a useful metaphor. However, it remains misadventure to apply it to the Victorian middle class without first recognising one crucial factor—that the middle class was a very, very broad group, stretching far up and down the income scale and encompassing professionals and tradespersons alike. Not all its inhabitants could afford to keep a non-working wife or daughter and not all daughters married. Consequently, a woman engaging in business and through this securing economic and social independence was not anathema to the Victorians. The next chapter will consider the practicalities of this and whether the obstacles to business outweighed the bridges.

2 Barriers and Bridges

Although campaigners promoted the plight of not-yet-married women as a justification for their entering into business, traditionalists tended to reserve this privilege for the widow. Until recently this was also the habit of historians, partly due to the vociferousness of some Victorian voices but also due to a lack of detailed study in this area. Hence, it has remained a common assumption that women in business, in any period before the twentieth century, would, apart from the odd anomaly, be widows and inheritors of businesses. Certainly plenty of examples of widow-proprietors can be found. They were seen to justifiably inherit businesses, but it is often overlooked by historians that it was also acceptable to early- and mid-Victorians to see widows set-up in new businesses, the funds for which were donated by friends, family and sometimes the anonymous benefactor. In 1865 *John Bull* carried just such a subscription request for establishing a venture. Headed 'struggle for existence', a Mr Lancelot Spence tells a sorry tale of a widow with eight children left destitute with the death of her husband, a clerk in a Government office.[1] Of course this could be an elaborate hoax but regardless of the widow's authenticity it demonstrates that public sentiment was such that widows could 'begin' in business and indeed, given their childcare commitments, that this was a sensible and respectable course of action.

It is important to consider why widow-proprietors were recognized more openly. Acknowledging women's involvement in business brought the more idealistic Victorian commentator into direct conflict with the prescribed role of women. As a consequence, popular sentiment tended to identify women with business only if dire circumstances had befallen her. This was commonly presented as widowhood and the notion that the businesswoman actually being synonymous with the reluctant widow was frequently voiced by the staunchest traditionalists. This stereotype was encouraged by writers such as J.D. Milne, whose analysis of the 1851 census occupational tables concluded, with no evidence but much professed experience, that:

> ... the individuals returned in this table are almost entirely widows, who on the death of their husbands have continued business for the support of themselves and their families. Glancing over the list of oc-

cupations, and referring to experience, the reader can corroborate this. These women-bakers, grocers, shop-keepers, general-dealers, innkeepers, keepers of lodgings, are, for the most part, widows of small tradesmen.[2]

Milne takes little account of their age, yet not all widows were middle aged or old. Nor does he consider whether they had in fact continued in their deceased husband's business or sold it off and set-up in a new trade. The link between widowhood and business was assumed and rested heavily on assumptions about what women could do and should do, not what they actually did. Such efforts represented an attempt to deal with reality. Ideologies proclaim roles often at odds with the necessities of daily life. The cherished stereotype of female dependency was, in the eyes of the conservative, threatened by the active working woman and woman in business. This necessitated an explanation for their deviation from the ideal prescribed role. As long as these women could be seen as victims, engaging in the commercial world out of sheer desperation, the ideals were upheld. Also, in practical terms the incidence of widows in business was not just a result of easier access to resources. In proportional terms, it was also a reflection that widows in the population generally were increasingly noticeable. Women outlived men in Victorian Britain. Furthermore, husbands tended to be older than wives. Hence, as the age profile of the population as a whole was getting older, more widows naturally followed.[3]

This along with the strength of contemporary rhetoric has had an enormous impact on the study of women in business by historians. Examples of women who fitted the stereotypes of caretaking widows have frequently been plucked from the archives and there has been a tendency to underplay the role of even widows in business by emphasising those cases where women are known to have hired foremen or were caretaking the business until the eldest son had completed his apprenticeship. Davidoff and Hall, for example, argued that widows were regarded as 'temporary incumbents of an enterprise', not expected to aspire beyond self-support.[4] This was not always the case. The promotion of business as an option for the insufficiently supported, not-yet-married or never-married woman has gone unnoticed and it has been assumed that the barriers to business for women other than the widow would have been impassable. These included the law, guilds, apprenticeship and training, the cost of setting up, restricted access to credit and commercial networks, and of course the growing availability of more genteel options for the investment of their funds in the form of stocks and bonds.

The law could certainly devastate the successes of businesswomen, particularly if they were married and their husband claimed their profits. The inferior legal position of women in this period is often presented as one of the major barriers against women participating in business. The position of wives under common law is held up as evidence of the impracticality of women engaging in trade. However this line of reasoning overlooks the rising proportion of women that did not marry. Nonetheless, it is true that as a *feme covert*, a married woman's property, alongside herself, came under the protection and influence of her husband. As Sir William Blackstone, author of *Commentaries on the Laws of England* wrote, 'By marriage the husband and wife are one person in the law: that is, the very being, or legal existence of the woman is suspended during the marriage, or at least is incorporated and consolidated into that of the husband'.[5] Wives, having no legal identity apart from their husband and no property under their control during marriage, could not enter into contracts or incur debts except as their husband's agent, and therefore could not sue or be sued.

However, Phillips' detailed analysis of legal treatise and practice has led her to argue that in terms of ability to trade, although coverture could be a great disability for married women, it was an entirely historically contingent doctrine. The definition, use and means of avoidance of coverture have varied greatly over time.[6] According to a treatise by Roper, by the early nineteenth century there were four main ways that a married woman could continue to trade and contract with others. Firstly, coverture could be suspended by a husband's absence. If he had been exiled, transported or had left the country for life, his wife was free to act as a single woman. This could however be undone by his pardon or return. The suspension of coverture did not apply to foreign husbands residing abroad by choice unless they were regarded as an 'alien enemy'. Secondly, the custom of London could treat a married woman as a *feme sole* for trading purposes. We will return to borough custom later in the chapter. Thirdly, a woman could secure agreement with her husband before or during marriage. Finally, she could operate on the basis of possessing equitable separate property.[7]

Developed over the centuries to correct the injustices and omissions of the common law, the equity courts had come to recognise a wife's right to property separate from her husband. By prenuptial agreements, marriage settlements, a woman or her family and friends could designate certain property as being her 'separate estate', free from her husband's common law rights of possession or control. The trustee was obliged to carry out the terms of the settlement or, in the absence of specific terms, to deal with the property according to the instructions of the married woman. Thus, a married woman with a separate estate in equity enjoyed virtually the same property rights as an unmarried woman. She could receive the income from her settled property and spend it as she pleased. She could make her separate property liable for debts that she incurred, and she could sue and be sued with respect to her separate property in the courts of equity.[8]

Critics have been quick to point out that the prospect of a 'separate estate' in equity was open only to the wealthiest women. However, Erickson has discovered that ordinary women also circumvented the more incapacitating aspects of coveture by means of marriage settlements of a simpler type. This had not previously been recognised by historians because the documents themselves—usually simple bonds—had not survived. However, the shadow of these settlements can be seen in probate accounts. These records offer a snapshot of an estate a year after all the debts of the deceased had been settled. The executor or administrator of a will was required by ecclesiastical law to file an account of their handling of the estate. It is possible to discern where a widow, filing her husband's estate, has deducted the amount of money for which she (or technically her sureties) had contracted before marriage. Erickson's examination of a sample of these probate accounts indicates that, at the very least, ten per cent of ordinary women employed pre-marital property settlements.[9]

Hence, the existence of marriage settlements, or their financial equivalents, even for women of the lower classes, challenges those arguments that suggest that the legal framework was an absolute subordinator of women. Furthermore, the common law framework was devised in medieval not Victorian times, when land constituted the chief form of property. The equity court system developed precisely because of the omissions under the common law, as new forms of property developed. Thus whatever the characteristics of the English legal system in this period, they cannot be said to be purely a tool of the Victorian domestic ideology. Indeed, a further caveat to the common law can be found in 'borough custom', the local regulations which often made provision for married women to own property for the purpose of trade if her husband agreed to it. If so, he forfeited his legal right to his wife's business assets. This converted the wife of a freeman from the status of *feme covert* into *feme sole merchant* with the legal rights of an independent trader.[10] Across Britain, such local customs could work in favour of businesswomen or against them. Their application was uneven, warns Wiskin, 'seeming to be as much concerned with local political and economic factors as issues of gender or fears of independent, 'masterless' women with the potential to disturb the stability of society'.[11] Although it has been argued that this right gradually fell into disuse, in the nineteenth century borough custom still held sway in London.[12] Furthermore, even under the common law, a wife did not need either borough custom or equity to be able to trade separately, if this had been expressly agreed before or during marriage.[13]

Nonetheless, the combination of trade and marriage did bring its problems. Mary Holl and Ann Turner set up as milliners in the late eighteenth century. Mary financed her entry into business with 250 guineas from her separate estate and £340 loaned to her by her husband, Joseph. She soon bought out her partner and was doing well enough by the end of the year to claim 60 guineas in net profit. She ran her business as a *feme sole*, separate and distinct from her husband. However, a couple of years later Mary's business began to fall on hard times and her husband, also in business, went bankrupt. Mary tendered a bill of sale for her stock in trade and effects to her principal creditor, Mr Clement, assuming she would be able to continue running the business. However, Mr Clement reached a separate accommodation with the assignees on Joseph's bankrupt commission and turned the bill of sale over to them. Mary's other creditors, who had not been included in this deal, became very agitated. They pointed out that as Mary had financed the business out of her own separate estate that they should be paid in full before Joseph's creditors. However the latter were not inclined to honour Mary's claim that she was running a separate trade. The dispute degenerated into a free for all in which both sets of creditors tried to seize as much of Mary's stock as possible.[14] Mary pleaded,

> Alas, alas, why wou'd you not put some confidence in me, your not do-
> ing so has undone both you and my self, you I fear, in the loss of your
> debt, or a great part of it, and me in the everlasting anguish of mind,
> in not fulfilling my engagements, so very separate from Mr. Holl, that
> many of my Creditors did not even know I was a married woman, and
> it was upon my Industry and the punctuality of my payments, that my
> Credit was founded.[15]

Given that she was a *feme sole*, she should only have been liable for the £340 originally put into the business by her husband, Joseph. In this case however, the category of *feme sole*, proved too weak to protect her.

Hence, it is true that 'there was a way in which the whole conception of profit was gendered'.[16] Husbands were barred under the *feme sole* rules from helping their wives with their trades on pain of becoming liable for the debts, yet they continued under common law to have the right of disposition of their wives' profits. *Feme sole* rules ensured that husbands could receive gain from their wives' trading activities without having to shoulder either the labour or the financial risk. But even when husbands refrained from taking their wives' profits, the expectation was that a woman's earnings would go towards family expenses. A man, on the other hand, had considerably more latitude to plough his profits back into his own business.[17] Nonetheless, not every wife fell foul of her husband's creditors. Stories such as Mary's outline the worst case scenario.

Many husbands welcomed their wives entrepreneurial efforts and recognized that it was far easier to juggle domestic demands alongside an enterprise of her own than if she worked as a paid employee (see Chapter 5). In his autobiography, William Hart praised his wife, Ann, for her willingness to work to support the household. An under foreman with the West India Dock Company, he and Ann produced seven surviving children.[18] Despite her successive confinements, Ann often worked on small business ventures either together with her husband or alone. For example, four years after their marriage, to improve their income, they moved from Shadwell to a house in St. Georges East from which Ann could run a small haberdashery shop. William continued to work at the docks and there is no mention of servants or additional help for Ann. Even with a third pregnancy and the care of two young children she continued, with some success, to sell haberdashery.[19]

Furthermore, when William was made redundant from the Docks on a pension of £30 a year, a sum far from sufficient to maintain his family, he was thankful that: 'the Lord kept me from great perplexity of mind. I had a good partner. She therefore set up a little school for children'.[20]

Arguments relying on the legal framework as a barrier to entry are misrepresentative not only in their emphasis on a homogenous experience for the married woman, which in reality was far more varied and complex, but also in their failure to address the relatively free legal position of single women, as well as widows. Spinsters fared better under the common law than married women because as a *feme sole* a single woman held rights to her own property. However, although some acknowledge that the law was not as great a hindrance as previously thought, it is still often assumed that those women that did enter into business were restricted to the 'feminine trades'. To a certain extent this is true, though it should not be described as 'typical'. In any regard, we need to move away from the tendency in the literature to be dismissive of such ventures. To be dismissive, is to disregard not only the skill that was demanded within these trades but also the independence that they provided their female masters. It seems strange, Sanderson commented in her study of Edinburgh's business women, that when women work by the needle historians dismiss this as a feminine occupation, whereas when men sew it is regarded as an occupation which gives identity and status, for example that of tailor or upholsterer.[21]

Lack of training, in the form of an apprenticeship to a freeman of a guild, would appear to have been a barrier to entry into traditional trades but was a declining one in this period. Glass' analysis of the admissions to the Freedom of the City of London indicates that apprenticeships declined significantly as a route to entry. In 1690, 86 per cent of admissions, that is 1,590 cases, were on the basis of a completed apprenticeship, this had fallen to 67 per cent (n = 755) by 1750 and to 53 per cent (n = 546) by 1800. Entrance by the alternative methods of patrimony and redemption increased over the period by 10.3 and 22.8 per cent respectively, to account for 17.7 and 29.5 per cent of admissions by 1800.[22] In addition, for many new trades, limited periods of training sufficed.[23] Nonetheless, since women had less to gain from the formalities of indenturing, they or their families may have been less interested in finding suitable placements. Some of the advantages of apprenticeship were not obtainable for girls. They could not usually gain the freedom of the corporation, nor did apprenticeship necessarily enhance their trading or political position as it did for men. This does not mean that women never engaged in these markets. Indeed largely restricted from the guilds and the advantages of collectivity, it has been argued, women were seen by men not as trading partners but as threats to their own position.[24]

In contrast, the various guilds often granted widows freeman status in view of their husbands service. However, lack of guild recognition for women other than widows did not, in reality, act as the great hindrance it might at first seem. Firstly, the guilds were only able to enforce their exclusiveness in a very arbitrary manner. Prior detailed several cases of this in Oxford, where women openly ran textile related businesses much to the annoyance of the Tailors and Mercer's Guilds. Furthermore, the duty of enforcing the London guilds' monopoly had already, by the early eighteenth century, devolved very largely upon individuals, neighbouring craftsmen or shopkeepers, who were prepared from indignation, malice or the prospect of reward, to bring proceedings against competitors who did not have freeman status. Although the ward-mote inquest formally presented those who followed trades or kept open shops without being free, the successful prosecution of an unfreeman depended upon the willingness of local inhabitants to come forward to give testimony. There were certain incentives not to testify. It was necessary for a freeman of the City to be temporarily disfranchised before he could bear witness in a City court. Unless the City guaranteed to renew his freedom free of charge at the close of the trial, he might be put to the expense of customary fees all over again.[25]

Furthermore, the influence of the traditional trade guilds was waning as new forms of consumer industry re-characterised the market place. This was particularly true of the textile trades where the advent of the woman's over-garment, the mantua and the increase in demand for ready-made clothing opened up new channels for female economic activity.[26] In addition, the economic benefits of admission to the freedom of a London Company had become far less evident than in former years. In the first half of the eighteenth century, most of the guilds passed through a difficult transition from necessary economic fraternities to wealthy proprietorial fellowships. During the transitional period, the freedom of the guilds offered neither the economic advantages of earlier centuries nor the honorific significance of more recent times. Yet few of the Companies were earning enough from the rents of their urban property to be able to ignore the proportion of their budget which they raised from their members by fees, fines and quarterage. According to Kellett, their books show the systematic advancement of freemen—even in some cases reluctant foreigners who had been coerced into joining the Company—through the various offices, each office involving the expenditure of large sums upon dubious privileges.[27]

However, the system was not abandoned. Rather, it was overhauled and made more flexible. In 1750, the Corporation introduced a system of controlled licensing of non-freemen. The surviving license books reveal Companies anxious to escape the limitations of the employment of journeymen without overthrowing guild regulation altogether.[28] In addition, coinciding with the Corporation's concession of Licence Books was the first of an extensive series of Acts clarifying and reinforcing the legal powers of most of the Companies that were still active in trade or craft regulation.[29] Therefore, in the early nineteenth century, at least on paper, the whole system of guild privilege remained. However, by mid-century most of the Companies had changed from bodies possessing a practical connection with their trade to corporations concerned primarily with the administration of their valuable freehold and trust estates and with sponsoring charitable and educational activities. Finally, in 1856 all laws and customs preventing persons other than freemen of the City of London from carrying on business by retail or exercising any handicraft were formally abolished.[30]

Even if guild exclusiveness and apprenticeship training were weakening barriers to entry for women, it has been argued that the cost of setting up in business was an increasing one. Attractive shop facilities, including glass windows, shop fixtures, and the like, were becoming more and more important. Consumers were coming to expect greater diversity in terms of stock, which necessitated large and costly inventories. Such rising costs probably made it harder for women to obtain the wherewithal to set up in business.[31] It may well have been increasingly costly to establish a business, but it cannot be said that women always lacked the financial means. Some women could be quite ambitious and resourceful. Arthur J. Munby recalled,

> . . . a handsome young woman of twenty-six, who, having begun life as a servant of all work, and then spent three years in voluntary prostitution amongst men of a class much above her own, retires with a little competence, and invests the earnings of her infamous trade in a respectable coffee house.'[32]

Furthermore, in the preceding century, women were able to act as a source of credit for the businesses of others, having made up 20 per cent of loan capital traded in towns.[33]

What of access to loans and credit? Were women taken less seriously? In her examination of the businesses of milliners and dressmakers in nineteenth-century Boston, America, Gamber argued that gender was bound to affect the nature of the relationship between debtor and creditor but not always negatively. She writes, ' . . . a curious blend of paternalism and economic self-interest characterised wholesalers' attitudes toward their customers. To be sure, these two qualities did not always meld together; businessmen were often torn between compassion and profit.'[34] Deeply embedded cultural assumptions influenced supposedly rational business behaviour. She continues, 'paternalism in business was more than a sugar coating for hard-boiled economic imperatives.'[35] This behaviour was no less evident in London at this time. As an anonymous draper described,

> . . . a poor woman, who had been left a widow, got her friends to advance her sufficient money to open a small shop, and she came to us for an assortment of cut lengths, and laid out upwards of two hundred pounds with us. We did our best for the widow, and everything she had—quarters of dozens of hosiery, and such goods—were all neatly papered up for her, and the descriptions outside plainly written in text hand, and a dozen yards of linen and similar goods put up into neat

rolls, ready for retailing, and this person became a steady customer to us afterwards.[36]

Wiskin pointed out that it is through the connections in 'middling' families we can see how women acquired monetary and related social capital. Her business reputation, which was essential for her to participate in networks of credit, depended not only on how well she conducted her business with customers and creditors, but on who she was and whom she knew, or to whom she was related. The foundations of her social capital could have been in a family businesses, were as a wife or daughter she learned more than bookkeeping and selling skills but also who paid promptly, who were good credit risks, whose word could be trusted. It was this intimate knowledge of business and her connections acquired across the lifecycle that enabled women to trade. They were part of the construction of her business persona.[37] However, Davidoff and Hall argued that it was more common for a woman to inherit or raise a lump sum of money, like the widow in the draper's shop earlier, than to establish a viable credit chain to support an ongoing enterprise. Banks, they argue, remained wary of lending to women so that their sources of credit continued to be mainly kin and friends well into the period when men were turning to other institutional sources. This general lack of commercial credibility, they argue, was an important factor in the limited scale of women's business operations.[38]

It is difficult to retrace the decision making process of creditors considering tradeswomen as potential borrowers. However, Newton examined the opinion books and character books of a variety of English joint stock banks in order to assess to what extent judgements about clients (regardless of gender) were made on subjective criteria such as reputation, social standing and virtue, as opposed to the objective criteria of financial statements and profits. Joint stock banks, from inception in 1826 until the 1870s, conducted business at a much localised level and on personalised terms. Opinion and character books were maintained as a method of reducing the risks associated with lending to customers. The information collected provided a means of assessing the creditworthiness of the individuals involved and, possibly, of the specific projects.[39] Newton adds, 'Directors of a typical pre-1860 joint stock bank—relatively small with few branches—were often themselves also businessmen, involved in local industries and commerce and were, therefore, a part of the fabric of immediate business networks.'[40] She argues, reputation and virtue were recognised as a form of warranty but that the language and perceptions contained in the bank archives differed from that of contemporaries in a non-business or non-banking environments. Hence, virtue related to the ability to make repayments rather than morality. She writes that despite discussions of potential borrowing customers' individual reputations for 'soundness' and trustworthiness, a clear and 'objective' assessment of the ability to repay was also being considered. Repayment was ultimately the most important criterion for bank managements and, in assessing this ability, both 'objective' and 'subjective' criteria were utilised.[41] Virtue was a proxy for the probity of the client.

Hence, if the 'reputation approach' was underpinned by more practical, pragmatic and objective judgements, businesswomen, assuming good credit histories and a sound businesses, would not have faced as great a difficulty in acquiring bank credit as initially thought. There is also some evidence that wholesalers exercised some generosity towards their female customers that were struggling. For example, the case of Mrs Gadderrer as recounted by her granddaughter:

> When my mother, Jane Gadderrer, was about seven years old, her father became surety for a man, who soon after went to America, and he had to pay a sum which left him almost penniless; which took such an effect on him, as he was strictly honourable, that he died in a few months after, leaving my grandmother involved in serious difficulties. A meeting of creditors took place, and they were very good and kind, particularly the firm of Hale and Co., ale brewers, of Redcross Street; who, knowing Mrs Gadderrer to be an honest as well as an industrious woman, prevailed on the rest to let her remain in the house for a year, to pay ready-money for what she wanted in, and see if, by instalments, she could pay off any of her late husband's debts. She succeeded, and soon cleared herself.[42]

Her grandmother continued successfully in business at the City Arms, Lombard Street for 10 further years until her death, when the business passed to her daughter, Jane. Personal reputation, honour and a history of making good on debts was a vital component of creditworthiness but manufacturers and wholesalers took these matters seriously, seeking detailed assurances before they would extend credit to struggling businesses or take on new stockists. They often did this by obtaining references from other members of the commercial community. This required businesswomen to have some sort of engagement with that community, whether through taking over the connections and networks of deceased family members or establishing new ones.[43]

It is also likely that women had access to local credit networks. Lemire argued that women habitually initiated many of the arrangements for petty borrowing. They worked as informal pawnbrokers, organised loans for friends, acted as agents for moneylenders and assessed risk in guaranteeing the character of potential creditors, male and female. Even in the face of increased legislation, some women persisted as informal pawnbrokers and, possibly, moneylenders as well. In addition, individual loans were commonly secured by pawning domestic artefacts over which women tended to exercise control.[44] However, legal and structural changes did impact on the organisation of small-scale credit as the nineteenth century progressed. There was an increasing effort to control and regulate lending, removing it from informal hands such as pledge women, petty pawnbrokers, and neighbourhood tradesmen and women, confining and regulating the profits on even minor loans. However, Lemire argues, although increasingly marginalized, independent petty traders continued to function on the margins of the formal commercial sector, offering credit from their front rooms or street corners.[45] Winstanley also argues that the mid-nineteenth century restrictions on legitimate pawnbrokers, obliging the recording of all transactions for inspection, controlling the charges and even business hours, resulted in the growth of illegal concerns. The increasing demand for small, short-term loans spawned many unsupervised 'dollyshops' and moneylenders, which threatened to undermine the licensed trade's existence.[46] It is likely that those women refused credit by official pawnbrokers would have been able to obtain it from these unofficial counterparts.

There is also some evidence that women created female economies of financial support through wills and inheritance. Hunt has highlighted the case of Eleanor Coade (1733–1821), one of the few women in trade from this period of history that still holds a reputation in present day. A lifelong spinster, Coade set up in the 1760s as a manufacturer of a type of tastefully modelled artificial stone that came to be called *coadestone*. When she died at almost 90 years of age she distributed her money among various charities and sixty-odd relatives and friends. Two-thirds of her bequests to individuals were to women, and more than half of these to spinsters and widows. Where she gave money to married women it was often in the form of trusts 'for their separate use' so that their husbands could not appropriate the money. In one case she actually ordained that if the woman died intestate the money would go to her daughters, not her husband or sons, thus ensuring it would stay in the female line into the next generation.[47]

Green found from an examination of a one in three sample ($n = 288$) of women's wills in London in 1830 that when it came to appointing a universal heir, or residual legatee, the tendency was to favour women over men. Sisters, daughters and nieces tended to be favoured to a greater extent than brothers, sons and nephews. However, closer inspection of the marital status of the testator revealed that spinsters tended to favour female heirs to a greater extent than did widows. Not surprisingly, as far as widows were concerned children, especially daughters, were the most important beneficiaries. For spinsters, the main beneficiaries were siblings, notably sisters, and their sister's children, especially nieces. Good female friends and trusted servants could also find themselves provided for. As Green reflects, the pattern of inheritance confirms the significance of kinship networks.[48] His tentative findings also lend some support for the existence of a female economy of financial support. Such bequests not only assisted female relatives in their chances of securing a husband, they also gave them an income to invest actively in business or more passively in bonds, stocks and shares.

In addition, women passed on skills and contacts and a specialised knowledge, of which they were proud and that they knew was worth something in terms of money and prestige, in relatively informal ways.[49] In the nineteenth century, however, the flow of trade and information increasingly extended beyond the reach of local neighbourhood networks. Women traders, in cultural terms at least, became more marginal. The growing prestige of larger networks, promoted by directories and other bourgeois forums, spelled a corresponding loss for local systems, which were often small scale and based on verbal transactions.[50] Indeed, Hunt argues, the real significance of town and trade directories is the way they highlight what women were not doing.[51] Very much in evidence in the directories, especially in the 'gazette' section, is a substantial 'industry' devoted to managing the junctions between manufacturing, marketing, finance, long-distance transport, law and government, and civic and commercial activism. Middling men monopolised virtually all this integrative work and at the same time benefited from the numerous benefits that accompanied it: trade opportunities, jobs in the local or national bureaucracy, cultural prestige, political power and connections, opportunities to learn new skills and access to 'insider' knowledge. In the directories, women held relative few positions in these areas, if any. Hence, Hunt argues that the assemblages of individuals exhibited in the directories, whether actual civic bodies or merely fictive groups of alphabetised names, were a powerful testimony to the complexity of relationships and symbolic power.[52] The directories also reveal another facet of the gendering of the market: the rise of men's civic associations. These had the further advantage of bypassing the more local, more feminine, more socially conglomerate and more tradition-bound networks of family, neighbourhood and church—precisely what supported the small-scale trading activities in which women could be found.[53] However, Wiskin has pointed out that many women had access to the new types of urban institution through the men in their families, households and businesses. These male connections brought back information which female proprietors could act upon, enabling them to make informed decisions about their enterprises. Announcements in contemporary newspapers, entries in urban directories and references in wills indicate that businesswomen conducted their enterprises in whole worlds, made of men and women traders.[54]

Furthermore historians of businesswomen have sometimes overlooked the more feminised networks, failing to see the support networks these women built around themselves. One of these networks, the household is investigated in Chapter 5. Other evidence has also been uncovered of women's attempts to organise, work and train collectively. *The Society of Industrious Females* was an organisation of 60 women who came together in London in 1832 to win for themselves 'a fair distribution of the products of our labour' through the co-operative production of clothing which they sold at Owen's Labour Exchange in Gray's Inn Road.[55] In addition, within Owenism, women were encouraged to participate in the regular classes on offer. In 1842, the 7th annual congress reported that 29 branches had 'social institutions' of which 8 seated over 1,000. In addition, 22 branches held regular classes, 9 held day schools, and 20 branches had libraries of their own.[56] Owenite women also organised classes for themselves, of which the best documented example was 'The Ladies Class', established by the women of the London A1 branch in 1844. The class began with a few women in March and quickly grew to some 60 members. It was self-governing, with its own elected executive who also sat on the local branch executive. Classes in reading, writing and arithmetic were reported to go so well that an advance into moral and physical science was urged.[57] While such forums were not the equivalent of the men's civic associations, they nonetheless offered women a means of passing on knowledge and information. Indeed, some men were made uneasy by the prevalence of such groups of women. For example, William Cobbett, who exclaimed, 'There are, in almost every considerable neighbourhood, a little squadron of she-commanders'.[58] In his book, *Advice to Young Men and (Incidentally) to Young Women, in the Middle and Higher Ranks of Life*, Cobbett warned,

> Women are a sisterhood. They make common cause on behalf of the sex; and, indeed, this is natural enough, when we consider the vast power that the law gives us over them. The law is for us, and they combine, wherever they can, to mitigate its effects. This is perfectly natural, and, to a certain extent, laudable, evincing fellow-feeling and public spirit: but when carried to the length of 'he sha'n't,' it is despotism on the one side, and slavery on the other. Watch, therefore, the incipient steps of encroachment . . .[59]

Even if businesswomen did have social capital, could establish credit-worthiness or could create women's networks, were they restricted by location? Were they on the margins of the marketplace? According to Wiskin and Barker they were not. From the eighteenth century onwards it was uncommon for women to be restricted to a specific quarter of an urban trading community. Businesswomen were central to urban society and to the operation and development of commerce in northern industrial towns. Women were actively involved in the 'public' world of work.[60] Furthermore, 'middling' women were especially unlikely to be banished to the periphery. They were not poor women who peddled goods from doorways or street corners. Businesswomen had to locate themselves were they could be easily found, with premises accessible to both their suppliers and customers. Genteel customers were also particularly unlikely to venture into streets away from the town centre. The choice of location was deliberate and was most closely tied to the nature of the business.[61]

Finally, it has been argued that even for those women that did have the means to operate an enterprise, the increasing number of alternative avenues for investment tended to deflect women from setting up in business.

These included the rise of relatively safe investments such as the various stock and annuity schemes that flowed from the foundation of the Bank of England in 1694. According to Davidoff and Hall, widows and spinsters formed the core of those investors requiring a steady income without administrative worries. They point to the variety of sources and types of income, including rents, which provided a living to those who wished for a 'genteel competence' not requiring active intervention.[62] Similarly, Earle's study of London has supported the rise of 'rent based income', arguing that it must have been regarded as a more genteel, domestic activity. Anecdotal examples of the 'landlady' are not too difficult to find. William Hart's diary makes reference to one such character:

> The landlady was an aged woman, a Mrs Clapton living in Ratcliff Highway. She accepted me directly without raising the rent. This I considered a blessing of god, as small houses were very much wanted, and several persons endeavoured to get it out of my hands. They would have given her more money, but the old lady stuck to her integrity and would not let them have it.[63]

Perhaps it is not surprising that she was an 'old' lady. Morris illustrated in his study of the male middle-class property cycle, that business*men* were willing to exchange the rewarding but risky rate of return on trade for the lower reward but greater stability of the unearned or higher rent income as they grew older.[64] This would suggest that as widows aged they would be less likely to opt for business than their younger single or married counterparts. It is important to recognise here that property leasing was not a purely domestic service. It was grounded in the commercial arena. A financial contract was entered into between the owner of the property and the tenant, often supported by various obligations of the landlady *or* landlord. Renting out property was a form of business activity, bringing women into the public sphere.[65] It is for this reason that we will revisit the role of women in property and accommodation provision later in the book (see Chapter 6).

Therefore, women did face barriers of entry into business but over time many of these barriers became more permeable and new bridges appeared in the form of new markets and opportunities. Start-up capital could be obtained from a number of sources and women were a significant source of credit both generally and to each other in this period. Although the law could be problematic, there were loopholes through which women could slip. Similarly, a lack of formal training should not be overstated as a barrier. However, a general lack of exposure and experience would certainly have been prohibitive, and it is here that a widow, reluctant or otherwise, would have had an advantage if she had been involved in her husband's business during his lifetime. Collectively, the evidence supports Barker's recent suggestion of a breakaway from a traditional historical consensus that independent women of businesses, particularly those deemed 'unfeminine', were insignificant and no more than an oddity. Rather, 'the woman of business might be subject to various constraints, but at the same time, she could be blessed with a number of freedoms, and a degree of independence, that set her apart from most other women and many men . . . '.[66] Yet there were barriers *within* business that limited her financial horizons. These related not to law but to law or credit markets but rather to notions of morality. Honour and duty were to be more important in women's business aspirations than profit. There are examples of business women, such as Mrs. Clapton, who clearly took this to the heart of their enterprise. Others may have dismissed such notions as social rhetoric to protect their femininity. Hence there may have been fewer barriers to entry and more bridges than historians first thought. In London businesses tended to be small and hence capital and labour needs were less onerous, customers were plentiful and borough custom allowed all women—widowed, married, or single—to engage in business. Furthermore, the marketplace was changing. The 'cathedral' of consumption enticed the middle classes into a domain where women had power, influence and a degree of control, a sometimes feminized marketplace within which businesswomen were well placed to capitalize.

3 Insuring Her Assets

The key focus of this chapter is to set women's businesses into a comparative context with those of men, using the same source. This is important because male proprietor's ventures were no more homogeneous than women's. It allows us to see a scale of enterprise with some gendered elements, rather than holding up an imaginary, standardized male enterprise as the benchmark norm. Having established that women could engage in business in the nineteenth century and that this was seen as suitable work by many Victorian commentators, actually revealing these women and the full diversity and extent of their enterprises is still challenging. In studies of businesswomen active in earlier centuries, historians have resorted to looking for shadows of their economic endeavours in advertising, general government statistics, and trade directories. All these sources have their benefits and provide us with valuable snapshots of women that operated businesses. However, there are serious shortcomings for each of these sources and consequently for any study based solely upon them. For example, in the case of newspaper advertisements, it was expensive for a proprietor to place a newspaper advertisement until well into the nineteenth century, rendering the costs prohibitive to a large part of the small business and self-employed population. Also, as will be touched on in the next chapter, it seems different 'Public' methods may well have been favoured in different marketplaces. Therefore, this material can provide us with interesting examples but this kind of evidence will remain anecdotal unless put into context by a more empirical study. Similarly, trade directories were biased in their compilation and coverage and the census descriptions and classifications even more so. Hence, any study of women in business in the nineteenth century must by necessity be innovative in its use of sources if it is to reveal the women hidden by the limitations of many sources.

Given that business was an avenue of income generation for women who found themselves unsupported by others, security against loss was essential for them. Women were not excluded by their gender from the opportunity to insure. As long as they paid their premiums their money was as good to the insurance company as any man's. Thus fire insurance records provide us with a detailed foundation to our picture of the businesswomen of

Victorian London. Surviving fire registers document ownership, construction and the value of businesses in the form of stock, utensils, fixtures and goods in trust—much more detailed business information than is available in other sources used for the study of women in business.

For those readers unfamiliar with insurance records, a brief background follows before moving into the findings of this study. Firstly, recognition that such records are of value in areas of historical enquiry beyond the history of the insurance business itself, developed as a result of the debate about the role of capital formation in industrialisation. The archives of the insurance industry are amongst the oldest and largest collections of business records in Great Britain. As insurance became widespread, particularly from the second half of the eighteenth century onwards, economic and social change was clearly reflected in the history and archives of the industry.[1] Indeed insurance is a function of these changes and especially wealth. In the words of Trebilcock:

> It stems from a change in the balance between the level of riches and the level of risks. It makes its most rapid strides when both riches and risks are growing in new ways. As economic prosperity advances, the potential for amassing property grows—but so too does the penalty for losing it. As property accumulates, so also does the risk to property.[2]

As Beresford points out: 'The economic historian, whose God is not always that of the big battalions, must be grateful that, when private records are lacking, the policy registers have survived to document such a wide range of capital investment.'[3]

Although not the oldest class of insurance, fire business was the earliest type of insurance to achieve corporate status. With the memory of the Great Fire of London (1666) still smouldering, Dr Nicholas Babon, a speculative builder, established the first fire office near the Royal Exchange in 1681. The Insurance Office for Houses on the Backside of the Royal Exchange was a mutual scheme for house insurance, guaranteed by a property investment fund. The trust deed allowed Babon's firm to insure up to 10,000 houses. In 1681, the Corporation of London also began to offer fire insurance, although it had withdrawn from the business by the following year. The Friendly Society for Securing Houses from Loss by Fire faired somewhat better, entering the scene in 1683 and issuing 23,000 policies before its demise in 1730. However, it was not until the Hand-in-Hand in 1696 that a lasting fire insurance business was founded.[4] This was followed by the Sun Fire Office in 1710 (the records of which are used in this study), the Union in 1714, the Westminster in 1717, the London in 1720, and the Royal Exchange in 1720. Together these constituted the first major wave of British fire insurance. The initiatives of the first wave were of three types: mutual societies like the Hand-in-Hand and the Union, unincorporated companies like the Sun (effectively extended partnerships) and privileged chartered monopolies like the Royal Exchange.

The fire offices were compelled to form their own fire brigade. This mostly consisted of watermen from the Thames who were clad in the distinctive livery of their company. The Sun Fire reassured its potential customers in its original proposal forms that there were 'thirty lusty able-body'd firemen who are cloath'd in blue liveries and having silver badges with the Sun mark upon their arms, and twenty able porters likewise, who are always ready to assist in quenching fires and removing goods having given bonds for their fidelity.'[5] It issued a badge or fire mark to be affixed to the building to confirm that it was insured. This had a rotund human face, surrounded by a halo of 16 rays, 8 direct and 8 wavy. It was wrought in lead and painted a bright golden colour. Its purpose was to prevent fraud by obtaining an insurance policy by indirect means after a house had been burned. As the fire brigade would not service a house unless a mark was affixed, a property was not considered to be secure until the mark was in position. It also provided advertising for the company. Eventually, the formal and lengthy titles of the insurance offices were replaced by the names of their marks.[6]

Agents appointed by the Sun Fire were responsible for the ordering of new business, the collection of premiums and the presentation of receipts to the head office. By 1786 there were as many as 123 agents, including a spinster and two widows.[7] Women were not uncommonly recruited. Indeed, in 1807 it was grudgingly admitted that Mrs Buchanan, their Glasgow agent, was 'very active and as attentive to the business as a female can possibly be expected to be'.[8] Male or female agents generally ran their agencies as a second line to their major occupation, usually some form of business activity. In the eighteenth century, small traders and retailers, local clerks and other small local business people typically took on the role. By the nineteenth century a broader range of people had become involved. Retailers, merchants, commission agents, teachers, surveyors of taxes, clerks in various professions including banks, estate agencies, railway and canal offices and so on were all recruited.

As in other insurance companies, the Sun Fire classified risk according to the established formula of Common Insurance, Hazardous Insurance and Doubly Hazardous Insurance. The first category covered brick and stone buildings not used for hazardous trades. The second covered timber and plaster buildings or brick and stone buildings housing hazardous trades. The final category covered timber and plaster buildings used for hazardous trades and all premises of sugar bakers, distillers, china and glass manufacturers and other dangerous trades. This classification system was generally followed until the late nineteenth century.[9] In addition, after 1825, a continuous stream of information about all classes of risk passed between the fire offices, ultimately culminating in the formation of a fire insurance tariff or cartel. From the 1850s these 'tariff offices' were publishing specifications and tariffs for warehouses and for corn, flax, woollen and cotton mills. By 1860 the offices had formed area committees, with twice yearly general meetings for all offices concerned in the tariffs. This sharing of expertise and underwriting experience effectively standardised fire insurance services across the metropolis.

The Sun Fire policy registers utilised for this chapter are held in the Guildhall Library, Corporation of London. They represent the head office compilations of orders for new insurance business and augmented renewals from all branches and agencies.[10] Until recently there has been limited use of these records, which is surprising given the key role the Sun Fire played in the London insurance market. As Jenkins noted,

> Of the many fire insurance records that survive undoubtedly of most interest are those relating to the Sun Fire Office, both because of their comprehensiveness and because of the dominance of that company. Even in 1830, with all the new formations and competitive pressures, the Sun was still almost twice as large, measured by premium income, as any other office . . . [11]

Along with the Phoenix (est. 1782) and the Royal Exchange (est. 1720), the Sun Fire dominated the fire insurance industry. At the start of the nineteenth century, its gross premium income at over £100,000 per annum was considerably larger than the fire business incomes of its rivals. The Sun Fire's secretary estimated in 1802 that his own office covered sums amounting to £79 million, compared to the Phoenix's £56.9 million and the Royal Exchange's £36.9 million.[12]

When it carried out a review of its industrial risks in the 1820s, the Sun Fire found that it had on its books property relating to such diverse trades as 'gingerbread bakers, bedstead upholders, oar makers, tallow melters and chandlers, lamp-black manufacturers and brushmakers'. Likewise it insured all types of shops and offices, theatres, churches, cloth halls, town halls, inns and brewhouses, schools and libraries.[13] The head office policy registers hold a vast amount of information about these different properties and their contents. Details of owners, tenants, partners, executors and occupations and places of residence are frequently recorded. Property contents, including livestock, libraries of books, clothing and wearing apparel, business and industrial stock, and machinery are specified. Many policies contain physical details of buildings insured, including numbers of storeys and rooms, and construction materials. Uses of property are also recorded, as well as details of heating and lighting methods and means of power. There are also of course the valuations of property and their contents for insurance purposes.[14]

We now turn to the utilization of this source for the study of female enterprise. Used alongside trade directories, the census, or newspapers, the fire policy registers of the Sun Fire provide detailed information on women's businesses. The registers are comprised of two un-indexed, handscribed series. The first contains 600,000 policies from all geographic locations taken out before 1793. From 1793 separate registers were maintained for London and the provinces, again un-indexed and hand-scribed. The surviving collection of this second series of policy registers end in 1863—hence the empirical elements of this study do not go beyond mid-century. However, there are over 1.3 million policies in the second series of registers (1793–1863). It was impractical within the confines of this study to review them all. Consequently, in order to establish a meaningful data-set and one with which record linkage could be undertaken with the census, full sample years were selected and all the policies taken out by women in these years were extracted. The sample years were chosen, subject to complete sets of volumes, to permit record linkage with the censuses of 1851 and 1861. In addition, in order to assess whether there were any radical differences in mid-nineteenth-century women's business policies to those in the preceding century, two mid-eighteenth-century sample dates were also selected—1747 and 1761. These were selected at as close to 100 year intervals to the nineteenth century dates as possible but subject to surviving volumes as there are volumes missing for many years including 1751.

In addition to extracting all the policies held by women for these four years, a five per cent sample of men's policies was also collected. This was achieved by the consecutive extraction of men's policies taken out in the month of October for each sample year. (There is no reason to assume that October was in any way an unusual month.) The sampling procedure adopted, whilst not as statistically optimal as a random sampling procedure, was a more practical one to adopt considering the hand scribed and un-indexed nature of the source. The resulting dataset of fire insurance policies numbered 33,440 policies in total, with 3,396, 7,157, 10,303 and 12,584 policies for 1747, 1761, 1851 and 1861 respectively. The collected samples for 1747 and 1761 ($n = 10,553$) included policies taken out by men and women from all locations as the Sun Fire did not separate London and the provinces into separate listings until 1793.[15] However once the samples had been extracted from the source those with a London address were separated out for the purposes of analysis. In turn, for each of the four years policies covering a business were extracted from the original dataset, producing 861 business policies for the mid-eighteenth century and 1,175 business policies for the mid-nineteenth century. These policies form the core of the evidence considered in this chapter.

The Sun Fire samples confirm that despite claims that women withdrew from business across the eighteenth century, even by the mid-nineteenth century London women can still be found operating and insuring enterprises of their own. Indeed, as consumers of fire insurance for both personal and business assets, women kept pace with the insurance industries massive expansion. The number of Sun Fire policies held by women increased from 126 in 1747 to 1,230 by 1861. In the mid-nineteenth century female policyholders held around ten per cent of all the Sun's London fire insurance policies. However there was a proportional shift in the nature of their policies. As regards coverage of business assets, the proportion of all women's policies explicitly of this nature halved from the mid-eighteenth to the mid-nineteenth century sample dates. Although this may reflect a declining participation in business, the true scale of this decline is by no means clear. This is because the relative decline in business policies, and thus any indication of declining business participation, is proportional not absolute. The dataset indicates a significant increase in the propensity to insure personal belongings, which is unsurprising given the changes to the consumer landscape over this period. This shift does not mean that there was a declining propensity to insure business assets. Indeed, there was a fivefold increase in the number of women's policies covering stock, utensils and fixtures across the sample dates. When we look at the dataset of male policyholders we see a similar story. Despite a sixfold increase in raw numbers of business policies taken out by men across the period, the proportion of their business to personal policies also fell. Some 72.5 per cent of men's policies covered stock, utensils and fixtures in 1747 but by 1861 this figure had fallen to 43.8 per cent. Hence, the proportion of policies covering business assets fell for both men and women across the period as the general need or desire to insure against fire increased.

Looking at those female headed policies that were explicitly covering business assets, by the mid-nineteenth century some 20 per cent still listed a business and covered stock, utensils and fixtures (*n* = 202 and 251). Even this significant finding of participation in enterprise is an underestimate of the true proportion of female policyholders engaged in business activities because many businesses required little in the way of stock, utensils and assets separate from the fixtures, fittings and personal belongings of a woman's personal household and hence her insurance policy for personal assets. For example, lodging house keeping and school keeping. It is possible that a move towards enterprises of this nature as the period progressed has contributed to a surface level picture of a decline in female enterprise, whereas it actually represents a shift towards ventures in which the business

Table 3.1 Overview of London Men's and Women's Policies Covering Business Assets.

Year	Male (5% sample)		Female (all)	
	n	%	*n*	%
1747	37	73	50	40
1761	96	67	131	42
1851	184	45	202	19
1861	224	44	251	20

Source: Sun Fire Policy registers, series 11,936, LGL.
Note: Expressed as percentage of total men's insurance policies in sample or all women's policies, including non-business.

connection could be downplayed—both by the proprietor herself and by the compilers of trade records such as directories. We will return to this discussion in Chapter 7 when we reflect on women's enterprise more broadly.

A further example of women whose endeavours were less obvious until we dig deeper into the sources were those women who rented out accommodation. Whilst captured here in the total dataset of female policyholders, they are not included in the 20 per cent who held a policy covering business assets, unless they also had an additional separate enterprise (see Chapter 6).[16] This activity was not seen as a trade and so was not listed in directories or described as such in other business records. However it was seen as an economic activity and its use was often extensive, extending to an empire of substantial property investment, with each accommodation requiring contracts and management. It was an activity often carried on alongside other business interests. However, although this was not a practice limited to women, in studies of women's economic agency it is often interpreted as a more passive form of economic activity. Yet it is difficult to imagine the property investors of today being downplayed in such a manner. Detailed, large-scale research into women's investment in leasehold and freehold property investment and their role in the private housing market as providers of rented accommodation is long overdue. We return to this form of enterprise in Chapter 6 which focuses on the business of accommodation.

Turning to the value of metropolitan women's businesses, it was the policyholder who valued the property proposed for insurance. In theory the value represented the replacement cost but historians of fire insurance have suggested that a kind of blanket cover was evolved. Deliberate undervaluation might have arisen from a simple desire to minimize premiums and duty rates. There is also the suggestion that the policyholder was expected to share the risk or spread the risk across numerous insurers, carefully avoiding accusations of fraud presumably. However, historians do not agree on the evidence for this.[17] It is unlikely, Cockerell and Green argue, that the valuations presented in the policy registers represent overvaluations. The tension between the insurer's desire for maximum available premiums but not over-evaluated payouts and the policyholders reluctance to pay excess premiums but desire to avoid loss by under-evaluation ensured that valuations were ordinarily realistic.[18]

Looking first at minimum and maximum valuations, Table 3.2 illustrates that the minimum value of a business policy held by a woman fell across the period 1747 to 1861, as it also did for male policyholders, reflecting the increasing accessibility of fire insurance. Adversity to risk ensured that it was in a woman's interests to insure her assets, however seemingly insignificant. This applied to men too and, combined with the declining cost of insurance, explains why very low value policies can be found on proprietors policies regardless of gender. The maximum value for a business policy also increased across the period, although 1761 seems to have been a year that saw some particularly high insurance valuations of women's businesses. The highest value policy held by a woman increased from £1,400 in 1747 to £10,250 in 1861, this was half that of the highest value men's policy.

Of course minimum and maximum values whilst representing the floors and ceilings of insurance values, and offering a proxy of capitalization, are outliers and are not therefore indicative of more general patterns. So, turning to all business policies and sorting by value we can see that both male and female policyholders are represented below £100 and above £3,000. However, just short of 80 per cent of women's business policies were below £500 in the mid-eighteenth century and just over 82 per cent by the mid-nineteenth. This compares to Barnet's finding of 88 per cent for 1820, based on all women's business policies with multiple insurers. However, whilst he found that 48 per cent were insuring for £100 or less, this study finds that only 29 per cent were in this lower range.[19] In addition, the differential between men's and women's policies valued between £100 and £499 is pretty steady across the period. It is in the proportion of policies valued below £100 that we can see a growing differential between male and female policyholders, although it is important to stress that men were still insuring businesses in this range, not just women. Indeed, Barnet's survey of all commercial insurance in 1820 estimated that the median valuation was £320 and that only 23 per cent of firms insured for over £1,000.[20] Approaching half of men's businesses were valued / capitalized between £100 and £499. Hence, taking the Sun Fire register's valuations as an indicator, some 60 per cent of women's businesses at mid-century were what can be described as comparably well capitalized at between £100 and £499. A further 15 per cent insured for even greater values.

At mid century, of those men's policies valued above £3,000, almost three quarters belonged to merchants, factors and brokers and those policies valued at £10,000 or above were exclusively held by such trades. The largest two non-merchant related valuations were for £9,700 and £8,000 on a tobacco manufactory and distillery respectively.[21] The remaining valuations fall back to £5,000 or below. Not only are valuations a snapshot in time but different trades required their proprietor to carry varying levels of stock. This could artificially inflate valuations in the merchant related trades, which were disproportionately inhabited by men. For these businesses, primarily about the flow of goods in and out of warehouses, we should remind ourselves that confusing the value of the stock for the value of the business is like confusing turnover with profit. A business may have a high turnover but be barely breaking even in terms of profits. Furthermore, actual carriage of stock may have varied throughout the year but it was in the policyholders interests to insure for the highest value of goods likely to be sat in warehouses in their name. Therefore, it seems sensible to treat the valuations of merchants and large factors and brokers (who are essentially merchants) with caution and as outliers to the general trend. Indeed, looking at Barnet's figures for 1820 again, he

Table 3.2 Minimum and Maximum Insurance Valuations on Men's And Women's Business Policies.

Year		Minimum		Maximum	
		£	%	£	%
1747					
	Men	100		2,900	
	Women	100	100	1,400	48
1761					
	Men	70		7,000	
	Women	40	57	9,000	129
1851					
	Men	10		15,000	
	Women	5	50	5,170	35
1861					
	Men	10		20,000	
	Women	3	30	10,250	51

Source: Sun Fire Policy registers, series 11,936, LGL.
Note: Percentage refers to the minimum/maximum valuation of women's policies expressed as a percentage of the minimum/maximum valuation of men's policies.

Table 3.3 Comparison of Insurance Valuations of Men's and Women's Policies (%).

Year		< 100	100 to 499	500 to 999	1,000 to 1,999	2,000 to 2,999	> 3,000
1747							
	Men	0	57	30	3	11	0
	Women	0	74	14	12	0	0
1761							
	Men	5	54	27	5	7	1
	Women	12	72	12	3	0	2
1851							
	Men	11	31	17	17	6	18
	Women	30	49	12	6	3	1
1861							
	Men	13	44	20	10	5	9
	Women	28	58	8	3	2	2

Source: Sun Fire Policy registers, series 11,936, LGL.

has calculated that if merchants, factors and wholesalers are excluded, women's average value of capital insured increase from 19 per cent to 32 per cent of that of all firms.[22]

It is important to draw a distinction between 'all firms' and the ventures of small and medium sized proprietors. Whereas at the beginning of the last quarter of the eighteenth century nearly a third of all manufacturing capital was accounted for by small and medium sized firms, half a century later this proportion had fallen to about one-sixth. However, the proportion insured by large firms increased very significantly, from under half to exactly two-thirds. Barnet argues that this suggests that smaller firms did not predominate in the London landscape as had previously been thought.[23] On the contrary, this does not automatically follow at all. It suggests that they did not predominate in terms of capital but in terms of numbers and physical presence they were still very much peppering the vista, providing livelihoods and serving markets. This difference in view is at least partly a result of the different interests of the two different projects. Barnet's study was more concerned with the idea of firms and where capital was concentrated, whereas this study is more interested in business proprietorship. In terms of the latter, proprietors of smaller to medium sized concerns were a dominant feature of London's economy and economic culture. However their share of capital, regardless of the gender of the proprietor, was in relative decline as the big battalions of business began to cast an increasing shadow across the metropolis.

Although we must be cautious with merchant valuations and acknowledge that women were far less likely than men to operate as merchants, factors or brokers, they could and sometimes did. For example, Rachel Hart described herself as a merchant and warehouse keeper. Her policy for 27 Houndsditch and 1 Duke Street was for £6,200 in total and £5,000 specifically on stock, utensils and fixtures.[24] Similarly, Emily Coales of Whitechapel described herself as a wine and spirit merchant. She insured stock, utensils and fixtures for £5,000, plus a further £2,000 on stock held in her dwelling house and £3,000 on stock held in a vault underneath it.[25] These two policies compare very favourable with the combined mid-century mean value for the 41 male merchants' policies at £3,806. There were six female merchants insuring stock, utensils and fixtures in the dataset. Their mean insurance value was £2,748; 72 per cent that of their male counterparts.

Hence, men were more likely to operate as merchants than women, pushing up the valuation of men's businesses overall. However generally, a significant proportion of women's businesses were similarly capitalized to many men's businesses and even female merchants were competitive with many of their male counterparts. Many women and men were operating in the same businesses, insuring their stock, utensils and fixtures in the same ranges of value. However, some men's businesses could be insured for much higher values than women's and a significant proportion of other men's businesses too. There are a number of causal factors to consider here.

This pattern could be a reflection of women's lesser access to the higher ranges of investment capital and hence that their business ventures had a sort of capital ceiling—a ceiling it needs to be added that they shared with many men's businesses. Another possible explanation is that proportionally women operated in different sectors to men and that some sectors contained ventures tending towards higher or lower capital values. Of course women may have chosen these sectors by default of their lesser access to capital or due to other factors such as experience and suitability to domestic circumstances. Their sector may be led by their relationship to capital or to other factors by varying degrees.

The use of a contingency table and the chi-square test (see appendices) corroborates the intuitive interpretation that gender did influence sector choice to a degree but the distribution of women's businesses across sectors was not static. The Sun Fire policies reveal a shift over time in the sectors in which women's businesses were most commonly located. The proportion of women's policies relating to traditional 'male' production trades, for example coach-building and ironmongery, remained constant at 15 per cent if the two sample years in each century are averaged. If the sample dates stand alone, the picture suggests more of a decline. Nonetheless, accounting for some 19 per cent of London women's business policies in 1851 and around 13 per cent in 1861, the proportion of women operating in such trades remained significant.[26] Although such ventures as grocery and eating house keeping also remained popular for women, by the nineteenth century the textile and clothing related trades were their most common sectors, which combining sample dates saw a 14 per cent increase over the period. By 1861 they accounted for almost 40 per cent of women's business policies.

Was the textile sector (including the sale, manufacture and laundry) less capitalized than other sectors? When looking at the valuation of men's business policies for 1851 in Table 3.5 we can see that their insurance valuations in textile related trades trailed far behind their ventures in other sectors – £15,680 compared to £140,924 for food, drink and entertainment related ventures, £62,040 for retailing ventures (other than those relating to the latter or textiles), and £90,000 on other businesses, largely production related (and not falling into textiles or food and drink). Indeed, men's textile related policies were responsible for only five per cent of their total insured values of £308,659. In terms of mean values, textile policies at £871 averaged less than half that of all men's business policies at £1,754. (Similarly for 1861, the mean for textile related policies was £639, 60 per cent of the mean for all businesses at £1,060.) Only 11 per cent of these male textile proprietors had policies valued over £2,000 and none of them had policies valued at over £10,000, rendering textiles the only sector which was not represented at this higher insurance valuation. The highest value textile policy held by a man was for £5,000. So clearly men's policies covering businesses in the textile sector were valued at significantly less than men's policies in other sectors. Textile related policies made up only

Table 3.4 Sector Distribution of Men's and Women's Business Policies (%).

Year	(a) Food, Drink and Hospitality	(b) Textiles and Clothing	(c) Other Retailing, not included in (a) or (b)	(d) Production not included in (a) or (b)	(e) Professional
1747					
Men	27	11	24	30	8
Women	30	18	32	16	4
1761					
Men	43	14	12	26	6
Women	29	29	27	13	2
1851					
Men	30	12	25	29	5
Women	22	37	23	17	1
1861					
Men	21	14	33	27	5
Women	25	38	24	12	2

Source: Sun Fire Policy registers, series 11,936, LGL.
Note: Includes small number of business policies that did not give specific SUF value. Policies taken out by professionals have been included here as setting up a practice did have a business element. The policies of professionals are not included in the other tables as women were largely excluded from the professions by the related organizing bodies.

Table 3.5 Insurance Valuations of Men's Business Policies by Sector, 1851 (%).

£ Value	Sector			
	(a) Food, Drink and Hospitality	(b) Textiles and Clothing	(c) Other Retailing, not included in (a) or (b)	(d) Production not included in (a) or (b)
• £50	13	22	0	10
• £500	46	61	45	49
• £1,000	68	78	61	64
• £2,000	72	89	77	83
> £2,000	28	11	23	17
• £5,000	81	100	90	99
> £10,000	13	0	7	1

Source: Sun Fire Policy registers, series 11,936, LGL.

10 per cent of all men's business policies in 1851. Yet for women this sector accounted for approaching 40 per cent of their policies. Hence, the lower capitalization of textile businesses relative to other businesses, regardless of gender, will have lowered women's overall capitalization by virtue of their greater tendency to set up enterprises in this area.

However as Table 3.4 reveals, although there are leanings, women's business policies were not mostly clustered in the textile sector. Therefore, without discounting the role of sector as a dampening influence on the relative capitalization of women's businesses in comparison to men's, we should consider complimentary explanations. The variation in the value of assets may also be a reflection of differing aspirations and motives for some male and female business proprietors. Rather than a 'failure' of female proprietors to expand their stock, utensils and fixtures, could we not instead be seeing a choice on the part of many women in business to keep their ventures small. This might be for personal reasons or to preserve flexibility, in order to respond quickly to changes in the market. In addition, there may have been a need or preference on the part of many businesswomen to put their profits into the familial purse rather than ploughing them back into their business. As long as a business provided an income, independence, and respectability in the community, size was not necessarily important. Indeed, one might argue that growing a larger business would have removed the suitability of operating a little enterprise in the eyes of contemporaries. Also, women in business may have preferred to invest any gains in an alternative form of income generation such as the rental property market or less active forms of investment such as bonds, stocks and shares. The varying values of women's business policies indicate that the motives, intentions and successes of metropolitan women in business were not homogenous. Some female proprietors will have been frustrated by access to credit, others will have been self-limiting.

Although the textile sector was significant for women entering into enterprise, it is clear that there were many other options. It would be reckless to interpret the significance of textiles as proof that to 'stitch' did become the defining activity. On closer inspection, many of these trades were in fact retail rather than manufacturing enterprises. In addition, many of the food, drink and hospitality trades had a heavy retailing component (e.g. leather seller, haberdasher, dealer in baby linen) and a further quarter of women's business policies related to other types of retailing (e.g. florist, music seller, stationer). In short, the Sun Fire registers suggest that by the nineteenth century, London's women in business were very much operating at the retail end of the supply chain.

It is clear from the insurance records that female proprietors were able to choose from a growing range of business opportunities. Whilst the number of distinct trades listed for men tripled over the period, the number for female policyholders more than quadrupled, increasing from 23 in 1747 to 107 by 1861. However, while the number of different trade types expanded, this influenced concentration levels very little. Around half of all women's business policies could be grouped into just ten trades in the nineteenth century sample dates. Although the clustering in what we can refer to as the 'popular' trades may seem intense, the level of concentration is actually less dense than in the eighteenth century—70 per cent in 1747 and 61 per cent in 1761. Clustering in popular trades suggests not just that some trades were easier to enter than others, but also that women probably followed the example of other women who had already been successful and that they reacted to market trends and opportunities. Nonetheless, although more frequently occurring, these popular trades individually represented a very small percentage of all women's business policies with the Sun Fire.

We can also see from Table 3.7 that men's policies tended to cluster too. At the mid-century sample dates 49 per cent of their policies related to just ten trades (45 and 53 per cent, respectively). There were also popular

Table 3.6 The Ten Most Popular Trades for Women Insuring Business Assets (%).

| | | 1851 | | | 1861 | |
| | | (a) As % of Popular Trades | (b) As % of All Women's Business Policies | | (c) As % of Popular Trades | (d) As % of All Women's Business Policies |
Ranking	Trade			Trade		
1	Milliner / Dressmaker	29	15	Milliner / Dressmaker	27	13
2	Chandler (all types)	15	7	Coffee House Keeper	12	6
3	Hosier / Haberdasher	12	6	Victualler	11	5
4	Victualler	11	6	Linen Draper	10	5
5	Grocer / Greengrocer	9	5	Laundry Keeper	10	5
6	Coffee House Keeper	6	3	Greengrocer / Grocer	8	4
7	Clothier	5	3	Chandler (all types)	7	4
8	Linen Draper	5	3	Stationer	5	2
9	Stationer	5	3	Tobacconist	5	2
10	Tobacconist	5	3	Hosier / Haberdasher	5	2
Total		100	54		100	48

Source: Sun Fire Policy registers, series 11,936, LGL.
Note: Percentages are rounded up to nearest whole.

Table 3.7 The Ten Most Popular Trades for Men Insuring Business Assets (%).

| | | 1851 | | | 1861 | |
| | | (a) As % of Popular Trades | (b) As % of All Women's Business Policies | | (c) As % of Popular Trades | (d) As % of All Women's Business Policies |
Ranking	Trade			Trade		
1	Merchant	31	14	Merchant	35	18
2	Victualler	13	6	Warehouseman	13	7
3	Warehouseman	12	5	Stationer	10	5
4	Hop Factor	11	5	Grocer / Greengrocer	9	5
5	Grocer / Greengrocer	6	3	Chandler (all types)	8	4
6	Watch / Clock Maker	6	3	Farmer	7	4
7	Bookseller	6	3	Tailor	6	3
8	Boot / Shoemaker	5	2	Victualler	5	3
9	Butcher	5	2	Boot / Shoemaker	5	3
10	Oil / Colourman	5	2	Tobacconist	3	2
Total		100	45		100	53

Source: Sun Fire Policy registers, series 11,936, LGL.
Note: Percentages are rounded up to nearest whole.

trades in common between male and female proprietors. Victualling and grocery were popular in both 1851 and 1861 and stationary and chandlery also made it on to the 1861 list of popular trades for both genders. There were key differences though. Merchants rather than milliner–dressmakers accounted for over 30 per cent of men in the popular trades and 16 per cent of all men's business policies. It is almost as if there was a direct swap between these activities, with the remainder fairly open to proprietors regardless of gender. In addition, whether considering the women identified in business generally or just half that clustered in the most popular trades, it is clear that we need to look beyond the needle to establish a truer picture of Victorian women's enterprises. At mid-century milliners and dressmakers accounted for around 14 per cent of all those women insuring business assets with the Sun Fire. This is significant but less than might be expected based on common assumptions about what businesswomen did, especially when one considers that this is a percentage based on a total sample that has so far excluded those women's policies that did not specifically insure stock, utensils, and fixtures but nonetheless were able to carry on a little enterprise using their private assets such as those involved in school keeping, lodging-house keeping and the business of accommodation (renting out houses). So why has it been so readily assumed that a woman in business would largely be restricted to the needle trades?

The dressmaker and milliner were emotive figures, popular in the contemporary imagination and reform efforts. Often lumped together with less skilled needle workers, they were caught up in an image of distress. This combined powerfully with a discourse of 'needs must' enterprise. Contemporary reformers often perceived few differences between seamstresses who stitched together pre-cut versions of men's shirts and pants, and dressmakers and milliners who designed and crafted individual garments for exacting customers.[27] There was a great deal of moral panic in the 1840s and 1860s over the exploitation of women in the needle trades, based not just on the exceptionally long hours and low wages experienced by many, but also assumptions about the vulnerability and powerlessness of dressmakers as women. What was in actuality a diverse group of trades and employments were represented as a social problem through the body of the 'distressed sempstress', the spirit of which is captured in the 1846 painting by Richard Redgrave *The Sempstress*. He was inspired not by observation but after reading Thomas Hood's celebrated poem *The Song of the Shirt* published in Punch in 1843:

> With fingers weary and worn,
> With eyelids heavy and red,
> A woman sat in unwomanly rags,
> Plying her needle and thread–
> Stitch! Stitch! Stitch!
> In poverty, hunger and dirt,
> And still with a voice of dolorous pitch
> She sang 'The Song of the Shirt.'
>   (T. Hood, *The Song of the Shirt*, 1843).[28]

This imagery was commonplace in early nineteenth-century fiction and drama, embodying the anxieties concerning the position of single women, women's work, and sexuality. Representations of the solitary needlewoman implied 'feminine saintliness and martyrdom', resting on her ability to resist the temptation of the wages of prostitution.[29] For many, the needlewoman personified the 'redundant woman'. However, the needle trades had many levels and the businesswoman milliner is a different creature to the jobbing sempstress.

A further reason why historians have attributed the needle trades a defining role in typologies of women in business is that the traditional sources disproportionately included these women's enterprises and not others. For example, the extensive London Post Office directory for 1851 lists 1,957 women engaged in the popular trades as identified by the Sun Fire registers. Milliners and dressmakers accounted for a much greater proportion of these women in the directory listings than in the insurance records—41 per cent compared to 29 per cent. This suggests that an examination of the trade directories alone would encourage the picture of women in business being chiefly engaged in the needle trades. It is the proportionate involvement of women in millinery and dressmaking, constituting 80 per cent of proprietors listed in the Directory that gives the surface-level impression that this trade of the needle was 'the' business of women. However, while a substantial number of proprietors did make their living in this fashion, many more did not. It is true, however, that retailing businesses related to the needle trades, such as haberdashery, hosiery and the retail clothing trades, were popular avenues for the female proprietor. Nonetheless, in addition to textiles women's business were also widely distributed across the hospitality and retailing trades and did have a presence in production trades outside of these realms too.

Given the legal and ideological restrictions of this period, and coming before the Married Women's Property Act, it is unlikely that men were hidden behind the women of the insurance policy registers.[30] Rather, it

Table 3.8 The Popular Trades of the Fire Insurance Policies as Represented in the London Post Office Directory, 1851 (%).

Trade	Sun Fire	Post Office Directory	Differential	Post Office Directory
	As % of Popular Trades			As % of Listings for Each Trade
Milliner / Dressmaker	29	41	−12	80
Chandler	15	2	13	10
Hosier / Haberdasher	12	5	7	17
Victualler / Coffee House Keeper	17	30	−13	9
Grocer / Greengrocer	9	8	1	7
Clothier	5	1	4	7
Linen Draper	5	2	3	5
Stationer	5	5	0	11
Tobacconist	5	7	2	14

Source: Sun Fire Policy registers, series 11,936, LGL.

is far more likely that more women than those identified here are hidden behind the names of male relatives. This was certainly found to be the case when linking between the policy registers and the Post Office Directory. The latter sometimes listed the business under a male name. There was a much greater imperative to engage in window dressing the business for a directory than for fire insurance, where misrepresentation of proprietorship could be taken as fraud. Also, of course, in linking the policies to the directory listings there is the possibility of time lag or of repeat subscription, neglecting amendment for changing circumstances such as the inheritance of a business.

Also, a surprising finding of this study was the relatively small number of female partnerships. It has been suggested that women could only survive the vagaries of business if they had a male or female partner, yet such partnerships were not commonly found in the Sun Fire policies. Most women insured their business assets with the Sun Fire Office independently, that is as the sole policyholder. This might be taken as a tentative indication that they were sole proprietors. Some 86 per cent were the sole policyholder at mid-century. A further nine per cent had a female only partner, and six per cent had a mixture of partners of either gender or unknown gender. However, even though the proportion of partnerships in 1851/1861 was small, it was double that in 1747/1761. This suggests either that partnerships were becoming more common, or more formalised. Nonetheless, on the whole the Sun Fire registers suggest that in terms of proprietorship women more often operated alone.

One area in which we know from multiple sources that partnerships were not uncommon was school keeping. Women who were enterprising in this way, however, are often hidden by the domestic. Only larger schools are listed in directories and because proprietors often used their personal assets to run their schools their businesses are cloaked in the fire insurance records behind their personal policies. They tended not to provide a separate valuation for stock, utensils and fixtures and to muddy the waters even further, did not always distinguish between the occupational label of the schoolmistress and school keeper. The policies need to be examined very closely to reveal the distinction, often indicated by a note about schoolroom furniture or musical instruments. Frequently these are mentioned but bundled into the valuation of household goods. For example, Mary Ann Bush insured household goods, including school furniture, for £770. A further £120 was put on her musical instruments.[31] Similarly, of the 28 policies taken out by women in this business area in 1851 and 1861, only two describe themselves explicitly as school keepers or owners. Yet on closer inspection of the 'schoolmistress' policies, school related fixtures and fittings are included and 11 policies made specific mention of musical instruments and sheet music, valuing them from as little as £88 up to £150.

The lowest valuation of school fittings and fixtures that can be identified is the policy for £15 belonging to Eleanor Tattersall for her school on Poland Street, near Oxford Street.[32] Perhaps a more common amount for a small school was Clara and Ellen Pykes' policy for £30 on school furniture and fixtures and £80 on musical instruments for the school in Great Prescott Street.[33] However, it must have been difficult even for the proprietors themselves to separate out the assets of the enterprise from their personal belongings. Total values insured ranged between £100 and £1,000, although the inclusion of a dwelling house could take this higher. For example, the Giblet sisters of Greville Place, Kilburn collectively insured their dwelling house for £1,500. Presumably it was substantial in proportions.[34]

Pulling together all these findings, this chapter has revealed that London's women in business were not that dissimilar to many of their male counterparts. Although in terms of overall averages they operated at a lower level of capitalization than did male proprietors. However, the overall average misrepresents the diversity of men's businesses, suggesting the majority were more highly capitalized than women's businesses, whereas there was a much greater degree of overlap than this. Also, it did partly depend on sector but also on the individual entrepreneur, regardless of gender. In addition, at the upper end of the scale women were less well represented because they were less likely to be merchants (and merchant's policies were inflated to allow for peak stock flows). Plus, some women's businesses such as schools or lodging houses were excluded from capitalization estimates because they were hidden behind their domestic assets, reducing overall estimates of businesswomen's capital values. The general tendency for household and business assets to overlap in the smaller, home-run enterprise tends to produce a dampened picture of the businesswoman and makes her appear less capitalized than her male counterparts overall.

All this suggests that more women ran businesses in the nineteenth century than is often recognized even by the fire insurance policies and that estimates of the capitalization of women's ventures are underestimates of the assets they invested and utilized. Ceilings and barriers did exist of course but it is important to recognize that some of these were self-imposed. Ambitions could be modest and business downplayed by the proprietor herself. Furthermore, their enterprises were not restricted to the needle trades and to 'stitch' was not their only option. However, it is the case that the manufacture, sale and laundry of food, drink, textiles and other personal and household accessories figured large in their entrepreneurial endeavours. In this sense, it can be said that women's business ventures in London roughly followed trends in women's work in the capital. According to the census, and not including domestic servants, almost 40 per cent of 'employed' women aged 20 or over in 1851 were persons engaged in 'entertaining, clothing, & performing personal offices for man' ($n = 128,049$).[35] This chapter has also highlighted that sources traditionally relied on to tell us about the makeup of a business community are heavily gendered. Only one-third of all the female insurers of business assets with the Sun Fire in 1851 ($n = 202$) could be located in the London Post Office Directory. The linkage of those women engaged in the popular trades faired only marginally better at 35 per cent. This low linkage rate will partly be due to the frequency with which people moved in this time period, especially in urban areas. However, it is also likely that many women's businesses simply did not make it into the trade directories, either because they were too small, too local, too new or perhaps, as with many men's businesses, they were too short lived. Not only do traditional sources under-represent the true level of economic agency of Victorian women, they present us with a skewed picture that leans heavily towards the needle trades.

However, the Sun Fire registers, like the extensive London Post Office Directory, cannot give us an accurate measure of the number of women engaged in business in nineteenth century London. The directories under-estimate because they do not include smaller concerns, those relying on local trade and word of mouth. It is also difficult to identify in them even the full number of women they do include because of the tendency to list partnerships in surname only. The Sun Fire records have their shortcomings too. Barnet has indicated that in the 1820s the insurance records suggest that the proportion of businesses run by women was not less than 7 per cent, with a further 1 per cent operating as co-proprietors.[36] However this estimate does not include the enterprises women carried on using only the private assets they had at their disposal, or hiding behind them. Such women had little advantage in declaring on their policies how effectively they were utilising their assets, as this may have resulted in higher insurance premiums. This suggests the estimate should be higher, although probably not exceeding 10 per cent.

This proportion is not insignificant, especially for a period in history for which it has been argued that women were pushed out of business and into the home. It also suggests that rather than dramatically declining, that women's involvement in business may have actually been fairly static from the late seventeenth century through to the mid-nineteenth. Women could still operate as merchants, manufacturers or in the genteel trades, but the majority were retailers of some description. Although in terms of overall capitalization their contribution was in relative decline, they continued to take up the role of proprietor and did so across a range of sectors and at a level of capitalization similar to many male proprietors. Indeed comparing their businesses with those of men, suggests that in addition to the influence of gender, we should allow for different types of historical entrepreneurship that may not always be gender specific. In this sense, the women studied here reflect the continuation of a distinct type of entrepreneurship—one characterized by self-employment or small business. This endured into the nineteenth century, despite the emergence of much larger, more intensively capitalized, less personal, forms of business entrepreneurship.

Many of the female, and some of the male, proprietors found in this study were survivalist entrepreneurs (at least their capitalization suggests this), others were more comfortable although still small. This type of small-scale, personal entrepreneurship is as much (if not more) about an independent livelihood than it is about capital accumulation, size or profit chasing. Many of these women (and men) may have only reluctantly thought of themselves as people of business and seen little in common with the big players, preferring to identify with their craft, service and personal reputation. Using other sources such as trade cards and record linkage with the census, we can now build upon this empirical foundation by considering how female proprietors presented themselves and their businesses externally to others and how their homes and households were an integral part of their very personal ventures.

4   Retailing Respectability

According to the fire insurance evidence, women in business in London were engaged in diverse enterprises but heavily, if not predominantly, involved in selling. Their ventures spanned a broad range of activities from food provision to clothing, to retailing all description of goods and services. We can now turn to other sources to learn more about how women positioned and marketed their businesses and by extension themselves. This chapter uses trade cards to explore the varied nature of their ventures in selling and also considers the nature, purpose and motivation behind this form of business communication.

The trade card was a very popular form of business promotion in this period, before a reduction in prices in the second half of the nineteenth century made newspaper advertising more accessible (for those businesses whose nature required advertising across a wider region). Classified newspaper advertising at mid-century does reveal some female business proprietors but these hardly leap from the page and instead where women are concerned the governess and lodging requests dominate. In the case of London, as with trade directories, the examples of female proprietors communicating with their public in newspapers are valuable but also create a narrative that is skewed toward those successful in the needle trades and larger establishments. An example of just such an establishment is that of Myra's Dress and Pattern Depot, a large establishment on Bedford Street in Covent Garden stocking everything from ball dresses to children's aprons.[1] Newspapers also carry interesting examples of correspondence-based businesses:

> Madame Valery's Neolin Hair Wash, for infallibly Restoring Gray Hair to its Natural colour in two or three weeks. In proof, Madame V. requires no payment until successful in those cases treated by herself. In bottles, 7s.6d.; packed for the country, 8s.6d. See Madame Valery's 'Treatise on the Hair', post free, 1s.—40, Wigmore-street, Cavendish-square, W.[2]

Goodness knows what colour of hair the purchaser really ended up with. Clearly not all female proprietors were as honourable as the dressmaker at the start of this book. A lady who professed to value the responsibility her trade allowed her, providing her with the opportunity to 'avoid inducing a wife to adopt a fashion that is foolish and will displease her husband, or one that is expensive, and which I know she cannot afford'.[3]

Walsh argues that newspaper advertising had very little importance for the sale of domestic products in London, despite the increase in newspaper circulation and general advertising therein from the eighteenth century. It was the shop that was the point of information and persuasion. The proprietor used trade cards, hand bills, façade and reputation to bring the customer to the premises. At this point they would begin marketing specific wares rather than the shop itself. In this sense it was the shop and proprietor that was branded rather than the goods provided.[4] Although the branding of products became more popular over time, the reputation of the proprietor remained the key well into the nineteenth century.

Similarly, in their comparison of English and French trade cards, Berg and Clifford found that they had a wider impact both in terms of the wider range of trades represented and the complexity of the messages conveyed. Newspaper advertising was only a small part of the wider world of commercial promotion and after the eighteenth century rarely carried images due to the cost of space. Trade cards in contrast combined image with text and used the tool of visual seductiveness. They were not a form of mass advertising but rather represented a form of closely targeted advertising. Sometimes given after a sale or as part of a bill, they were used to reinforce messages about the shop and to encourage repeat custom. Also, distributed in the local area, they focussed tightly on the target audience. Passed on to friends and family, they had a cumulative impact, disseminating knowledge about the shop, its image, reputation and wares from existing to potential customers.[5] In this sense, trade cards were integral to the consumption network, communicating an early notion of brand value and group membership.

Nonetheless, despite these advantages, it should be acknowledged that the surviving 'collected' examples are still themselves limited, tending to hail largely from the turn of the century up to the middle years, with examples thereafter very rarely collected. Those examined for this study are drawn from the Banks, Heal, Guildhall and John Johnson collections. The latter were collected by chance rather than design but the Sarah Banks and Ambrose Heal collections were constructed on aesthetic principles. Some are dated and others have been approximately dated by the collector or archivist based on contextual detail such as the form of address, style of decoration and so on. Of course these dates are tentative and in any regard are snap shots both in the life of a trade card that could be circulated and recycled over longer periods and also for a business that could have a long duration. In many ways, the more successful the trade card, the more successful the business. Trade cards were an expense and are not related to the disposable flyers thrust at the passerby on today's streets. They were given out very selectively and some historians have likened them to souvenirs or gifts of the shopping experience.[6]

Originally paper, printed from plates engraved by local craftsmen, on a practical level the trade card served as an aide-memoir for customers, an invoice, a receipt form and often a price list.[7] Furthermore, when a proprietor invoiced a customer, it was common practice to include a copy of the trade card on the billhead. This printed-paper version of the trade card was an all-purpose jotter, bearing the proprietors name and address—or before the introduction of street numbering, a long-winded indication of where he or she was to be found. The paper later became a card, and the term *trade card* came into being. The earliest trade cards were printed by letterpress from type but the introduction of commercial engraving, and later lithography, allowed almost unlimited pictorial and decorative treatments. Hogarth, Bartolozzi and Bewick were among the great names that accepted commissions to work on trade cards. However, the decorative conventions adopted by trade engravers became more or less standardised. As with the stock block of the letterpress printer, stock images appeared, copied from one to another.[8] With advances in printing and literacy, single sheet posters or bills, also referred to as broadsides, also became an extremely common form of advertising.[9]

Trade cards and billheads varied enormously in their level of illustration and detail depending on the nature of the trade, the target clientele and the coffers of the proprietor. In addition, they frequently utilised textual description to communicate the proprietor's good standing, their good connection, the quality of their stock, the extent of their skill, breadth of their experience, and crucially the respectability of their clientele. Sometimes this was in the form of poetry:

Female
Reform Bill
Ladies
If you wish to *buy*,
Cheaper than ever, go and try,
Babb's (High Holborn).
That's the place,
To suit your *Purse*, and Charm your *Face*.
The Largest Stock in London's there,
The Newest Patterns, *rich* and *rare*.
Bonnets.
Tuscans, Dunstables, Silks and Straws.
Caps.
Lace, Tulle, Blond, Appliqué, and Gauze;
Habit shirts, Collars, Canzoves, Capes
Of every kind, and various shapes,
In English style, all British made,

As patronised by
Queen Adelaide.
An endless choice will there be found.
One shilling each, and some *One Pound*.
Then thither hasten, in a trice,
for now they sell at *Wholesale Price*.
Now *ladies*! *now*—your *attention fix*.
For Babb's 296,
HIGH HOLBORN.
Dealers and Milliners supplied on the very Lowest Terms.[10]

This mode of advertising was more common than newspaper advertisements due to the heavy duties imposed on newspapers and the extra charge for advertisements. Indeed, until the repeal of the stamp duty in 1855, few people purchased newspapers for themselves. As Sampson states,

> . . . many news vendors' chief duty was to lend *The Times* out for a penny per hour, while a second or third day's newspaper was considered quite a luxury by those whom business or habit compelled to stay at home, and therefore who were unable to glance over the news—generally while some impatient person was scowling waiting his turn—at the tavern, bar or coffee-house.[11]

Furthermore, such taxes acted as a considerable check to the number of notices appearing in the press. In addition, a very heavy tax was charged upon every notice published in a purchasable paper. According to Sampson, until 1833 this was no less than 3s and 6d upon each advertisement, irrespective of length, content or subject matter. The total abolition of this advertisement duty did not take place until 1853.[12] Hence, it was not until the second half of the nineteenth century that circulation of the penny paper took off and advertising therein became a major mode of promotion. Accordingly, the newspaper advertisement, until this time, was an accessible means of business promotion only for the most established of proprietors.

Even a cursory glance at the lists of surviving trade cards held in the British Museum; Guildhall Library, Corporation of London; and the Bodleian Library, Oxford reveals the variety in scale and scope of metropolitan women's enterprises. The prevalence of trade cards for women engaged in the more popular trades identified by the insurance records (see Chapter 3), supports the notion that there was some clustering. Nonetheless, the great variety in content and style of their trade cards reveals not only differences in the taste of the female proprietors but also in the messages they chose to convey to the marketplace.

Turning first to women engaged in dressmaking, millinery and the clothing trades generally, it is not difficult to find examples. However, it is important to recognize that the needle trades had many levels. High-class dressmaking and millinery offered skilled work and business opportunities to women from professional, clerical or trading families. Unlike seamstresses who stitched but did not cut, dressmakers fashioned gowns to suit the 'sartorial and psychological needs' of individual patrons. In a period when the fit of a garment, as opposed to merely its fabric or trimmings, distinguished the aspirational woman from the 'puckered, gaping, baggy masses', the skill of the dressmaker was paramount. They were designers as well as craftswomen, charged with transforming a variety of raw materials (straw, wire, silk and so on) into a number of different shapes and arranging numerous trimmings in pleasing combinations.[13] *The Young Tradesman* advised,

> The Dress-Maker must be an expert anatomist; and must, if judiciously chosen, have a name of French [de]termination; she must know how to hide all defects in the proportions of the body, and must be able to mould the shape of stays that, while she corrects the body, she may not interfere with the pleasures of the palate.[14]

Not all proprietors went so far as to take up a French name but the successful dressmaker did require many skills, including not only talent but also tact, as customers frequently expected more from a dress than it was capable of giving.[15] However, milliners and dressmakers needed not only to be skilled but also to be able to keep up with the ever-changing, often ridiculed fashions.[16] Figure 4:1 is an anonymous cartoon etching from 1828 entitled *Hurrah for the Bonnets So Big*. The commentary beneath reads,

> It having been represented to the City Authorities that Temple Bar was not wide enough for the Ladies Bonnets to pass through with convenience to the fair sex; the Court of Common Gown-sellers ordered the side arches to be widened to six feet four, but they are still too narrow, & the Ladies are obliged at the imminent danger of their lives to pass through the Centre Arch intended for carriages only.[17]

Ultimately, however, it is important to recognise that dressmakers and milliners were not merely responding to the fancies of their customers. They themselves played an active part in the ever-changing fashion cycle, in doing so ensuring a demand for their services. As *The Young Tradesman* wrote in 1839:

> Dress is a thing subject to almost daily fluctuation, so that a history of the ladies' dresses in England, for merely half a dozen years, would furnish matter for a bulky volume; we shall therefore not attempt it, but merely observe that the best, and, perhaps, the only excuse for such continual change in the empire of dress, is the opportunity which that

change offers of employment to those persons who would otherwise have no immediate claim upon the rich and opulent; and thus, what would be retained in their coffers, is now scattered in a variety of ways amongst the community in the purchase of luxurious dress, and in the alterations which fashion is continually introducing.[18]

Many milliners and dressmakers were aspiring woman. Engaging in a trade with perceived prospects, they were far less likely to have been motivated by a calamity such as widowhood. Rather, requiring a lengthy four to five year apprenticeship, these trades provided a strategy for survival and independence from a young working age. A good business head was essential for success, and even at mid-century the more enterprising of them kept a woman agent in Paris who had 'nothing else to do but watch the Motions of the Fashions, and procure Intelligence of their Changes; which she signifies to her Principles.' Many London milliners also made trips to Paris themselves.[19]

Hence, the conditions of business and prospects for these women varied across the needle trades. Even within the niches there existed a range of experiences. Women could also turn to the retail drapery trade, which also picked up the expanding business in ready-made items. The trade card collections reveal that such female proprietors were numerous. A particularly elaborate design is found on that of Cheapside linen draper, Hannah Dore. However, women like Hannah had to withstand fierce competition

Figure 4.1 Hurrah for the Bonnets So Big.

from the substantial draperies, which would eventually become the early department stores. One method of promotion was window dressing. This was essential for drapers and many clothing and textile trades, especially for those establishments aiming for a better class of customer. As one draper recalled,

> We used to be very lavish with our goods in window dressing. As for example, delicate goods, such as white or pink silks, which ought to have been kept inviolably fresh and nice, were often strung up for the sake of effect, resulting in creasing, and putting out of condition goods that afterwards needed 'tingeing' of another description before they could get sold.[20]

Similarly, *The Young Tradesman; or, Book of English Trades* proclaimed,

> We believe there is no trade in England, in which more efforts are made to captivate the public, and more especially the ladies, by a display of goods; and in London this display is carried to a most costly and sumptuous extent. In most of the principal streets of the metropolis, shawls, muslins, pieces for ladies' dresses, and a variety of other goods, are shown with the assistance of mirrors, and at night by chandeliers, aided by the brilliancy which gaslights afford in a way almost dazzling to a stranger, as many of those poetical fictions of which we read in the Arabian nights' entertainment.[21]

The shop front could be used to proclaim financial security and good taste, and became a focus of attention for retailers not just of drapery, linen and textile goods but all sorts of different wares.[22]

Drapery and other substantial shops were often open till late at night and the lamp lit shopping thoroughfares were the marvel of many a tourist. One such traveller by the name of Lichtenberg described the view from Cheapside to Fleet Street: On both sides, tall houses with plate-glass windows. The lower floors consist of shops and 'seem to be made entirely of glass'. The light of thousands of candles sparkled on 'the silverware, engravings, books, clocks, glass, pewter, paintings, women's finery, modish and otherwise, gold, precious stones, steel-work, end endless coffee-rooms and lottery offices'. The street looks as though it were illuminated for some festivity, they remarked, 'with gay-coloured spirits; the confectioners dazzle your eyes with the candelabra and tickle your nose'.[23]

The installation of glazed windows allowed the permanent display of goods and enticed the customer into the seclusion offered inside the shop from the noise and bustle of the street. Once inside, the glazed window also enabled the shopkeeper to sell to a captive audience. This captive audience enabled London's drapers to transact so much daily business 'as almost to exceed belief'.[24] Of course many drapers shops were not the

Figure 4.2 Trade card of Hannah Dove.

grand establishments found along Oxford Street and other major thoroughfares. Nonetheless, the importance of window dressing, glazing and a plentiful stock meant that this trade could be costly to operate in.[25]

In contrast, haberdashery often attracted shoppers with a smaller purse than those who entered into the emporium of the draper. When an aspiring mid-nineteenth-century draper opened a haberdashery section in his shop, he soon became concerned about the effects on the gentility of his establishment. He wrote that there was a rather embarrassing drawback to this branch of trade. 'My object was to cultivate the trade generally, that we should do the best class possible; but as many of our new customers were of a ragged and dirty appearance, the shop, when several of this class of persons were in it, presented the appearance of one where the very lowest trade was carried on', he lamented.[26]

Yet for women, haberdashery remained a not un-genteel trade and often provided a respectable front to a much broader business. Pinchbeck noted from her survey of advertisements and trade directories that notices were common from haberdashers, who traded in stuffs and drugs as well as small wares, silk mercers, woollen and linen drapers.[27] Hosiery items also found their way into haberdashers.[28] Hosiers dealt in stockings, braces, belts, purses, watch chins, waistcoats, drawers and petticoats and sometimes combined with hatters and gloves. For example, the businesses promoted by the trade cards of Elizabeth Dent and Mary Rippon[29] and the rather elaborate trade card of Ann James a Soho based 'Hosier, Haberdasher and Worsted Maker'.

Although the illustration on Ann's trade card was probably not a limited edition but rather one chosen from a selection at a printers; it will nonetheless have been picked to convey a visual message about the type of establishment she saw herself as running—extensive and substantial. Indeed, she offers both wholesale and retail services and alludes to a broad stock. However, the business of pins, ribbons, threads and hosiery could also be carried on at a smaller scale along the minor streets, were rents, rooms and shops were cheaper, and was therefore not restricted to the major thoroughfares. The materials were familiar to every woman and if she chose not to engage in wholesale herself, she could restrict her sales to an essentially, although not totally, female economy.

As the nineteenth century progressed haberdashers and hosiers, like the milliners, dressmakers and drapers, also increasingly stocked ready-made items of clothing, although their main function was to provide materials for the home production of clothing, for the clothing and footwear production trades, and for household furnishings. And for some, the business of fancy dress or masquerade clothing provision was a viable venture, particularly during the Season. For example, Anne Dawson of Pall Mall combined millinery with fancy dress provision and counted Her Royal Highness the Princess of Wales amongst her clientele. Based on Pall Mall, two of her receipts have survived, one for £5 6s 6d and another for £9 2s 8d, both substantial

sums for party ware.[30] It would seem that the trade for specialist clothing was plentiful enough to support entire establishments devoted to this
demand alone. The trade card of Mrs Sowden of 8 Gerrard Street, Soho,
reveals that the partygoer could there delight in the choice of the 'most
farcical, comical, droll unaccountable, inimitable and irresistible MASKS
by the REAL MAKER, a stock which she had only recently replenished'.
Her shop, Opera House Masquerade, claimed to entice even the nobility
and gentry with its breadth of costumes, shepherd's crooks, flower baskets,
forks, rakes, hat feathers and promotional poetry:

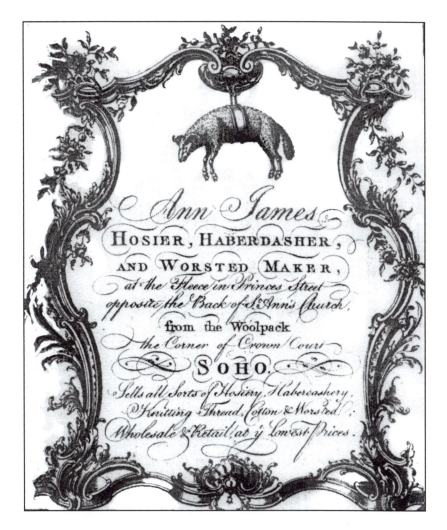

Figure 4.3 Trade card of Ann James.

Come ye Sons of glee and Fun,
See all other Shops out done;
Fie for Shame why must we press ye,
To come to such a Shop to dress ye
The Charge is small which must entice,
You'll ne'er complain of Sowden's Price.[31]

In its early days the ready-made trade and the women in it sometimes found themselves the object of ridicule. Yet in reality these businesses had to be robust enough to survive the fluctuations in demand in the London market-place caused by the season. Those based in the West End were particularly affected.

Textiles and clothing were not the only trades that London women operated in or that were influenced by the season. Women were also, as the rhyme goes, butchers, bakers and candlestick makers. Figure 4.4 is an example of the latter. It is the trade card of Sarah Hind, a 'Wax, Spermaceti & Tallow Chandler'. In addition, the preparation of food for sale was also a popular activity. Pastry cooks, confectioners and a great variety of other food related activities made their way into the insurance records and can be found in the trade card collections. The strong association of women with domestic victuals provision secured them a commercial niche doing the same things for sale.[32] Pinchbeck suggested that the grocery and provision trades were businesses that women could manage perhaps more easily than others.[33] No doubt many ventures of this kind were small scale, targeting a very local clientele. Nonetheless, examples of the more ambitious proprietor can be found. For example, cook and confectioner, Elizabeth Debatt. whose trade card provided an extensive list of her production range: 'Soups, French Pies, Made Dishes, Savoury Patties, Jellies, Blancmanges . . . NB. Dinners & Turtles Dress'd at Home & ABROAD. Ice Creams, Soups sent out. Routs & Ball Suppers Served up in the Greatest Perfection.'[34] Her repertoire was extensive and no doubt so too was her client list. In addition, although primarily a retailer, they did retain some processing responsibilities—blending, sorting, and cleaning—and as dealers in bulk, in addition to breaking down consignments of products for their own shop or branch of shops, many grocers also acted as wholesalers for other shops.

Until the mid-nineteenth century because many of their goods were imported, the customers of grocers tended to be restricted to the middling and higher income groups, making this a particularly attractive trade to the more class conscious proprietor. Tea, coffee, sugar and cocoa were luxury goods, only gaining a foothold in the basic diet as the nineteenth century progressed, when tea and sugar in particular began to form an important part of the urban diet of all classes. The grocers' primary stock consisted of spices, dried fruits and condiments.[35] From the mid-nineteenth century, sweetened tea became the main form of liquid refreshment, altering the clientele of the grocer. In addition, the second half of the nineteenth century brought mass production and semi-processing of common foodstuffs. Furthermore, this also brought competition from the plethora of general shopkeepers who could then stock packages of tea and other products.[36] Blackman writes that all sorts of shopkeepers took on some of the grocer's lines. Shopkeepers took advantage of the almost daily sales they could make of some items, particularly sugar and tea. Furthermore, the advent of blended and packaged teas enabled many shopkeepers, large and small, to stock one or two types or brands of tea without having themselves to be a specialist in tea blending and carry large stocks of several teas.[37]

In London, as demand increased, some women also opted to specialise in the retailing of particular grocery products. It was most common to specialise in tea and coffee and Figure 4.5 is the trade card of Helena Noble, a 'Tea Dealer and Grocer'. Based at 209 High Holborn, her business, probably inherited from her late husband William Noble, was in a prime location. A major thoroughfare like this must have meant significant passing trade in addition to her regular customers. Similarly, chocolate had always had an exclusive market and women often inhabited this niche of specialist retailers. An example of this is the 1812 trade card of Madame Rose promoting her chocolate, cocoa and coffee retail business.[38] Different specialisms such as these were regarded as conferring different levels of gentility. Pinchbeck noticed that the tea shop or tea warehouse, where coffee, chocolate and sugar were frequently sold as well, was also a business much favoured by women, 'since it was not only lucrative, but was the most "genteel" of all the provision trades. Even haberdashers and milliners advertised "fresh Teas of the highest Flavour"'.[39] However, from a practical point of view, the range

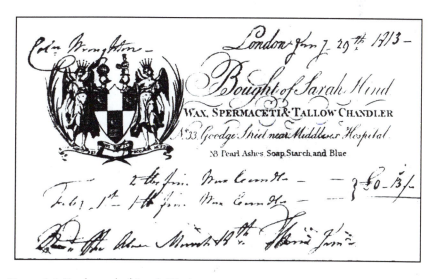

Figure 4.4 Trade card of Sarah Hind.

of goods grocers or specialist dealers carried probably largely depended on the location of their premises. On the major thoroughfares there was sufficient trade and variety of custom to permit a grocer to specialise, and thereby attract a particular type of customer.

Grocers also increasingly stocked other provisions such as dairy products and Italian warehouse goods (sago, gelatines, tapioca, macaroni, vermicelli). Some retailers redefined themselves as 'grocer and provisions dealers'. In addition, grocers in quieter areas, serving a local clientele, tended to stock a wide range of wares and other items such as soaps, candles and lamp oil. In this way, grocers shared in the household goods market also inhabited by tallow chandlers, oil and colourmen, chemists, ironmongers and hardware sellers. Indeed, in the second half of the nineteenth century, these broader suppliers would eventually eclipse the rigidly specialised grocer's shop.[40] Tobacco retailers also crossed over into this market as well. For example, Elizabeth Gallaway sold tobacco and snuff followed by 'perfumery; turnery; candles; soap; starch; blue &c. on the most reasonable terms.'[41] Women could also make their way in the wholesale end of the tobacco trade and even pipe making. Mary Bourguignon and her son operated as wholesale tobacconists and snuff makers from their King Street warehouse. Sarah Greenland promoted brotherly love on her trade card promoting her tobacco pipe making business. Her workshop, located at number 60 Lower East Smith Field, even manufactured pipes for exportation.

Most female grocers and provision dealers undoubtedly made a living, although securing a place in the better class of market no doubt required good service, reputation and capital investment in the premises. By the turn of the century, plate glass for windows was available in panes of up to two feet high. However, particularly for smaller general grocers and provisions dealers, selling through the un-glazed window, allowing direct contact with the customer on the street may have been an effective mechanism that they were reluctant to abandon. Certain trades chose not to enclose well into the century, despite the fact that the technology of glass manufacture had put panes of glass within the reach of the most humble shopkeepers.[42]

At the lowest end of the provision trade was the chandler, regarded as dealing with the lowest order of customer. There were many examples of female chandlers, or petty general shopkeepers, in the insurance registers (see Chapter 3). However, dealing mainly in a very local trade many will not have needed trade cards. Very little capital was needed to set up in this end of the provisions trade. Schwarz cites the case of John O'Neill, an Irish born shoemaker who had saved £10 and used it to buy a chandler's shop in 1842. O'Neill recalled that 'we soon found out that a chandler's shop was no sinecure; but a comfortless drudgery, where one is obliged to be servant and liable to the abuse of the most degraded'. Furthermore, he noted, ' . . . the profits, if articles are honestly sold to your customers, are so small, and in some cases, are actual losses, that there is not a living to be got at it'. He added a note of caution: 'while the keeping of the chandler's shop is marked

Figure 4.5 Trade card of Mary Bourguignon & Son.

Figure 4.6 Trade card of Sarah Greenland.

out as fair game for all the swindlers in the neighbourhood. If he refuses to give credit, the shop is avoided, as if marked with a plague spot . . . .'[43]

Selling to your customers for cash alone was for many retailers nearly impossible but the offer of credit did also have real advantages. It not only facilitated sales; it also helped to create a bond between buyer and seller, tying the one to the other. On a more mundane level, it enabled the trader to hold a smaller reserve of cash in the shop.[44] The dangers of extended or indiscriminate credit were widely recognised but most trade manuals and journals nonetheless openly recommended its adoption. Credit had obvious advantages for the customer. Indeed the possession of a 'book' among the middle classes, the amount of credit allowed and the ease with which it was obtained became status symbols in their own right. To be denied credit was one of the worst blows that could be inflicted upon a respectable, and by implication thrifty and independent, successful middle-class family. To be refused was viewed as a slur on their character. Credit worthiness implied financial soundness and moral probity.[45]

Another trade that was less than genteel was that of the laundry keeper. The laundry industry was an important part of the nineteenth-century shift in the economy toward services. A great many Victorian families with more pretensions than money had inadequate space, staff, and facilities to do much washing at home. Even such a careful housekeeper as Eliza Warren, whose 1867 publication *How I Managed My House on Two Hundred Pounds a Year* was the domestic bible of many middle-class women, budgeted 10 pounds a year for washing.[46] Cramped urban dwellings—often tiny single rooms in the case of the growing numbers of single women working and living on their own—made washing at home very difficult and consequently increased the work of professional laundresses. The demand for laundry work was particularly heavy in London, and stemmed from the high concentration in the metropolis of wealthy households, lodgers, and large institutions such as government offices, hotels and shipping lines.[47]

The work of a laundress could be carried on across a lifetime. The necessary skills were widespread and the necessary equipment was basic and easily acquired. As Simonton has written, laundry offers a caricature of women's domestic work. She adds, 'The notion of moral worth tied up with clean, white laundry helps to explain the persistence of women's association with their laundry and the way it acted as a form of display.'[48] It is only a short step from this to women's work in commercial laundry. For this reason the provision of laundry services was a trade often turned to in times of adversity. Indeed, contributing to the purchase of an item of laundry equipment, such as a mangle, was one of the neighbourly strategies employed to help a widow support herself and her children.

Small workshop laundries, often called hand laundries even though many used some small machinery, predominated throughout central London.[49] The provision of laundry services was dominated by married women and widows and was one of the only trades in which women dominated in which spinsters were a minority. Malcolmson undertook an examination of the 1861 census enumerators' books for three London communities in which laundry work was the most important female occupation—the Potteries, and Jennings Buildings in Kensington, and Kensal New Town, a detached portion of Chelsea.[50] She found that between 51.1 per cent and 61.4 per cent of all laundresses were married women.[51] Especially when performed as homework, laundry services could be fitted around domestic responsibilities. The income could supplement and sometimes sustain a family and was an obvious choice for widows with children. Setting-up was not costly as an old mangle could be purchased for about a pound and the labour of family members including children could be utilised.[52]

However, if a woman ran her own laundry business, a good business head was as important as a good ironing technique if a profit was to be realised. Assertive debt collection was a reality to be faced. One daughter of a laundress described how, when they got to the door of their client, Mrs Moody in Thames Street: 'We wedged our feet in the front door lest it be shut in our faces without the washing money; and our emotions were divided between the agonizing uncertainty of Mrs. Moody's finances and the inexpressible relief of the day behind us'.[53] Daughters and occasionally other female relatives were a great asset to self-employed laundresses. Many mother-and-daughter teams worked until midnight or even all through the night during the busy season. In addition, children could help in washing, mangling and ironing, with the youngest members of the household sorting and packaging bundles of clothes, fetching and carrying.[54] Nonetheless, aspects of this trade required great skill, especially ironing.

An ironer needed to have the ability to gauge the correct temperature for pressing a particular fabric, the skill to avoid scorching the garment, the attentiveness to avoid soiling the clothes with soot and starch residue, and the strength to polish garments to the required gloss.[55] An assortment of irons was an important investment. Flatirons came in many sizes and designs, from tiny crimping and finishing irons for finishing intricate garments to large weighty goose irons for the heaviest fabrics. They all needed to be constantly reheated. Flatirons were propped up against the fire on a metal stand suspended from the firebars, or by being placed face down upon a stove. In the late nineteenth century many laundries and independent laundresses installed specially constructed iron stoves, which heated irons without making them dirty.[56] Not only did ironing require skill and dexterity, so broad was the know-how needed in all aspects of the trade that in 1817 S. Christopher penned a guide—*Cleaning and scouring. A Manual for dyers and laundresses, and for domestic use*—providing detailed instructions and clearly distinguishing between the English and French method.[57]

Throughout the Victorian period washers in full-time work earned 2s. to 2s. 6d. per day. Ironers, who were generally pieceworkers, earned from 3s. to 3s. and 6d. However, in all types of laundry work, individual earnings could vary widely, and where work was paid by the piece, a premium was placed on youth, strength, quickness and dexterity. Occasionally keeping a small laundry could be relatively lucrative, earning enough to avoid working on the Sunday, or even enough to employ another woman.[58] Pinchbeck, reminded her readers of Mitford's novel, *Our Village*, in which the most prosperous pair in the village were a farmer and his wife, a laundress, 'with twenty times more work than she can do, unrivalled in flounces and shirt frills, and such delicacies of the craft.'[59] However, the work was hard and permeated domestic life in such a way as to make a mockery of the Victorian preference for the separation of home and work space:

> The week began with the obnoxious, stale smell of many families' dirty laundry—the piles of clothes providing temporary messy playhouses for the youngest children. There soon followed the smell of soap, bleach, bluing, and starch mingled with steam, puddles of soapy water interspersed with unsteady islands of loose bricks or old mats, and the high temperatures—often reaching ninety degrees Fahrenheit and converting the family kitchen into a Turkish bath. Dripping clothes democratically dampened the heads and shoulders of all. Later in the week the heated atmosphere shifted to the parlor-ironing room where the coke or gas stove used to heat the irons maintained the temperature and added noxious fumes, fumes confined indoors by the closed windows that guarded against the laundress's enemy—the so-called London smuts. The thonk of heavy wooden box mangle, the hiss of irons, the thwack of the dolly, the slosh of washing, the quiet swish of linen on washboards and of scrubbing brushes on heavy fabrics, the splash of seeming oceans of water, mingled with muttered curses—these were the lullabies of the laundrywoman's child.[60]

Even towards the end of the nineteenth century, laundering services were influenced by domestic folklore, even in commercial premises. Laundry had to be washed early in the week. To wash on Monday was to be virtuous but she 'who washes on Friday is half a slut; Who that wash on Saturday is a slut to the bone', wrote the *Laundry Record* in a poem it printed called 'The Right Day for Washing'. Even the offer of cheaper rates by laundry keepers would not induce the public to depart from this ancient custom. Almost everywhere, the early part of the week was occupied with the collection, sorting, marking, soaking, washing, mangling, blueing, and starching of laundry, while the later part of the week was devoted to ironing, airing, folding, packing, and, finally, delivering the finished product.[61]

Of course, only extreme adversity would drive a woman of above the lowest levels of the middling classes, even a daughter of trade, into this avenue of income generation, unless the work could be carried out by employees, such as was the case with Mr and Mrs Nicholson's Thames Bank Laundry in Chelsea. A self-proclaimed 'extensive and superior laundry', the Thames Bank offered customer references to attest to its quality of service. If its picture is anything to go by, the Nicholson's must have employed a significant number of women, probably engaged about specialised tasks.

Another service women offered was the provision of food, drink and hospitality in the form of inns, taverns, public houses, coffee houses and bath houses (bagnios)—a business area with a strong retail component. The atmosphere and character provided in the establishment was as important to the customer as the products available for their consumption. Occasionally the proprietor was also a producer and brewed their own beer, although this was increasingly taken over by larger breweries. Food production did however remain on the premises. In the eighteenth century, the keeping of inns and alehouses was considered a very proper and suitable business for women and partnerships with husbands were common. For example, at the end of the century, Joseph Ashford and his wife Jane ran the City Arms at 1 Lombard Street—a business they had inherited from Jane's widowed mother. Mary Ann, their daughter, writes,

> My grandmother left a will, and bequeathed all she had to her only surviving daughter: the executor was a Mr. Tyce, a tobacconist, of Exchange Alley: and it was my grandmother's desire that the business should be given up, and everything sold, and the money placed to what she had in the bank; and her daughter to be put to some genteel business. But as the house was in full trade, and selling the goodwill had not then become a practice. Mr. Tyce did not trouble himself about it.[62]

Figure 4.7 Trade card of Mr and Mrs Nicholson's Thames Bank Laundry.

But women could also maintain their independence by operating as a licensed victualler. For example, the 1795 trade card of Mary Warner, the proprietor of the *One Castle* in Highgate.[63] Pinchbeck noted that eighteenth-century lists of licencees showed how large was the proportion of inns managed by women, and these appear to have included all types, from the small village alehouse to the busy hostelries which supplied the needs of travellers and accommodated numerous passengers by stage coach.[64] Thus Deborah Gooding ran the Chelmsford Machine fly on the lucrative Essex to London route in 1790. The run terminated at the Bull, Aldgate, also run by a widow, 'the all powerful Ann Nelson who had found means of making her name known on almost every road out of London'.[65]

However, inns were becoming less respectable and increasingly stratified by rank and status, seriously constraining women's activities and creating a dilemma for those who owned and managed them. Similarly, the arrival of the railways diminished business, while remaining livery stables became more closely associated with the 'masculine monopoly of horse culture'.[66] By 1800, more and more public houses were being bought up by breweries turning the publican into a retailer. The usual consequence of the larger scale, more rationalized, centralized marketing which followed, write Davidoff and Hall, produced the crop of male managers, clerks and agents, under whose authority many public houses were run.[67] However, the London breweries, according to Girouard, did not start buying up pubs in large numbers until the 1880s and 1890s. Until then, most publicans held their pubs on long leases from non-brewing ground landlords and quite a few freeholders. Brewery-owned pubs were usually leased to tenants on 20- or 30-year leases. The system of installing managers rather than tenants was until the 1880s still rarely used by the brewers, although common enough with the publicans who owned more than one pub themselves.[68]

Legislation of the 1830s creating a category of unlicensed beer shops provided opportunities for women but at the lowest end of a trade that was increasingly being differentiated by the social rank of its clientele. By the 1850s, public drinking places had become specialized and stratified by class, rendering public houses 'anathema to genteel or even respectable femininity'.[69] On the other hand, the possibility of renting premises from another landlord or brewery meant that inns and public houses could be taken up without much capital. Davidoff and Hall add that undoubtedly this option remained an important part of the lower middle-class service trades in particular where women were employed as family members. Indeed, they add, women might be deliberately sought as employees in their capacity to provide a home-like atmosphere and control disorderly behaviour.[70]

Coffee houses, which played a large part in London's social life, also had their share of female proprietors. Although still in evidence in the nineteenth century, these were a more common feature of eighteenth-century London. Lillywhite has revealed that widow coffee-house proprietors were commonplace and their establishments frequently bore their marital status. For example, *Widow Turnbull's Coffee House* on Red Lion street, *The Widow's Coffee House* on Devereux Court, and *Widow Prat's Coffee House* in 'Cat-Eaton' Street.[71] Spinsters and married women also operated in the coffee-house trade. Mrs Needham was based on London Bridge and in 1790, Mrs Hudson kept a coffee house in Covent Garden.[72] Sometimes alongside food and beverages, rooms were also available. Rose Clinch proprietor of the *Spread Eagle Tavern and Coffee House* on the Strand, also promoted her 'genteel accommodations' for gentlemen and families.[73] Similarly, *Goodwin's Coffee House*, on Water Lane by the Custom House, was run by Jane Goodwin, whose trade card informs the reader that she has 'spared no expense to have the best accommodations with a Stock of the best Wines, Brandy, Rum and neat as can be imported Wholesale & Retail. Dinners every day on the most Reasonable Terms.'[74]

At the lower end of this trade were the coffee stalls. Mayhew estimated that there were over 300 such stalls on the streets of London in the mid-nineteenth century. The number had quickly increased after the duty on coffee was reduced from 1s. to 6d. per pound in 1824.[75] He suggested that 'to commence as a coffee-stall keeper in a moderate manner requires about 5l. capital. The truck costs 2l., and the other utensils and materials 3l. The expense of the cans is near upon 16s. each. The stock-money is a few shillings.'[76] He estimated that the average coffee-stall keeper cleared 1l. per week, with actual takings double this. However, competition was intense and success depended on the quality of the pitch secured as some thoroughfares brought more business than others.[77]

The other 'houses of refreshment' were the bath houses, the bagnios, many of which had coffee rooms attached, 'thereby attracting a coffee-house following and character'. For example, that belonging to Mrs Eddowes in St James Street,[78] and also the *Turk's Head Bagnio* run by Alice Neal.[79] The bagnios, like some public houses, let out rooms to prostitutes and their clients and consequently had a reputation for disrepute rather than respectability. Bagnio keeper, Minna Wood, took out a fire insurance policy on her establishment at 9 Hanover Court, Long Acre, Covent Garden in 1851. The policy was valued at £300. Her entry in the census enumerator's returns records records her profession as 'brothel keeper'. On census night Minna, her young servant Bridget, and Georgina Bloomfeld (a young dressmaker perhaps moonlighting as a prostitute) had opened the house for business. A widower and his two sons, Michael and Moses Israel were recorded in the premises and with no relationship to the head of household listed they were presumably customers.[80]

In addition to textiles, provisions, laundry services and food, drink and hospitality, trade cards survive of women engaged in what might be regarded as heavier or more masculine production trades. There were coopers, wheelwrights, distillers, turners, carpenters, saddlers, engine, lathe and toolmakers, sale makers, rope and twine manufacturers, pewterers, iron boiler manufacturers, market gardeners and so on. For example,

Mary Alderson was a pewterer on Great Marlborough Street and Anne Pilton, a widow wire-worker in Piccadilly. Both cards are simple and to the point.[81] In the Newgate area of London, Margaret Smith's more decorative card promotes her business making and selling a broad variety of coffins and plates.[82] A trade in which reputation was an important competitive element. Martha Banting, a shoeing and jobbing smith, 'most earnestly solicits a continuance of their support' from her customers now that her son has left the business.[83] These are isolated examples. However, there does seem to have been particular production areas that women were more likely to find a niche. These included the furniture and upholstery trades and printing, publishing and engraving. For example, Julia Booth was an engraver and printer in the 1820s based at Saint Andrew's Hill, Doctors Commons,[84] as was Mrs Cook[85] and Hannah Cross from Leadenhall Street.[86] Furthermore, returning to the fire insurance policies of the previous chapter, the 1851 Sun Fire policy registers revealed three publishers, Anne Tatham of Covent Garden, Mrs Lucinda Tallis of Warwick Street, and Laura Bunet D_ of Oxford Street, and an 'engraver, printer and stationer' and the 1861 registers contained *Illustrate London News* publisher, widow Anne Ingram, in 1861.[87] Women were also found in printing and this was a trade that widows frequently continued in after the death of their husband. For example, Elizabeth Cluer who announced 'to all shopkeepers and others' that she would be continuing the business 'having the same Hands to act for her, as her late Husband employ'd for many years'.[88]

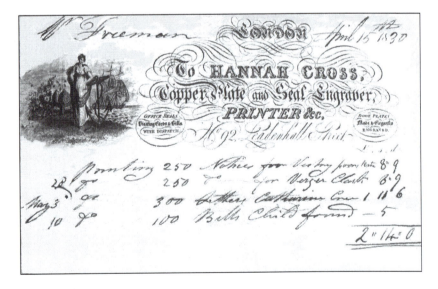

Figure 4.8 Trade card of Hannah Cross.

Similarly, there were numerous little pamphlet shops in important thoroughfares that were often kept by women. Often a profitable situation, they sold all kinds of newspapers and journals, almanacs, parliamentary speeches, plays and pamphlets of all sorts.[89] The stationery trade seems to have attracted single women in addition to the married and widowed, perhaps because the culture of letter writing among educated women bred a knowledge of paper products sufficient to make this a suitable choice of business. Elizabeth Dartnell's shop near St. Martin's Lane[90] and Elizabeth Fielding's on Broad street, 'behind the Royal Exchange', were both well positioned. In addition, Sophia Sewell's shop on the Norland Road included music and toys alongside stationery.[91] Print selling was also popular and good business could be made. Mrs Mary Parkes took out two insurance policies with a combined value of £6,170 on the stock, utensils and fixtures in her shop at 22 Golden Square.[92] News vending was also an option for women. Mrs. Sophia Bain of Duke Street, Westminster took out an insurance policy for £150 on her business assets in 1851.[93] The businesses of both Mary and Sophia were sizeable and respectable enough to secure entries in the Post Office London Directory.

Figure 4.9 Trade card of Elizabeth Fielding.

Pinchbeck wrote that for women who had no special skill or technical training and yet had to earn a living, retail shopkeeping was the easiest recourse. Wives, widows and single women alike, were shopkeepers in various branches of trade. She continued,

> Apart from the large number of general shopkeepers in country and small market towns, the most popular businesses with women, to judge from their advertisements, were those dealing with some kind of drapery, books and stationery, grocery and other branches of the provision trades. Notices from haberdashers, who traded in stuffs and drugs as well as small wares, silk mercers, woollen and linen drapers are common, and sometimes two or more of these branches were combined . . . Occasionally such businesses were conducted in partnership either with a man or another woman.[94]

However, the cost of space in London, both in terms of land values and rates, was a pressing problem. By the 1870s an acre of land in the City was valued at £14,520 compared to a suburban acre of £726.[95] With wage levels also higher in London than elsewhere, competition from the provinces and abroad was acute, particularly when the railways brought major towns within easy reach of the London market.[96] Shops on Bond Street, St James' Street or important city thoroughfares were costly to occupy. For example, Lipsham, a St. James Street confectioner, paid £400 a year in rents and rates; Reynard, a New Bond Street tailor, paid £375 a year in rents and rates. Shops on the Strand, Coventry Street, Piccadilly, Regent Street and Oxford Street were also expensive. However, rents fell sharply off these main thoroughfares and in less fashionable areas, where a tradesman or woman could rent good facilities for £100 or less.[97]

Small neighbourhood shopkeepers, the kind not always making it into the trade directories, often lived and traded from cellars and ground floor rooms. This mitigated the costs associated with separate premises and glazing. They often carried only small volumes of stock and many did not require warehousing facilities. Shops were fitted with counters, showcases, shelving, cupboards, containers, cash boxes, weights and measures and the tools related to the processing and production functions associated with the trade. The capital invested in furnishings and equipment naturally varied among trades and within them with respect to the size of the shop and the quality of its trade. Although a minimum investment in furnishing a high street shop was likely to have been in the region of about £150, smaller, local retails could set up with much less.[98]

Numerous different types of retail outlets co-existed. Shopkeepers deployed different methods to sell their wares depending upon their type of customer and the type of wares. Selling within shops could take many forms, ranging from speedy processing of payment over a simple counter to a concentration on service and comfort for the customer. Some streets served a more fashionable clientele than others. For those tradeswomen aiming to appeal to high-class customers, the position of their shop was a crucial factor. The location of a shop on a particular street signalled to potential customers to whom the level of market was intended. The value of this for retailers was that they maximised their chances of dealing only with customers who were interested in their wares and could afford their prices. The level of the shop was also signalled by the design of the shop front, the goods placed on show and the dress and manner of the assistants. Shopping hours varied by location, but most shops were open from 12 to 16 hours a day, and longer on Fridays and Saturdays. In London, shops normally opened for business on Sunday mornings as well. They prepared for opening around 6 a.m. and very few closed before 7 p.m. and many not until 10 p.m. Generally speaking, they opened earlier and closed later in the summer than the winter. Those that catered for the working class were open longer than those that serviced the middle and upper classes.[99]

The skill of selling was not limited to those retailing goods and trade services. The women who opted for the business of schoolkeeping also needed to promote their educational and boarding service, their respectability and their curriculum. These businesses could range in size considerably, beginning with the modest offerings of Ann Hart when her husband was made redundant from the West India Dock Company.[100] Surviving trade card collections reveal many such women: Mrs Barber, Mrs Chassaing, Mrs Delatre, Mrs Howes, Mrs Luck, Mrs Meall, Mrs Meeson and Mrs Naisby,[101] Mrs Beeby, Mrs Brown, Mrs Drake, Mrs Pemberton, Mrs Pritchard and Mrs Rogers[102]. The list could go on.

Although schoolkeeping has not always been recognized as entrepreneurial by historians, this aspect of its nature was not lost on contemporaries some of whom felt that it outweighed the desire to educate. Hence, women in this area had to carefully guard against accusations of self-interested profiteering.[103] Yet there can be no doubt that the activity of schoolkeeping was a business. A reputation for standards and respectability needed to be maintained and school fees collected from an aspiring if not always cash liquid clientele. Although often run from the home in the case of smaller ventures like Ann Hart's, many women set up impressive establishments. The more educated could form quite expensive and organised schools, taking out trade cards like that for Miss Ravenscroft's French and English Establishment of Brunswick Place. Spotting a gap in the market, the enterprising proprietor even offered evening classes for ladies (Figure 4.10). London offered fashionable girls' schools aplenty, the larger more successful ones drawing in girls from outside London as well as more locally. Word of mouth and recommendation were key, but competition was fierce and location, curriculum, fees and ethos were promoted frequently to attract pupils and also retain them by competing with other advertising schools.[104]

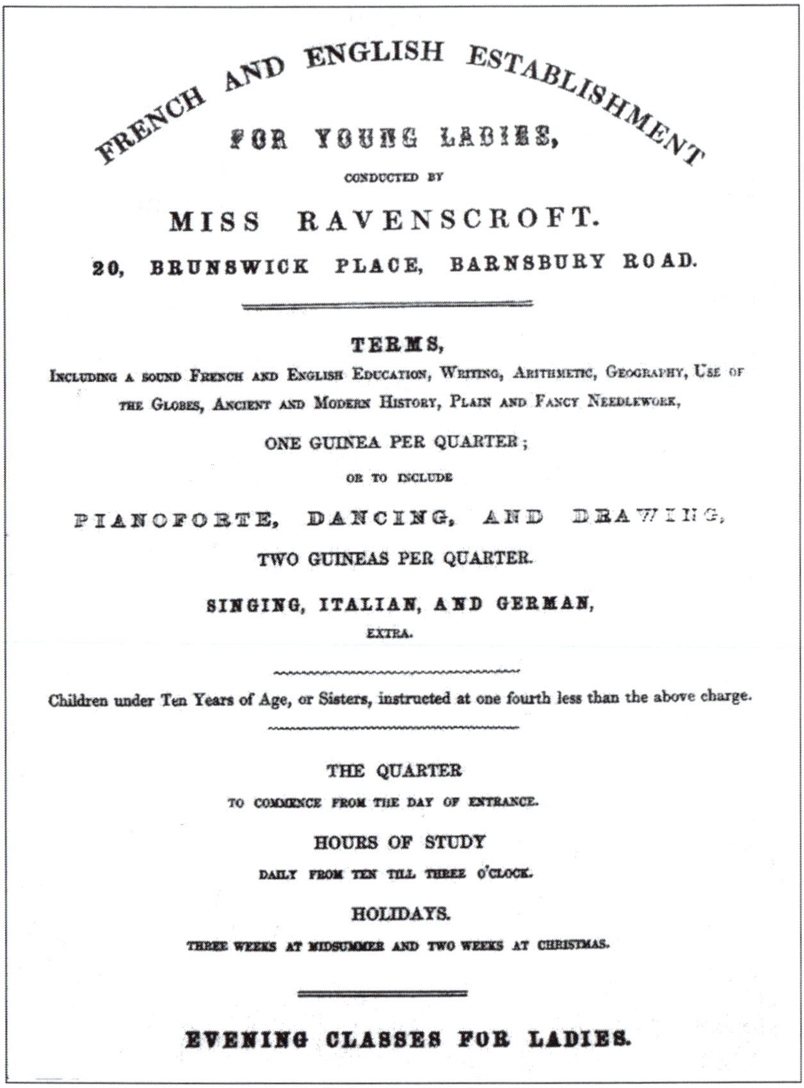

FRENCH AND ENGLISH ESTABLISHMENT

FOR YOUNG LADIES,

CONDUCTED BY

MISS RAVENSCROFT.

20, BRUNSWICK PLACE, BARNSBURY ROAD.

TERMS,

Including a sound French and English Education, Writing, Arithmetic, Geography, Use of the Globes, Ancient and Modern History, Plain and Fancy Needlework,

ONE GUINEA PER QUARTER;

OR TO INCLUDE

PIANOFORTE, DANCING, AND DRAWING,

TWO GUINEAS PER QUARTER.

SINGING, ITALIAN, AND GERMAN,

EXTRA.

Children under Ten Years of Age, or Sisters, instructed at one fourth less than the above charge.

THE QUARTER

TO COMMENCE FROM THE DAY OF ENTRANCE.

HOURS OF STUDY

DAILY FROM TEN TILL THREE O'CLOCK.

HOLIDAYS.

THREE WEEKS AT MIDSUMMER AND TWO WEEKS AT CHRISTMAS.

EVENING CLASSES FOR LADIES.

Figure 4.10 Miss Ravenscroft's French and English Establishment.

Not all schools will have advertised or even been included in directory listings but an examination of the Post Office London Directory gives us an indication of the sheer numbers in which women turned to the business of schoolkeeping in the nineteenth century. In 1851, there were 747 private schools listed. Female proprietors can be identified for 59 per cent (n = 438) of these. It must be stressed that even this is an underestimate as the directory will have excluded some of the smaller, less expensive day schools. Of the female schoolkeepers that are identified, 40 per cent used the prefix 'Mrs', and so like Ann were either married women seeking an extra income or were widowed. A further 46 per cent were operated by spinsters, attesting to the popularity of this avenue for the unmarried woman. The Directory also indicates that partnerships were popular with some 14 per cent of those listed run in combination with other women. The trade cards indicate a similar story. It is not difficult to find examples of partnerships, for example that of Mrs Pritchard and Miss Wakefield recently relocated from Wellclose Square to Islington.[105] Possibly these women were related. Susan Skedd found that marriage did not always curtail women's involvement.[106] Furthermore, less ambitious day schools required only small premises and had a modest student intake, making it a possible second business for a family like the Hart's. It was the boarding school that demanded a larger home or more substantial capital outlay on premises. Hence, many started small and either extended premises or moved to a larger house if they secured enough students.[107]

Finally, although this study and others have found that businesswomen in London used trade cards to entice customers to their premises, it is worth noting that Barker's findings for Manchester, Leeds and Sheffield, of plentiful newspaper examples but few surviving trade cards, led her to conclude that newspaper advertising was more important outside of London.[108] However, comparing her analysis of the newspaper texts with the trade cards studied here reveals that many similar messages were conveyed. For example, there was a heavy focus on reputation and obtaining public approval. Polite, deferential language was used, giving thanks for 'favours' received and expressing the hope of attracting 'public patronage'. The need for announcements often prompted the need for the advertisement such as the arrival of new stock, change of address, or change in the composition of ownership. In addition, just as on the trade cards, the businesswomen described and defined themselves not in terms of marital status but in terms of their occupation.[109] The purpose served by newspapers in the northern industrial towns and trade cards in the metropolis seems to have been a similar one. Barker herself reflects that the form of advertising chosen by businesswomen was perhaps a reflection of the greater distances into town that many provincial customers travelled.[110] Certainly, it is clear that businesswomen selected the best means available in their local economies to convey their existence unashamedly.

Through their trade cards, businesswomen sent out very clear messages about the type of customer they hoped to attract. For example, Amelia Brady of Little Russell Street, Covent Garden, informed her 'ladies' of the availability of rich court and fancy dresses available in her rooms.[111] Mrs Bean informed prospective customers that she was a court dress-maker to 'Her Royal Highness, The Duchess of Kent and also the Princess Charlotte of Saxe Coburg by special appointment'.[112] Similarly, the trade

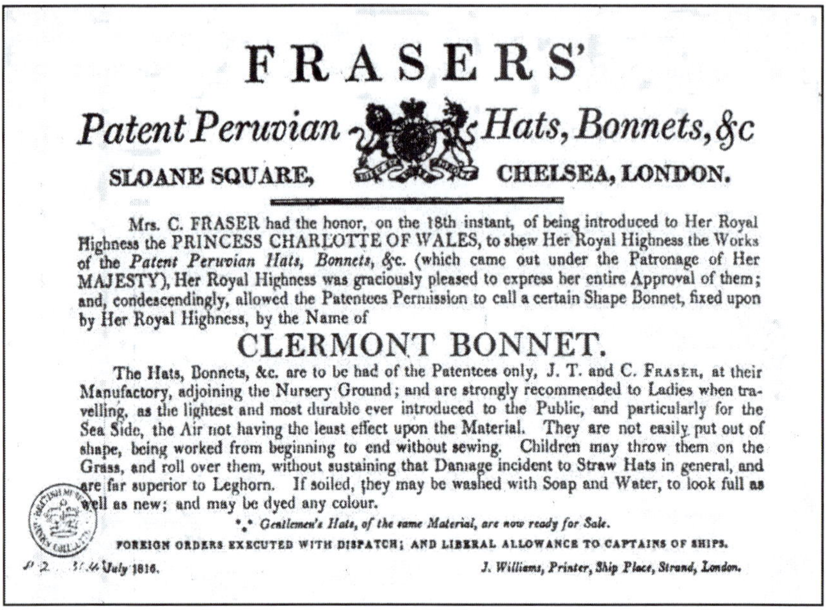

Figure 4.11 Advertisement for Frasers' Patent Peruvian Hats, Bonnets &c.

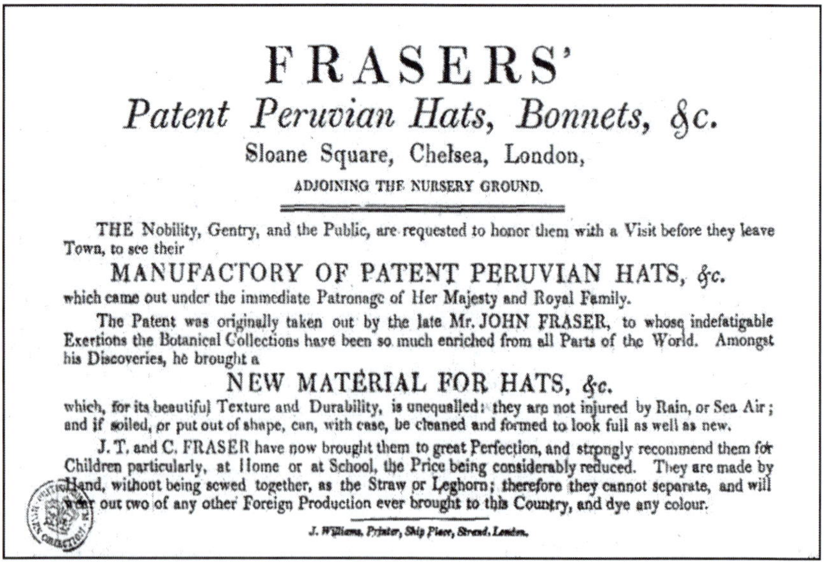

Figure 4.12 Advertisement for Frasers' Patent Peruvian Hats, Bonnets &c.

card of Mrs Russell tells us that she was milliner and dressmaker 'to Her Majesty & Royal Family'.[113] Trade cards like these reveal that name dropping was a vital component of nineteenth-century retail practice. This tactic, drawing on the cult of personality, conveyed not only messages about the standing of the clientele but also the respectability of the business and proprietor. The cards portrayed intimate connections and confidences and articulated the standing of the proprietor in a hierarchical marketplace. Mrs Fraser of *Frasers' Patent Peruvian Hats, Bonnets, &c* of Sloane Square, Chelsea, was very keen to inform clientele her that she had displayed her wares for the benefit of Princess Charlotte, who 'was graciously pleased to express her entire Approval of them'.[114]

Meanwhile, other cards were pitched at quite a different audience to the woman aspiring to be the prudent financial manager. In order to create the right appearance, most middle-class women who struggled in the £150 to £300 income range needed to be functional and thrifty. If the economic ideal was the efficient direction of production, writes Loeb, then the womanly ideal was the 'beneficient ordering of consumption'.[115] For example, Susan Dolland's 'reasonable rates' indicate that her target clientele was probably from the more thrifty ranks.[116] Others conveyed the more modest quality of their clientele and products simply by the frugality of their cards—small, limited in detail and poorly printed.

In London trade cards were a vital component in the selling process. They were an integral tool for proprietors in securing the benefits of the growth of consumption and the feminization of consumption. Used by a wide cross section of businesses, trade cards could persuade, inform and cajole the customer. As Berg and Clifford argued, for the consumer the use of the trade card was part of the skill of identifying networks of goods and the lifestyles that framed them.[117] Closely targeted advertising, they were for encouraging personal connection and loyalty; they reinforced both the skills of shopping and selling and gave respectability to the process and quality of both acts.

Hence, rather than 'to stitch' it was the ability 'to sell' that defined London women's survival in business. Wives, widows and single women alike were shopkeepers in various branches of trade. They operated at different levels, catering to a very varied clientele in terms of both taste and budget. They clustered in the areas for which they were the best prepared, particularly textiles and provisions, areas in which they had received some training, formally or informally, or in which their experience in the household had schooled them. They promoted their businesses and their personal respectability through their trade cards, in so doing attracting customers who were in turn concerned to communicate their own respectability through the items they purchased and who and where they purchased them from. Particularly in the textile trades but to some extent in other areas too, female proprietors were able to harness the ideology of separate spheres to their own advantage. They operated across the trades, many offering a genteel shopping environment, laden with ritual and symbolic meaning, where their predominantly female clientele could exercise consumption choices and, through the act of purchasing goods, bolster an air of respectability for themselves. The retailing activities of London's independent women thus provided for the economic agency of other women as well as their own social status and mobility. Trade cards could be expensive to produce and operated as a targeted form of advertising. Hence, the relative absence of these women in other forms of historical record may well in part reflect the proprietors' own desire to entertain a restricted audience of customers. By doing so, London's female proprietors were able to sustain an appearance unsullied by the murky seas of wider commerce.[118]

5 A Household of Enterprise

Fire insurance and family were two of the most important mechanisms for spreading risk and insuring personal and business survival. Such risk protection was especially vital for London's women in business because they were often engaging in economic enterprise because other means of support such as alternative 'suitable' paid employment or marriage were undesirable or unavailable to them. Responsible for their own survival in terms of both social position and economic well-being, the stronger the network of support these women were connected to through some manner of reciprocity, the greater their chances of surviving the impact of economic shocks. Although fire insurance records can tell us about the financial assets of women's businesses and trade cards can reveal something of their public nature, it was the home and household that provided the fuel for the endeavour—human capital, credit and connections. Women's enterprises were often carried on from within their home and the inhabitants of their household were inevitably connected to their business activities in some manner. Children, siblings, cousins, residential servants and employees all had their part to play in ensuring the success of the business and the network of support and survival that it fed into. Furthermore, extended family and non-familial members of the household forged connections between one household network and another, thus fuelling larger local networks.

For this reason this chapter will focus on the household of the female business proprietor. This is not a straightforward undertaking but relies on record linkage between the original hand scribed fire insurance policies of the Sun Fire Office and the microfilm copies of the hand scribed census enumerator's reports. Although the insurance policies provide good linkage information, house numbers were not always included in the census and spelling variation can also make the matching of individuals a slow and painstaking exercise. Since the data for this study was collected, far more census years have come online and this should greatly speed up similar endeavours in the future. Not least because it will eliminate the need to first identify the census district of the address given in the insurance records and from there the corresponding microfilm spool reference and position on the microfilm itself. This study specifically uses record linkage between the insurance records and the census for 1851 and 1861. It then also draws comparisons with other studies of female headed households in London and the United Kingdom. The results demonstrate the benefits of connecting home and business in studies of female enterprise. After all, it was here in the home, where the business of making a living and keeping family and reputation intact was centred, that the web of responsibilities, promises, favours, allegiances and contacts began to be spun.

Some readers may not be familiar with the census as a historical source. The first census, taken in 1801, was merely a headcount. Local overseers of the poor and clergymen were asked to provide John Rickman, a clerk of the House of Commons, with the totals of persons living in their parishes. The censuses of 1811 to 1831 were very similar. However, in 1840 Rickman died whilst making arrangements for the census of the following year. Responsibility then eventually passed to three commissioners, the most important being T.H. Lister, the Registrar General. As head of the General Register Office (GRO), Lister was responsible for the national system of vital registration, set up in England and Wales in 1837. These registration districts, also referred to as superintendent registrar's districts, were subsequently adopted as the administrative units for census taking and were numbered one to 11. London is division one. Each district was divided into sub-districts, and each sub-district into enumeration districts. Enumeration districts varied in size and could consist of several small places, an entire civil parish, or only part of a large civil parish.[1]

In the week preceding census night the enumerator delivered forms to all the households in the area to which he had been assigned. A householder was obliged to complete the form ready for collection by the enumerator on the Monday after the census night. It was the duty of the enumerator to complete any blank forms by asking the householder information. A householder was anyone who rented or owned a dwelling. Everyone who slept in their house on census night was to be included, even if it was not his or her permanent home. Those absent from the home due to work were to be included in the house to which they would normally return on the morning after they had finished their shift. Those individuals travelling were to be enumerated in the house in which they would be staying at the next stop of their journey.[2] The information given on the census forms was then copied by the enumerator into a book, several of which were bound together into folders, and given to the registrar for checking. The books were then sent to the census office in Craig's Court, London where they were checked again. The books formed the raw material from which the clerks in the Census Office tabulated the number of people in the country, their occupations, marital status and so on. Although the original householder forms were destroyed, the enumerators' books still survive, providing a wealth of information on individuals and their households.

Although people moved frequently in this time period and in addition, addresses in the census were not always entered as a precise house number and street name. This can make locating individuals problematic.

Nonetheless the details supplied on the Sun Fire insurance policies extracted for this study can be linked to a sufficient number of census returns to shed light on the household of the female business proprietor.

The 453 London women's insurance policies with the Sun Fire in 1851 and 1861 covered a startling array of activities as varied as horse-slaughtering, leather pipe manufacture and fancy dress provision. Linking the personal details on these policies with the census enumerators returns for the corresponding year in which the policy was taken out reveals whether these proprietors were the head of their household; the size of their household; their marital status and age; whether they resided with siblings or children; and if live-in servants, employees, boarders and lodgers lived in the household. However, within the confines of this study it was impractical to search for all of the women identified in the fire insurance records and instead two groups of women were selected for linkage. Together these women constituted around 60 per cent of the business dataset, making a sizeable linkage sample. The first of these two groups was those women engaged in the ten most popular trades ($n = 224$). This first group had in itself constituted half of all the women in business and although we want to avoid suggesting too great a homogeneity amongst businesswomen, we do want to look for common trends. In addition, for comparative purposes, the households of women engaged in specifically manufacturing trades outside of the food and textiles sectors were selected for linkage. These trades would have been seen as more typically men's business. The overall linkage success rate was almost 60 per cent, producing a detailed and significant sample ($n = 156$) of businesswomen's households at mid-century in the metropolis.

Beyond the case study, looking at the business proprietor in the context of her household is new territory. Because of the limitations of other sources it is by this avenue that we need to travel to systematically test common assumptions made about women in business in the nineteenth century. For example, it was often argued that if a woman was in business then she would most likely be at least approaching middle age and also widowed and indeed that it would have been by the death of her spouse that she came into the role of proprietor. Furthermore, she would usually be regarded as a temporary incumbent of an enterprise, caretaking the business until it could be sold or passed on to an adult son. The research presented in this chapter reveals that these stereotypes have some truth in their application to women engaged in the manufacturing and typically 'male' trades but much less so for the other businesses they operated in and of course it is in the latter that most female proprietors were found (see Chapter 3).

The households of the linked Sun Fire proprietors were spread across three-quarters of the 36 London census registration districts, although there was substantial clustering. Popular districts included Whitechapel, Shoreditch, Pancras, Marylebone, and Westminster. (Of course they may as much reflect the variable competitiveness of Sun Fire agents across the districts.) The average size of these households was 4.3 residents and in greater than 80 per cent

Table 5.1 Linkage Results for Sun Fire Popular and Manufacturing Trade Female Proprietors, 1851/1861.

	Policies *n*	Linked *n*	Linked %
Milliners & dressmakers	63	36	57
Chandlers	24	14	58
Haberdasher & hosiers	18	11	61
Grocers & greengrocers	19	12	63
Linen drapers	17	8	47
Victuallers	24	16	33
Coffee-house keepers	20	11	55
Tobacconists	11	6	55
Stationers	11	4	36
Clothiers	5	3	60
Laundry keepers	12	8	67
Manufacturing trades	51	27	53
Total	275	156	56

Source: Sun Fire Policy registers, series 11,936, LGL; Census returns for 1851/1861.

of cases the linked female proprietor was also the head of the household. This is not especially shocking. If the assumption holds that the majority of women in business were unsupported by other parties, then it is not surprising that they headed their own household. However, as Gordon and Nair remind us, who retained headship of the household was not just a matter of formal record in a census: it had practical implications in terms of freedoms and responsibilities. Furthermore, if the same designation is to be taken as meaningful when the household head is a man, its significance should be preserved when applied to a woman.[3] When the picture is broken down to examine household status by business it becomes apparent that a number of trades, in this study at least, were only carried on by women who were heads of households. These included the activities of the coffee-house keeper, tobacconist, linen draper and stationer. Several more were dominated, if not held exclusively, by women who were household heads, for example, chandlers and grocers.

Comparative data on female headed households is not plentiful. The limited data gathered has been part of larger studies encompassing general household structure, directed by different research questions to those addressed here. Nonetheless, there are six studies (all based on census samples) from which we can extract data for comparative purposes. For London there is Chaplin's general sample (*n* = 765), Lee's Irish sample (*n* = 132) and Clarke's Bethnal Green

Table 5.2 Extracted Data from Other Household Studies, 1851.

Author of Study	Total Households	Female-Headed Households		Location of Study
	n	*n*	%	
Gordon & Nair	232	53	23[a]	Glasgow
Chaplin	3,964	765	19.3	London
Lees	761	132	17	London (Irish)
Clarke	1,012	139	13.7	London (Bethnal Green)
Fraser	980	131	13.4	Cardiff
Anderson	1,241	221	17.8	Preston

Source:

E. Gordon and G. Nair, 'The myth of the Victorian patriarchal family', *The History of the Family*, 7, 1 (2002), Tables 2 to 6.
D. Chaplin, 'The structure of London households in 1851', unpublished paper, Western Michigan University, 1975, Table 2; Quoted in L. Hollen Lees, *Exiles of Erin. Irish Migrants in Victorian London*, Manchester, 1979, Appendix B, Table A4.
L. Hollen Lees, *Exiles of Erin. Irish Migrants in Victorian London,* Manchester, 1979, Appendix B, Table A4, pp. 130–131, 134–136.
M.A. Clarke, *Household and Family in Bethnal Green, 1851–71. The Effects of Social and Economic Change*, PhD thesis, University of Cambridge, 1986, Tables 2.7, 3.5, 3.7, 3.18, 3.23, 3.24, 3.25, and pp. 75, 82, 99, 100.
C.G. Fraser, *The Household and Family Structure of Mid-Nineteenth Century Cardiff in Comparative Perspective*, PhD thesis, University of Wales, Cardiff, 1988, Tables 3.2, 3.5, 4.3, 6.1, 6.2, 6.3, 6.4, 6.15, 7.11, and pp. 84, 136, 261, 272.
M. Anderson, *Family Structure in Nineteenth Century Lancashire,* Cambridge, 1971, Tables 10, 13, 17, and pp. 43, 46, 47.
[a]On streets housing the lower middle-class the proportion was higher at 29 per cent.

sample (*n* = 139) of female headed households. In addition, Fraser provides a sample of female headed households in Cardiff (*n* = 131) and Anderson gives us a sample of female headed Preston households (*n* = 221). Finally, Gordon and Nair's research provides a small but detailed sample of middle-class Glasgow households headed by women (*n* = 53). It is this latter sample that most closely matches the population of this study. Their examination of the census revealed that a considerable and rising proportion of households on middle-class streets in Glasgow were headed by women and note that this reality is at odds with the picture of the Victorian household organised around and subordinate to the paterfamilias.[4]

There are some interesting similarities and differences between the households of the Sun Fire businesswomen and those of female headed households across London and Britain generally. Although it was very far from the case that widows accounted for the majority of Sun Fire women, they did make up a significant proportion. They constituted 64 per cent of the

popular trade proprietors and 78 per cent of the manufacturing trade proprietors. The barriers to entry in the latter in terms of training, experience
and often capital, would have been more difficult to overcome for unmarried women without prior exposure to the business. However, even among
the manufacturing proprietors the proportion of widows in the Sun Fire
dataset was lower than that identified in studies of female headed households in Bethnal Green and Preston, although similar to that for London's
Irish community and female headed households in Glasgow and Cardiff.
Furthermore, with the exception of Bethnal Green and Glasgow, married
women were much more prevalent in the other studies than among the Sun
Fire businesswomen. However, the Sun Fire registers did reveal married
women running their own businesses (nine per cent). For example: victualler Elizabeth Booth, haberdasher Susan Richards and stationer Mary Ann
Harrison. The whereabouts of their husbands is unknown.[5]

We can compare the widowed or married Sun Fire women with the
proportion of proprietors using the 'Mrs' prefix in the Post Office London Directory. In 1851, 72 per cent of the female proprietors listed in the
directory under the popular trades (as identified by the Sun Fire policies)
used the designation 'Mrs'. This compares to 66 per cent in the insurance
registers. This suggests that spinsters were generally under-represented in
the London Post Office Directory listings. Yet looking at the two sources
together one can see that in none of the popular trades were spinsters
excluded. If not found in the Sun Fire policies, they are included in the

Table 5.3 Comparison of Marital Status of Household Heads, 1851 (%).

	Married	*Widowed*	*Spinsters*
Sun Fire popular proprietors	9.3	63.6	26.6
Sun Fire manufactur- ing proprietors	8.5	77.2	14.4
Gordon & Nair (Glasgow)	2.1	77.0	20.8
Chaplin (London)	18.4	63.8	17.8
Lees (London, Irish)	14.4	78.8	6.8
Clarke (Bethnal Green, London)	5.8	87.1	7.2
Fraser (Cardiff)	23.8	64.0	12.0
Anderson (Preston)		85.5	

Source: Sun Fire Policy registers, series 11,936, LGL; Census returns for 1851/1861.
Also see Table 5.2 for source of the studies.
Note: No data given on the proportion of married women or spinsters in Anderson's study
but presumably some portion of 14.5 per cent each.

directory listings and visa versa. Also, although a substantial proportion of proprietors in the directories used the prefix 'Mrs', the assumption that they were all widows is too hasty. Some will have been married and some will have borrowed the title for a greater cloak of respectability in trades where single status might be especially compromised, for example, lodging house keeping. In any regard, few women's positions were static. It was possible to engage in business at different stages in the marital lifecycle. A tradeswoman could be operating her own business whilst moving from the position of daughter, to independent spinster and on to wife and widow. Of course, all women did not pass through all of these stages. Nor is it likely that all women continued in the same trade, or in trade throughout their life. Rather they will have entered and exited as their circumstances dictated.

Marital status does seem to have had some influence on the value of stock, utensils, fixtures, livestock and goods in trust that female proprietors insured. Combining the dates and linkage groups, spinsters were both more likely to insure below £50 and above £500. Although more commonly operating at the extremes, they were less likely than married or widowed proprietors to insure assets above £200. Looking at the popular trades specifically and taking 1851 and 1861 separately, 50 and almost 70 per cent of spinsters and half of married female proprietors held policies for over £50 but under £200 in value. None of the popular trade spinster-proprietors' policies fell below £50 in 1861, although in 1851 16 per cent did. In the same year, the proportion of widow's policies falling below this level of £50 was 35 per cent. In 1861 it was only widows' policies that inhabited this lower end of the value scale. Similarly, only widows held policies for £500 or more. Hence, in the popular trades, at least for 1861, it was the widow-proprietor who operated at the extremes. Hence, the image of the wealthy widow-proprietor did have some real-life counterparts but so too did the image of the poorer widow thrown back on the mercy of the market on the death of her spouse. It was in the manufacturing trades that married and widowed proprietors' policies tended to be larger. In the popular trades alone, rather than being at the extreme ends, the spinster-proprietors seem to have operated somewhere in the middle. In 1851, 53 per cent of spinsters held policies between £100 and £299 in value. The corresponding figure for married women was 33 per cent and for widows it was 28 per cent. In the 1861 policies, spinsters faired even better and were more likely to be in the £200 to £499 range. Of course, although these valuations of business assets can be taken as an indication of the size and success of their businesses, as already discussed in Chapter 3, in trades such as victualling and coffee-house keeping there was a significant degree of overlap between private and business assets. This means that the valuations for female policyholders operating in these trades could be variably undervalued.

Table 5.4 Comparison of the Proportion of Married or Widowed Women in the Sun Fire Polices and Post Office London Directory Listings, 1851.

Popular Trades	Sun Fire Married or Widowed Women %	Post Office Directory Women with 'Mrs' Prefix %
Milliner & dressmaker	50	54
Chandler	86	89
Haberdasher & hosier	57	67
Victualler	100	88
Grocer & greengrocer	88	91
Coffee-house keeper	75	84
Clothier	67	67
Linen draper	80	90
Stationer	100	70
Tobacconist	67	78

Source: Sun Fire Policy registers, series 11,936, LGL; Census returns for 1851/1861.

Returning to the comparative data on female headed households, with widows and married women less well represented amongst businesswomen than among female household heads generally, we can see that business proprietorship enable spinsters to be independent and to take responsibility for a household. Constituting 20.5 per cent of Sun Fire proprietors, this is higher than that for all the other samples except for middle-class households in Glasgow. This might partly be a reflection of the significant degree to which women outnumbered men in London. Indeed, in 1851 between the ages of 20 and 40 there were 119 women to every 100 men of this age. Those between 40 and 60 years of age exceeded men by 116 to 100 and between 60 and 80, by 137 to 100.[6] By default or choice, a substantial number of these women must have turned to the economic marketplace and small business for their survival.

Table 5.5 Valuation of Stock, Utensils, Fixtures by Marital Status (%).

Marital Status	Value Range in £s			
	< 50 %	≥ 50 < 200 %	≥ 200 < 500 %	≥ 500 %
Married	0	50	42	9
Widowed	8	50	37	6
Spinster	25	52	19	12

Source: Sun Fire Policy registers, series 11,936, LGL; Census returns for 1851/1861.

Table 5.6 Comparison of Mean Age of Female Household Heads.

	Mean Age
Sun Fire popular proprietors	45
Sun Fire manufacturing proprietors	54
Gordon & Nair (Glasgow)	49.5[a]
Chaplin (London)	
Lees (London, Irish)	
Clarke (Bethnal Green, London)	
Fraser (Cardiff)	47.4
Anderson (Preston)	

Source: Sun Fire Policy registers, series 11,936, LGL; Census returns for 1851/1861. Also see Table 5.2 for source of the studies.
[a]Figure for unmarried female household heads only. No data given on the mean age of female household heads in the studies by Chaplin, Lees or Clarke.

The mean age of all female proprietors in the manufacturing trades was 10 years older than in the popular trades. However, the late age at which women could be found operating businesses of varying types is particularly striking, suggesting that women might be active in business until quite late in their lifecycle (and in this period of course there was no mandatory retirement or pension). Overall, the mean age for all the linked proprietors was 49.5. This matches that found in Gordon and Nair's Glasgow sample for unmarried female-household heads and is just two years older than the mean age of the women in Fraser's Cardiff sample.

In the popular trades, the oldest of the 65 women linked in the 1851 census was an 84-year-old widow-dressmaker called Abriah Reynolds.[7] In 1861, the oldest proprietor was also a widow, 69-year-old laundress Elizabeth Baldwin.[8] The youngest women in each year were spinsters aged 19 and 24-year-old, respectively. Unmarried businesswomen clustered in the 20 to 39 age group in 1851, although in 1861, they were more evenly spread across the 20 to 49 age range. Their widowed counterparts fell most heavily in the 40 to 69 age group in 1851 but the narrower 40 to 59 age range in 1861. Half of all married proprietors were aged between 50 and 59 in 1851 but fell in the lower age range of 30 to 39 in 1861. As 70 and 80 per cent of the women who were below 29 years of age in 1851 and 1861 were also spinsters, this suggests that young women in business could be aspirational. They used small business as a means of securing themselves a livelihood should the prospect of Prince Charming and the possibility of marriage not come along, and devising a means of supplementary economic support for the future household if it did. Of course some will have chosen not to marry. Furthermore, the activities of these younger, single women were not restricted to dressmaking and millinery; rather their efforts were spread across a range of trades. To 'stitch' was not their only option. Indeed, across a variety of trades, the youngest proprietors were below 30 years of age.

The age distribution of manufacturing proprietors was a little different to that for those engaged in the popular trades. Whereas in the popular trades 50 and 48 per cent of the women were aged 45 or under, only 24 and 11 per cent of manufacturing proprietors respectively fell into this range. The women in manufacturing did still span a broad age range, with the oldest being a 76-year-old widow and the youngest 31-years-old. However a mean age for spinsters of 50 and 53 is high. Yet despite their advancing age, given the narrow range and nature of their trades—upholstery, chair making, and shoe manufacture—it is not necessarily the case that these women will have inherited their businesses. Rather they illustrate the limited options in terms of manufacturing activity for never married women seeking to enter into business. (See appendices for tables breaking down the age of proprietors by business type and marital status.)

Turning now to the other inhabitants of the London businesswomen's households, we can test some of the other commonly asserted stereotypes. Contemporaries propagated the notion that unsupported women, or distressed gentlewomen as they were sometimes referred to, frequently cohabited with their sisters. Furthermore, it was often asserted that women thrown on their own resources who then engaged in business seldom did so alone. Rather, they gathered in numbers to brave the dangerous public sphere of the commercial world. In such cases, sisters were presented as the ideal helpmates. We know anecdotally that this did happen but the extent of this sisterly combination risks being exaggerated.

Only Gordon and Nair's Glasgow sample offers us comparative data here. It seems that living with a sister was much more common in middle-class Glasgow women's households than in those of London's female proprietors. While 31.3 per cent of the Glasgow sample cohabited with a sister, the comparable figure for the Sun Fire proprietors was 11.7 per cent. Taking the popular trade proprietors separately, the proportion was a little higher at 15.5 per cent. However, on closer inspection, five of these 20 proprietors were in fact still living in the parental household and were not yet, at any rate, matching the profile of the poor and lonely spinster sisters. Furthermore, in 45 per cent of these cases, where the Sun women cohabited with a sister(s), the female proprietor was a dressmaker or milliner. This supports other evidence, for example that furnished by trade cards,[9] that in the needle trades sisters did often support each other. The most famous examples are the female siblings of engraver and painter, William Hogarth.[10] Nonetheless, standing back to view the women in the ten most popular trades collectively, only 11 per cent of those cohabiting with sisters also shared a trade with those siblings. Furthermore, only two manufacturing proprietors resided in a household with a sister and in neither of these cases did the sisters share the same trade. In the manufacturing trades it was more common for proprietors to be living in the same house-hold as their brothers. For example, Lucy and George Walter who operated a boot and shoemaking business together at 29 Chalton Street in Somers town;[11] and Margery and Joseph Hall, wood cutters and dealers, who took out two substantial policies with the Sun Fire for a collective £1,900.[12] Hence, the extent to which the combination of both trade sharing or busi-ness partnership and cohabitation dominated the work-life experience of the female business proprietor should not be overstated. This does not of course mean that sisters did not help each other in other ways—providing contacts, credit, labour in the form of nieces and nephews, even acting as customers themselves.

In addition, London's businesswomen were often able to draw on other forms of assistance such as servants. The late eighteenth century and nine-teenth century saw a widespread increase in domestic service. This was partly linked to a rise in the number of prosperous households in expand-ing urban areas. Most servant keepers were upper and middle-class. How-ever, in the early nineteenth century, up to a third of the English lower middle-class was without servants as was 15 per cent of the better-off mid-dle-class.[13] Indeed, in London generally at this time, it was estimated that a third of households had only one servant and a quarter had two.[14]

In the case of victuallers and coffee-house keepers examined here, the numbers of house servants, as opposed to 'employees,' are difficult to dis-tinguish. The nature of these trades meant that the duties of servants could cover both the domestic and business needs of the household. This over-lap makes classification difficult, as the use of occupational descriptions in the census was not necessarily consistent. In order to better estimate the number of residential employees in coffee-house keeping and victualling, 'servants' and 'general purpose servants' have been counted as 'employees' in this study, leaving only 'house servants' in the calculations of house-holds with servants in the table. In other trades the designation of 'servant' and 'house servant' is less fluid and the distinction between employees and domestic servants more obvious. If those servants and general purpose ser-vants of coffee- and victual house keepers also treated as employees are double counted as domestic servants, the proportion of popular trade pro-prietors with servants in 1851 reaches 55 per cent, (36 out of 65). The figure for 1861 is 41 per cent (26 out of 64). Combining the sample dates, residential domestic servants were present in the households of almost half of the popular trade proprietors and 22 per cent of the manufacturing pro-prietors. This is a significant finding.

The majority of proprietors had one young, female, servant. Indeed domestic service was highly gendered and the typical live-in domestic ser-vant was typically young, female and single. The latter characteristic was partly a reflection of living in another's household and certainly an issue of accommodation. It would seem that few households with servants tolerated the spouses of servants who were independent of the household. Simonton

Figure 5.1 Trade card of Mary & Ann Hogarth.

noted that marriage altered the mistress-servant relationship, and created a conflict of interest. So much so that in 1851 London only two per cent of servants were married.[15] Servants living in the household of female business proprietors, as studied here, were overwhelmingly young females with only five male servants recorded out of 52 in 1851 and two out of 30 in 1861. Some servant girls were as young as 12 or 13. Nevertheless, the existence of unmarried female servants over 50 suggests that domestic service could become a long-term career path.[16]

Businesswomen were much more likely to have servants living in their households than female household heads generally. Servants were reported in only 3.6 per cent of female headed households in the Bethnal Green sample and eight and 19 per cent of the Preston and Cardiff households respectively. This finding supports that of Higgs, which revealed that in mid-nineteenth century Rochdale it was also the shopkeepers, innkeepers and small traders generally who constituted the typical servant employers.[17] He found that households headed by retailers in 1851, 1861 and 1871 contained between a quarter and a third of all servants.[18]

The number of servants hired for wages was related to wealth. Higgs has estimated that room and board was worth about 5s of wages for a servant. Although the cost of retaining domestic servants was offset for the proprietor by the provision of room and board, wages for servants were relatively good and had risen steeply over the decades. In England, wages for a general servant were £9.5 annually at the end of the 1830s. By the 1890s they had doubled.[19] *The Economist and General Adviser* in 1825 estimated that the retention of a full-time, live-in servant only became possible at an income of £200 to £250 a year, where there was a family to be maintained. It suggested that a single lady or widow might afford a servant at a considerably lower income.[20] In the same year, Samuel and Sarah Adams' *The Complete Servant* estimated that such a woman, with an income of £100 a year, could keep a young maid at a low salary of between five to 10 guineas a year. To hire a better servant maid at about 10 or 12 guineas would require an income of £150 to £180 a year. And a 'servant maid of all work', costing from 12 to 14 guineas was attainable for those with a yearly income of

Table 5.7 Servants Residing in Female Headed Households (%).

	Servants
Sun Fire popular proprietors	38.7
Sun Fire manufacturing proprietors	22.2
Gordon & Nair (Glasgow)	
Chaplin (London)	
Lees (London, Irish)	6[a]
Clarke (Bethnal Green, London)	3.6
Fraser (Cardiff)	19
Anderson (Preston)	8[b]

Source: Sun Fire Policy registers, series 11,936, LGL; Census returns for 1851/1861. Also see Table 5.2 for source of the studies.
Note: No data was given on this topic in Gordon and Nair's study. [a]Figure applies to all households. No separate data was given for female headed households. [b]Apprentices and servants combined. See M. Anderson, *Family Structure in Nineteenth Century Lancashire*, Cambridge, 1971, Table 10, p. 46. No separate data was given on servants.

£200. For those households with young children and requiring two maids, an income of at least £300 a year was necessary.[21] By 1861, Mrs Beeton was informing her readers that a housekeeper was to have between £18 and £40 a year, a cook between £12 and £26, an upper house maid between £10 and £17 and a maid-of-all-work between £7 and £11, with tea, sugar and beer in each case.[22] Placing this in some context, contemporary Dudley Baxter estimated in 1868 that a lower middle-class income could range from below £100 to £300 and a middle-class income from £300 to £1,000.[23] Although the fire insurance valuations are not a direct indicator of the wealth of the proprietors and hence their ability to retain servants, they do provide a means of reflection. The value of stock, utensils, fixtures and livestock insured by proprietors does appear to have had a bearing on whether they had any servants in their household on the night of the census. In 1851 and 1861, some 73 and 77 per cent of policyholders with valuations of £100 or less did not retain servants and of those retaining servants, 73 and 60 per cent held a policy for over £100.

In the context of this study, there were certain advantages to having residential servants. They were at their mistress's beck and call and could assist at a moment's notice. Furthermore, servants were certainly a means of providing childcare for female business proprietors. Some 38 per cent of those popular trade proprietor's households that included children under the age of 14 also employed a servant. One of which, victualler Dorothy Genge, a 33-year-old widow, specifically employed a 'nursemaid' for her four young children: George, Jane, Clara and Charles. Her nursemaid was the presumably lively 71-year-old Maria Hart, herself also a widow.[24] It was not uncommon however for 'servants of all work' to share some responsibility for the children of the house, in addition to cleaning, cooking, washing, ironing, food shopping and so on. The employment of servants was for many businesswomen one of several 'strategies' enabling them to juggle their work, time and domestic commitments. The retention of a servant meant that a proprietor could maximise her income generating opportunities, providing that is that the revenue she created outweighed the cost of retaining a servant. In addition, servants often provided services to the business itself. Beyond this, of course, as social beings they provided links to other families, previous employers, and siblings in useful trades.

Before moving on to the next section it is worth noting that domestic service was often under-recorded, since servants were not always reported separately in household returns. Many were relatives, which complicated perceptions of them as workers or family members. For example, in 1851, Ellen Town, a 23-year-old spinster was fulfilling the role of 'housekeeper' for her sister, coffee-house keeper Julia Town.[25] And in 1861, Ellen Gracefield performed the duties of a general servant in her sister Sarah Burton's household.[26] No doubt many contributions went unrecorded. Evidence for this is found in other sources. For example, in the *Life of a Licensed Victualler's Daughter*, Mary Ann Ashford recounts for the reader the comments of a potential employer, Mrs Pearce of 10 Lambeth Terrace: 'The lady, who was a clergyman's widow, said she gave £7 a year to a housemaid, but if I would take the place as servant-of-all-work for a time, she would give at the rate of nine guineas a year, as part of her family was absent'.[27] Servants and relatives were clearly interchangeable on some level.

The combination of business proprietorship with motherhood is a noticeable finding of this study. Just under one-third of Sun Fire proprietors had children below the age of 14 living in the same household (n = 43). Indeed, as Murphy found in her study of Midwestern US women, motherhood may well have encouraged women to seek self-employment or small business proprietorship opportunities.[28] The desire for additional income but the need for flexibility in hours and effort will have made this form of income generation particularly attractive to mothers or guardians of young children. In addition, as children grew in size and increased in dexterity they could be incorporated into the enterprise, creating more household revenue and solving child-care problems.

Lone motherhood was not rare at this time. From the eighteenth to the early nineteenth century, around nine per cent of British households with children were estimated to have been headed by women. By the mid-nineteenth century lone parents headed about 19 per cent of families and women made up about two-thirds of lone parents, that is 13 per cent of households headed by women.[29] The presence of children in the home, regardless of parentage, must have shaped the decisions their mothers or female guardians made about the best way to earn an income or the type of business within which to engage in order to provide for themselves and their household. The significant percentage of Sun Fire proprietors with small children supports the argument that business was a popular option for the lone mother. Often undertaken from the home, proprietorship could be dovetailed with childcare in a way that paid work outside the home could not. However, in a period of high child employment within and outside of the home or in other households, the image of very large numbers of resident children requiring full maintenance should not be overstated.

Although there was no comparative household headship data at the time of writing, it is clear that the households of London s businesswomen also often included residential employees. Around a third of the Sun Fire women had such household members. Many seemed to have operated with one or two residential employees. However, there were exceptions such as Martha Phillips, a substantial grocer with a policy valued at £4,400, who had six assistants in her household on the census night. All were men and all were aged below 30 years of age.[30] The gender composition of Martha's employees was unusual. There were 101 employees in total in the homes of the popular trade proprietors, 76 per cent of whom were female (n = 72).[31] Dressmakers and milliners employed 56 per cent of these. In contrast, three of the four manufacturing trade employees were male. Employees offered similar networking benefits to servants and housing residential staff brought with it a certain responsibility of care, binding the ties of reciprocity even tighter.

In addition, there were often non-residential employees. The census returns sometimes contained a separate note as to the total number of the proprietor's employees. Examples included the policy of widow Jane Feamont, a chandler. It noted: 'employs 7 men and 3 women'. None of these were resident in her household.[32] Similarly, the entry for spinster Elizabeth Wise, a dressmaker, included the comment: 'employs 7 women', although only four female employees were resident on the night of the census.[33] Such additions to the census returns were even more frequent for those proprietors engaged in manufacturing. Examples included: the entry for bookbinder Susannah Armstrong, which reads 'employs 3 men, 1 boy and 1 woman'.[34] Across whip manufacturer Elizabeth Simpson's was scrawled 'employing 2 men'[35] and on Hannah Fairburn's, a wool and cotton card machine maker, 'employing 7 men'.[36] In manufacturing, perhaps because of the predominance of male employees, who having completed their training might be married and have their own household, employees were more separate from the domestic household of the proprietor. Respectability would also have been an issue for the spinster-proprietor, discouraging the residence of male employees.

It should be acknowledged that, as was the case with domestic service, there was a trade-off between familial and non-familial employees in the households of female proprietors. Family members sometimes took on the role of employee, though their contribution is often difficult to trace. For example, in 1861, 41 per cent (12 of the 29) older female children were recorded as being in the same trade as their mother-proprietors. Of these, three were described as assistants to the proprietor, usually their mother or aunt. Anne Longfoot, 19-years-old, was employed as a shop assistant in her aunt's linen and haberdashery shop on the Vauxhall Bridge Road.[37] Coffee-house keeper, Martha Dowsell, benefited from the labour of her 28-year-old daughter, Ann, who was described literally as 'assistant to mother'.[38] And Sarah and Martha Cune worked as a clear slancher and a collar ironer, respectively in their mother's, Hannah, laundry service business. Their sister, Lizzie, was recorded as a bookkeeper. It is not clear whether she provided this service to her mother alone. No doubt her skills were extremely helpful.[39] The evidence of such families suggests the household network of support on which London's female proprietors could call.

Returning to commonly held stereotypes of women in business, it has often been suggested that women in business would be caretakers waiting for their sons to come of age and take over the reigns. If this was the case we would expect to find ample evidence of younger sons and young adult sons working alongside their mothers in preparation. However, only five of the older male children of the popular trade proprietors were occupied in the same trade as his mother: In 1851, unmarried, 24-year-old, Charles Guillian worked as a clerk for his mother Christiana Guillian, proprietor of

Guillian's Hotel on Albermarle Street, Picadilly. She held a sizeable insurance policy valuing her stock, utensils and fixtures at £2,000. Edward Lawrance, aged 23, worked as the 'manager' in his mother, Maria's, clothing business. His 18-year-old brother, Charles, was an assistant.[40] Catherine Rebbeck held a policy against her licensed victualling business, the Coopers Arms in Saffron Hill. She was assisted by George, her 20-year-old unmarried son.[41] Similarly, 14-year-old William Kaye was an assistant to his mother, Maria, a hosier.[42] In 1861, only 20-year-old, Walter Lock shared the trade of his mother. He was her barman at The Gun Tavern on Shoreditch High Street. His older brother, Robert, worked elsewhere as a rate clerk.[43]

In the manufacturing trades, sons do seem to have been more useful to mothers. Indeed in 1861 all the older children sharing a trade with their mothers were male. Perhaps it was here in the manufacturing trades that the image of the widow-caretaker derived. Having presumably inherited her deceased husband's business, she kept it going until her sons came of age and could release her from this task. However, there is a caveat. The linkage reveals that five of the eight sons and one nephew were well past their coming of age: John Bower, 32-year-old, worked as an 'engineer' alongside his mother Agnes.[44] Thomas Huntley, 38-years-old, an engraver and printer, worked alongside his mother Elizabeth, also an 'engraver and printer', on New Bond Street.[45] James Dean was 27 and a journeyman bookbinder residing with his aunt, Susannah Armstrong, a bookbinder employing '3 men, 1 boy and 1 woman' at her workshop on Villiers Street.[46] There was also 40-year-old Joseph who worked alongside his mother Mary Draper on Great Titchfield Street, Marylebone.[47] And there was George Tubbs, son of Mary Ann, a Rose Lane ship chandler, who at age 30 was still described as her 'assistant'.[48] Therefore, whilst it is clear that widows could gain the support of their sons in their businesses, the records investigated here can not support the argument that the widows were in the main temporary caretakers of enterprises.

In contrast, there were actually marginally more female children to male (57 female to 41 male) and the majority of resident children who were over the age of 30 were female. Examples included: Abriah Reynolds, a dressmaker, was kept company in trade and home by her unmarried, 44-year-old daughter, Mary.[49] Sarah Bradshaw, a 34-year-old family governess, lived with her mother, stationer Harriet Bradshaw.[50] Finally, Susannah Brown, a 43-year-old widow and 'milkman', resided with her also widowed mother, chandler Ann Arrowsmith.[51] This supports the argument that unmarried daughters tended to remain at home, assisting and caring for their surviving parents. They often remained in the family household until the death of their parents and were then free to set up on their own as a household head.[52] Furthermore, it would seem that mothers and adult daughters found mutual benefit in cohabiting, collectively securing an income and home, and of course the respectability that came with this limited independence.

Each acted as the moral guardian of the other. Their presence acted as a surety for the other woman's respectability and good conduct.

Hence, gender aside, it was common to find offspring aged 14 or over living in the female proprietors households—62.3 per cent ($n = 97$), conveying certain advantages. In addition to providing childcare for younger children, they could be utilised within the enterprise and so could reduce the costs of running a business. Although many of these older children were assistants or 'in training', surprisingly, apprentices were found in only four of the households linked in the census. Only two of these were in the trade of the proprietor, rather than of a husband or another resident party. In both cases, the business proprietors who had apprentices operated in the needle trades and had only one apprentice each. Lydia Fry, 17-years-old, was apprenticed to Ann Boxall, a widow-milliner in Soho and 16-year-old Jane Morley was apprenticed to Jane and Ann Giddings, dressmakers and milliners.[53] The small number of apprentices is even more surprising given that many milliner-dressmakers had up to eight assistants resident on the night of the census.[54] No doubt their board was in lieu of higher wages. In contrast, board for apprentices was a costly addition to employment costs. Furthermore, outside of the needle trades, apprentices were much more likely to be found in the manufacturing trades than among tobacconists, stationers and coffee-house keepers. Yet, this study found only one in the records of the linked production trade proprietors: 18-year-old William Woolcott, a whip manufacturer's apprentice.[55] One explanation for this is that over the course of the nineteenth century there was a growing tendency not to offer room and board to apprentices and this may partly account for their absence from the household on the eve of the census. Perhaps also, the use of children or nieces and nephews as juniors in the business meant that formal apprentices were less needed. Thirdly, apprentices were not common to every trade and less so at the retailing end of the spectrum towards which many women's businesses seem to have gravitated.

Finally we can consider lodgers and visitors. A higher percentage of Sun Fire proprietors had lodgers in their homes than did female household heads in other studies of London. In contrast, outside of London female headed households were approximately twice as likely to supplement their income in this way, supporting the argument that there was a trade-off between taking in lodgers and the availability of other income generation strategies. Interestingly, this combination of income generation strategies may not have been utilised to the same extent by women engaged in manufacturing, although the sample is admittedly small. In 1851, only whip manufacturer Elizabeth Simpson of Hosier Lane, West Smithfield, had a lodger in her household on the eve of the census. Her lodger was Mary Hutt, a 75-year-old widow in receipt of parish poor relief.[56] In 1861, 22 per cent had a lodger. One of these women was Maria Stockdale of Poplar whose policy named her as a rigger but whose census returns record her as a lodging house keeper. Perhaps this was a new venture for her because

Table 5.8 Children Residing in Female Headed Households (%).

	Age < 14 Years	Age >14 Years
Sun Fire popular proprietors	33.4	41.9
Sun Fire manufacturing proprietors	28.4	82.7
Gordon & Nair (Glasgow)		
Chaplin (London)		
Lees (London, Irish)	75[a]	
Clarke (Bethnal Green, London)	57[b]	
Fraser (Cardiff)		
Anderson (Preston)	31[c]	

Source: Sun Fire Policy registers, series 11,936, LGL; Census returns for 1851/1861. Also see Table 5.2 for source of the studies.
Note: [a]Figure relates to widowed household heads only. Lees states that 'three quarters of widoes who headed households lived with unmarried children'. See L. Hollen Lees, *Exiles of Erin. Irish Migrants in Victorian London,* Manchester, 1979, p. 131. [b]Figure relates to proportion of widows with co-residing children of all ages. See M.A. Clarke, *Household and Family in Bethnal Green, 1851-71. The Effects of Social and Economic Change,* PhD thesis, University of Cambridge, 1986, pp. 82, 123. [c]Figure relates to proportion of widows with co-residing children of all ages. See M. Anderson, *Family Structure in Nineteenth Century Lancashire,* Cambridge, 1971, Table 17, p. 55.

one of her lodgers was a '1st mate mercantile marine', suggesting that she still had ties with the seafaring community.[57] The other proprietor who also kept lodgers was Charlotte Walter, a cork cutter. Her insurance policy on her Drury Lane business was for a substantial £300. Alongside her three sons and one daughter, she also had room for a lodger, Emily Hull, a 22-year-old spinster.[58] Generally in London, rather than choosing between taking in lodgers or engaging in public sphere business, female proprietors utilised the provision of lodgings as a means of diversifying household income. Some 28 households had lodgers. Although it was usual to accommodate only one or two lodgers there were exceptions. Esther Goatley, widow-proprietor of the coffee rooms at 37 Bermondsey Street, accommodated five lodgers, in addition to two sons, a son-in-law and a daughter.[59] Taking in lodgers in this way could help women to retain their independent household and extended their networks of contacts and acquaintances.

In addition to household members present on the night of the census, the enumerator's returns also recorded the personal details of any visitors. This information provides a narrow inroad into the networks and contacts of female business proprietors. Thus, we find our milliners entertaining fellow proprietors on the eve of the census. In 1851, widow Elizabeth Jones and spinster Ann Vaughan were both visited by dressmakers. Harriet Stiffs, also unmarried, received a visit from William Owen, a silk mercer.[60] In 1861,

Table 5.9 Provision of Lodgings by Female Household Heads (%).

	Lodgers	*Mean Household Size*
Sun Fire popular proprietors	21.8	4.6
Sun Fire manufacturing proprietors	14.1	4.0
Gordon & Nair (Glasgow)		6.3
Chaplin (London)	4.8[a]	
Lees (London, Irish)	18.5[b]	5.6[c]
Clarke (Bethnal Green, London)	5.0	4.17
Fraser (Cardiff)	35.1	2.69
Anderson (Preston)	33.0	

Source: Sun Fire Policy registers, series 11,936, LGL; Census returns for 1851/1861. Also see Table 5.2 for source of the studies.
Note: No data was given on this topic in Gordon and Nair's study. [a,b]A separate figure could not be extracted for female-headed households alone. Hence, this figure relates to all households. [c]No separate figure was given for female-headed households. Mean for all households was 3.7. Mean for middle-class Irish households was 5.6. See L. Hollen Lees, *Exiles of Erin. Irish Migrants in Victorian London*, Manchester, 1979, p. 136.

Mary Ann Corrie of 12 Grafton Road, Kentish Town, was visited by Sarah Parsons, described as a lacewoman.[61] Other proprietors received visitors from unrelated trades, such as Martha Sharp and Harriet Hitchinson who received respectively; Lucy Nunn, a waistcoat maker and James Purcell, a plasterer. These visits would also have provided an opportunity to discuss the general issues and experiences of business life. Strikingly however, there were no visitors–in–trade in any of the manufacturing trade households. Possibly coincidence, possibly women that engaged in these trades were more isolated. In millinery, dressmaking and to some degree in haberdashery and hosiery and aspects of drapery, proprietors could operate almost within a female economy. Their employees and servants were female, the majority of their clientele were female, and a significant number of female proprietors also engaged in wholesale. Perhaps businesswomen in the needle trades in particular, operated a network incorporating fellow dressmakers and milliners, assistants, lace women, and possibly those active in the linen and hosiery and haberdashery trades. They called upon each other for business, advice and friendship and no doubt exchanged information on materials, markets, wholesalers, other workers and of course clientele. Certainly, in general, on one night alone, and an important night to be at home at that, the Sun Fire proprietors were convening with both men and women to discuss issues of common concern. Such meetings no doubt encouraged the sharing of customer and wholesale contacts, credit sources and general business acumen, whilst also influencing the nature of the household itself. As Gordon and Nair said, the comings and goings of lodgers, servants and visitors, as well as changes within the family, reveal the household less as a static grouping and more of an ever-changing kaleidoscope of forms.[62]

In concluding this chapter the most obvious point to make is that in the mid-nineteenth century the boundary between spheres of home and work was not absolute for those women involved in business. Furthermore, there was a clear link between independence in income generation and independence in domestic living arrangements. Lone middle-class women often headed their own households and business proprietorship was one means of making this possible. They were able to keep servants and employees and support an extended family of both male and female relatives. As Gordon and Nair argued for women in Glasgow, although the conventional view of these women sees them as essentially passive, not as agents of their own destiny, this is clearly too simplistic. These women demonstrate that that they were free to choose their own friends, pursue their own interests and take up causes or occupations of their own choosing. Indeed many such women consciously rejected social protection and others around them could see that widows and spinsters did not invariably live under the wing of male social and economic protection. Indeed they often offered such protection to others. 'All women knew legions of lone women: all women could reasonably expect to be lone women at some stage. Such women could enjoy considerable social independence without sacrificing respectability.'[63] The freedom and responsibilities of household headship may have led women to business proprietorship or the proprietorship may have enabled the setting up of their own independent household. It was precisely the possibility of overlapping domestic living with small business activity that made this avenue an accessible and attractive one for women. Yet it is this very overlap between home and business that whilst beneficial to them has also often hidden their efforts from view. Their activities crossed the boundary of household and market, blurring their business identities. Similarly, the inhabitants of their households were not separate from the economic agency of these women. The London businesswoman usually inhabited, and often headed, a socially rich household that was multi-generational, combined familial with non-familial members, and which offered a support system that made her economic agency possible. Such reciprocal relationships will have extended beyond the domestic, not just providing a pool of flexible labour to the enterprise but also offering opportunities for credit, motivation, and the budding tentacles of a wider network outside the walls of their home and business.

6 Property, Home and Business

The preceding chapters have revealed the diversity of women's enterprises and the significance of retailing in the nature of their endeavours. Examining their household circumstances more closely has revealed the predominance of household headship and the household support network, which like fire insurance offered some protection against risk, but in addition also increased the burden of responsibility. Although the strong marriage between home and business aided women in their enterprises, it has also hidden many of them from view. Not only under-represented in traditional business sources, the cloak of domesticity has downgraded their economic activities by leading to interpretations of their activities as being merely minor extensions of the private sphere. This has particularly been true for women engaged in the business of accommodation. Many of the women who operated in this sector, and the diversity of enterprises within it, have been hidden. In turn, historians have prized out these women in only limited contexts—for example the seaside landlady, the landlady in literature and the petty provision of boarding and lodging.[1]

The nature of lodging house keeping will be examined later in this chapter but first let us consider another type of landlady, one who let out houses, tenements and commercial properties. Although the most removed from the cloak of domesticity, this activity has still been labelled as passive investment, underplaying the involvement and interest that many women took in their property affairs. In addition, property and other types of business are not mutually exclusive. The former often supplemented the latter for business proprietors, male or female. The fire insurance policy registers are a very useful source for unveiling women active in property. The woman who let property, like her male counterpart, would have suffered a significant blow to her investment and her income stream should a fire have destroyed her buildings and forced her tenants to move on. Hence, in addition to insuring the buildings themselves, many insured against the loss of rent should fire render their premises unfit for habitation. The Sun Fire policies thus provide us with a dataset of insurance coverage of rents on rooms, tenements, houses and workshops.

Taken together, out of a possible 2,289 London policies with the Sun Fire Office held by women in both 1851 and 1861, 28 per cent (n = 630) covered property in addition to their dwelling houses. Some 68 per cent (n = 429) of these insured one or two additional properties (with 48.4 per cent insuring only one). A further 18 per cent insured three or four properties (n = 73 and n = 43 policies, respectively). Some 10 per cent of policies insured between five and 10 additional properties (n = 65) and three per cent insured between 11 and 20 (n = 18). There were two policyholders with more properties than this. The greatest number of additional properties was 28. These were insured by widow Rebecca Gordon of Albany Road, Camberwell in 1851 for £2,200.[2] Her policy was exceptional. Some 66 per cent of policyholders insured their additional properties for between £200 and £1,000, with a further 12 per cent having policies valued between £1,000 and £1,500.[3]

However, despite insuring the most properties, Rebecca's was not the highest value policy. In 1861, spinster Elizabeth Trotter of Eaton Place, Belgravia insured 18 houses for a total of £14,560. This included: 12 cottages for £1,320; a house including stables and outhouses for £5,400; a house including brewhouse and outbuildings for £2,270; a further house for £400 and two farms for £2,680 and £1,380 respectively.[4] In comparison, in the same year, Emma Atkins of St Martins Lane insured 37 Church Street, Soho, which she let in tenements for just £25.[5] Widows seem to have been more likely to hold the larger policies. Of the 40 women with policies valued at £2,000 and above, 50 per cent were widows, 23 per cent were spinsters and eight per cent were married women. The remaining 20 per cent were held by women whose marital status was not recorded on the insurance policy.

Sometimes policies contain details on the itemized rents to be insured, usually in addition to a separate value for the property itself. Although many women were insuring rent on just one or two properties, some established sizeable portfolios. Maria Hardy and Eliza Ann Johnson insured rent on 16 and 17 properties, respectively. Maria owned numbers 15 to 30 inclusive on Thornton Street, insuring the rent on each house for nine

Table 6.1 Number of Properties Insured by Men and Women with Sun Fire Office (%).

	Number of Properties in addition to Dwelling House (1851/1861)				
	1–2	*3–4*	*5–10*	*> 10*	*Total n*
Men	65	15	14	6	246
Women	68	18	10	4	630

Source: Sun Fire Policy registers, series 11,936, LGL.
Note: Table relates to number of properties additional to their dwelling house. The dataset of male policyholders consists of a five per cent sample of all male policyholders in each year.

Table 6.2 Insurance Valuation Range of Men's and Women's Property (%).

	1851/1861	
Value Range in £s	*Men*	*Women*
< 200	7	9
200 – 499	39	37
500 – 999	31	29
1,000 – 1,499	14	12
1,500 – 1,999	4	5
2,000 – 2,999	2	3
3,000 – 4,999	2	2
5,000 – 9,999	0.8	1
≥ 10,000	0.8	0.3
No value given	0.8	3

Source: Sun Fire Policy registers, series 11,936, LGL.
Note: Excludes value of dwelling house.

months at a combined value of £200.[6] Eliza insured £24 of rent on a house in Tenter Street and £28 each on 14 houses in Scarborough Street. She also insured a rent of £84 on numbers 6 and 7 St. Mark Street, bringing her rental income to £500.[7] This was relatively high. 1n 1861, although 27 per cent of those insuring rents were covering sums above £200, around half were covering rents valued below £100. This reinforces the supplemental nature of this income raising strategy.

Although not every policyholder went to the trouble of itemizing individual rents, many did make mention of to whom they let the property and for what purpose that occupier used the premises. The words 'in the occupation of', 'let to', or 'in the tenure of' were common, closely followed by the trade. For example, Margaret Wilson let her property to 'a dealer in cats and dogs meat'.[8] This was not superfluous information. The information was relevant because the activity carried on within the premises influence the setting of the premium, with more hazardous trades with a greater risk of fire carrying higher premiums. As for property insurers that did not make specific reference to rents or occupants, it should not be read that they did not rent out their properties (although some will not have done) but rather that for many their tenants engaged in non-hazardous trades or were not engaging in trade within the premises.

Letting properties was a strategy used by some to supplement other business activities. In 1851, 11 per cent of women's policies covering property (in addition to their dwelling house) also listed a business. Allowing that other policyholders will have insured their other businesses on separate policies or even with other insurers, this supports Thomas Cubitt's reflection that small landlords belonged to 'a little, shop-keeping class of persons who have saved a little money in business'.[9] The women of trade and property identified here operated in 40 different types of trade, spanning all sectors of the economy. Perhaps they were progressing along the cycle of exchange between trade and property that Morris found for businessmen.[10] Certainly managing a host of properties and tenants was a different type of business to many others. Nonetheless it still retained a strong business element. Not all will have opted for or been able to afford an agent or manager. The suggestion that most women will have handed over their business to the management of others is limited, anecdotal and probably most accurately applies to the upper levels of the broad and varied middle-classes. Crucially, this type of activity was not just accessed by married women, for whom it is a more convincing argument that their affairs were managed, but also spinsters and widows. Also, as Phillips' comparison of property ownership between London and the provinces has shown, property ownership for women already in business could function as a manifest sign of creditworthiness. It not only spread the risk for women in business but also gave them increased access to credit, which has always been a contentious issue in discussions of women's access to business. Property letting was not in itself a specifically gendered practice and can instead be interpreted as a classic case of portfolio diversification. Rather than a sign of women's withdrawal, or even exclusion, from business, letting property can be seen as a reaction to difficult economic circumstances.[11]

Hence, property need not in itself have been a specifically gendered practice but one that reflected economic as well as social conditions and also made sound business sense. These arguments are further reinforced when we compare the Sun Fire's female policyholders with a sample of male policyholders. A quarter of these men, in comparison to 28 per cent of women, insured property in addition to their dwelling house. Similarly, women were also slightly more likely to list a trade in their policy than their male counterparts at 30 per cent compared to 26 per cent. Thus the Sun Fire policies suggest that businesswomen were a little more likely to be diversifying their portfolios than businessmen. However, the difference is small. Similarly, most male property investors, like the women studied here, were insuring a small handful of properties. Some 65 per cent of male headed policies and 68 per cent of female headed policies insured one or two houses, with 80 and 86 per cent, respectively covering up to four properties. Women were also only very marginally less likely to insure greater than 10 properties and 36 per cent of the male policyholders that did so were actually builders and so this was their trade rather than an additional or alternative business activity. Similarly, in terms of the insurance values placed on these additional properties, again the gender of the policyholder appears to have had little bearing. Seven per cent of men's and nine per cent of women's policies were insuring property valued below £200. Three quarters insured for above £200 but below £1,000. Finally, female policyholders were marginally more likely to insure properties valued above £2,000 at nine per cent compared to six per cent of male policyholders.

This gender comparison of insurers of property suggests that men and women in London had a similar propensity to invest in property, with only a very slightly higher propensity for women to do so. Similarly women were a little more likely (four per cent differential) to enter into trade and property than their male counterparts but the margin is small. These findings, along with the similar breakdown in numbers of properties held and the values of property portfolios insured, suggests that property as an investment and potential income strategy was broadly gender neutral in the metropolis. It also suggests that interpretations of this strategy as more economically passive and therefore more suitable for women and more preferred by women should be treated with caution until more substantial studies have produced data on this.

Boarding and lodging has also been downplayed and interpreted as a 'needs-must' activity and essentially passive in nature. Yet women engaged in this type of accommodation provision in different ways, on varying scales and to a variable clientele. The level of homely comfort and attention they offered in return for money ranged from the simple provision of a bed to the services of a surrogate mother. Furthermore, women who operated such enterprises, with the exception of those who operated at the very lowest end of the market in terms of gentility, turned the Victorian notion of the ideal woman on its head. They remained the angel in the house but opened their house to the public. They became guardians of morals and manners to the migrating young workers and provided respectable homes for the unmarried man, the annuitant, and indeed anyone who could not afford their own establishment or did not want the associated expense of upkeeping one—servants, rates, repairs. Hence, London's nineteenth-century businesswoman was not just a seller of goods and garments but also of space and sobriety.

High migration into urban areas in the nineteenth century created a pressing need for suitable lodgings and it was argued that capable persons were needed to keep the overflowing houses of accommodation in order.[12] At the same time, there was an increasing recognition that many women wanted employment, particularly in the low middle-classes. It was argued by some that such women could set up lodging houses, free from the dirt and ding of many of the 'Infernal Wen's' establishments.[13] 'Women of education', it was suggested, could undertake the management and working of houses, providing men and women with cleanliness, wholesome food, and the 'atmosphere of refinement' which the presence of ladies would ensure.[14] 'Why should not women avail themselves of this combination of circumstances to develop a little enterprise?' asked Elizabeth Kingsbury. In this way, lodging-house keeping, she argued, would cure the enforced idleness of the daughters of the middle-class, 'decayed gentlewomen truly', the 'dry rot' of unused energy having consumed them.[15] It could provide a suitable outlet for those female talents that 'find their proper sphere in business'.[16] Furthermore, it was a 'woman's business', she argued, to enable all people to attain to the human rights of physical comfort and mental culture:

> It is her duty to save the masses from the too great strain that is now put upon them, by taking a fair share of the world's labour upon herself, it is her privilege to resign the luxury of the body and to claim the luxury of the soul, her glory to renounce the position of receiver and to claim the nobler place of the giver.[17]

Well before Kingsbury, commentators promoted the provision of accommodation as a suitable survival strategy for such women. At the turn of the century, Pricilla Wakefield argued that daughters of tradesmen could turn their hands to 'the management of public houses for the reception of travellers, labourers and the single'.[18] Regarded as not only domestic in nature but also involving an element of moral guidance, lodging house keeping enabled women to earn a living without compromising their social position.[19] This notion that women had a unique moral mission to perform was popular with anti-feminists as well as feminists. Its ideological function was highly ambiguous. In the hands of anti-feminists, it usually served merely to buttress sentimental dogmas of domestic womanhood. Among feminists it led to a celebration of female moral superiority, which jostled uneasily with arguments against the concept of an innate femininity.[20] The two ideas sometimes found expression in the same piece of writing, as is the case with Kingsbury's piece. Such attempts displayed an unresolved tension between the desire to minimise sexual difference and the need to re-assert it in women's favour.

As an extension of domestic management, lodging house keeping, was presented as a logical and easy step. The necessary skills could be learned within the family home, it was argued. This underplayed the business acumen needed to make such enterprises successful, especially for those who went beyond the provision of a room to the setting-up of a lodging house. Monies earned needed to exceed expenses paid and some amount of capital would have been needed to set-up in business on a sufficient scale to ensure sufficient revenue. However, proponents of this type of enterprise, anxious that women should not be put off, allayed their readers concerns by pointing out the futility of money spent 'about toilets, entertainments and the various expenses incurred in the attempt to "establish" girls'.[21] Rather, they argued that investment in a lodging house would provide greater security and: 'if ordinary intelligence were brought to bear in the management, a fair percentage might be confidently looked for'.[22]

Although presented as 'suitable', the provision of boarding and lodging represented a conundrum. It replicated the feminine model of the woman carrying out domestic tasks in her home yet gentility was increasingly associated with privacy. Hence, letting rooms could be perceived as resulting in a loss of status. In the words of Davidoff, privacy was necessary for genteel status because it kept the family free from the taint of the marketplace. In addition, the provision of boarding and lodging was a gendered activity. The term 'landlord' meant to own property and collect rent, whereas to be a 'landlady' was interpreted as providing rooms and services for cash. This meant that the relationship of landladies and lodgers was problematic, especially in the provision of personal services. Basic services included 'attendance, light and firing', with attendance entailing cleaning, carrying water and coal, emptying slops such as waste water and chamber pots, making fires, and running errands. There was a certain ambiguity involved in extracting payment for such services that would often have been provided by mothers, wives and other female relatives under different circumstances.[23]

In order to obtain some measure of the number of women engaged in lodging house keeping in the nineteenth century, albeit an under-enumeration, we can turn to the listings of London's most comprehensive directory, the Post Office Directory. At the turn of the 1870s, 1,401 lodging houses were listed, 40.4 per cent of which had a female proprietor (*n* = 566). However, it would seem that this was not their hey-day. Some 20 years earlier, perhaps in response to the increased number of visitors to the Capital attracted by The Great Exhibition of 1851, considerably more—53 per cent of lodging houses—were listed under a female proprietor (*n* = 401). This is undoubtedly an under-estimate as many proprietors were listed without a title or first name and so it is impossible to distinguish their gender, particularly for those operating in partnerships. However, Walton's analysis of the 1871 census returns for Blackpool revealed only three unmarried men as lodging house keepers. Certainly in the seaside resort, lodging house keeping was a woman's business, whether married or single.[24] However married couples sometimes did engage in this enterprise together in London. For example, the surviving trade card of Mr and Mrs Josland promoted their commercial and private establishment, Providence House, situated near the Royal Exchange.[25]

The form that the London Post Office Directory listings take, often listing only by surname for partnerships and male proprietors, obstructs our view of the married couples providing 'houses of accommodation' in the metropolis. Without record linkage, it is not possible to decipher how many of these establishments were run in partnership with or solely by a wife. Furthermore, although 80 per cent of the female lodging house keepers were described as 'Mrs' in the mid-century listings respectively (*n* = 452 and 324), it is impossible without record linkage to decipher the proportion of these women who were still married or widowed. It is also difficult to know how many of the marital status prefixes were truthful reflections of women's marital status. Although a suitable activity, inviting paying strangers into your home represented a challenge to a woman's respectability, particularly if she was unmarried. The term 'Mrs' communicated a certain level of propriety and so conferred some protection on the reputation of the lodging house keeper and of course on her establishment. Similarly, in husband–wife partnerships the husband may have had an additional occupation. His inclusion in advertisements may have provided an extra layer or respectability for what was primarily his wife's enterprise and her efforts could supplement his income.

Dickens warns of the dangers of being compromised in 'The boarding house' in *Sketches by Boz*. Mr Tibbs' pension being insufficient, his spouse uses a legacy of 700*l* to take and furnish a tolerable house on Great Coram Street. Two female servants and a boy are engaged and gentleman and ladies moved in. One night Mrs Tibbs and a gentleman guest bump into each other as they investigate strange noises. They hear her maid Agnes possibly plotting to set the house on fire but fearing they will be discovered are forced to hide in the drawing room. Unfortunately they are discovered there by the other guests who are also investigating the strange night time disruptions and their activities are assumed dishonourable. This compromising situation leads to the closure of the lodging house and the separation of Mr and Mrs Tibbs by mutual consent.[26]

Despite such scaremongering, accommodation remained a popular area of business activity for women. However given the limitations of trade directories, we need to look for further detail and depth in other sources. We can turn to fire insurance policy registers but need to look at the broader dataset of all female policyholders rather than just business policies. Female policyholders engaged specifically in lodging house keeping usually did not define their assets as business assets (stock, utensils and fixtures) but rather as personal ones. This is because their business assets were essentially the same as their private assets—a dwelling house, furniture, mirrors, and books—the quality depending on the type of establishment. Furthermore, it was not necessarily in a proprietor's interests to declare the business use of their private assets, emphasizing the hidden nature of some types of female enterprise. Therefore, while this source does not provide the opportunity to gauge the extent of women's involvement in this business, we can use it to find out more about range and nature of their lodging ventures.

Only a small proportion of the lodging house keepers from the Sun Fire registers were included in the Post Office Directory listings. These included: Mrs Wilby of 44 Watling Street; Mrs Peters Brotherson of 17 and 18 Francis Inn, Holborn; Miss Johnstone of 16 Norfolk Street, Strand and Mrs Sheppard of 7 Arundell Street, Strand. All of these women held substantial insurance policies valued between £800 and £1,500.[27] The other lodging house keepers who did not make it into the London Post Office Directory held policies that were valued between £150 and £600. This suggests that many establishments run by women were small and relied on word-of-mouth advertising rather than directories. This reinforces the notion that nineteenth-century trade directories provided partial coverage of the businesses in the communities they purported to cover. The numbers of women engaged in lodging house keeping or any other trade were under-represented in their listings. They tended to include larger establishments on the better streets in the better parts of town. In the 1851 Post Office Directory some 60 female lodging house keepers (15 per cent) operated from the area of the Strand alone. None of the lodging houses listed as operated by women were located in the south of London and only 22 gave addresses in the east or north (six per cent). Central and western districts (including Marylebone) accounted for 44 per cent and 47 per cent of proprietors, respectively (*n* = 175 and 190).[28] In contrast, the lodging house keepers located in the Sun Fire registers were distributed more widely. The central and western districts accounted for 64 per cent of houses (*n* = 16) but the northern, southern and eastern districts were also represented.[29] This suggests that while a significant proportion of women operated from the more respectable parts of London, many others occupied what might be described as more marginal space. Rather than tourists and fine gentlemen and ladies, they catered to a local clientele with a more limited budget.

Similarly, the lodging house keepers extracted from the insurance registers insured their assets for a wide range of values.[30] The lowest value policy was £100 and the highest £1,500. However the proportion of the women insuring assets below £300, between £300 and £499, and between £500 and £999 was fairly evenly spread. In regards to assets above £1,000 in value, the proportion is likely inflated. It seems plausible that 1851 being the year of the Great Exhibition, a number of additional women might well have opened up their otherwise private homes to paying guests for a brief period when there was a particularly high demand for accommodation. This highlights the flexible and accessible nature of this business and that not all women engaged in it were victims of circumstance. Rather, many proprietors were opportunists. For example, the trade card of Miss Killick reveals that not only did she create a hierarchy of bedrooms with corresponding staggered pricing but that she charged extra for more than one person in the room. In addition, male guests were charged 1s more than female guests for attendance and linen.[31] The proportion insuring above £500 is far greater than for women's business policies generally at 60 per cent compared to 22 per cent. This is partly due to

Table 6.3 Insurance Valuations of Female Lodging House Keepers Policies (%).

Year	Value Range in £s			
	< 300	300–499	500–999	> 1,000
1851	20	20	30	30
1861	33	40	27	0

Source: Sun Fire Policy registers, series 11,936, LGL.
Note: Valuations contain combination of dwelling houses and household goods. Inclusion of 1861 for comparison demonstrates that the Great Exhibition of 1851 may have had an impact.

lodging house keepers' greater propensity to insure dwelling houses, boosting the overall value of their policies.

To learn more about these women and their enterprises we need to link their insurance policies to their census returns. As the previous chapter revealed, nominal linkage between the Sun Fire Office policies and the census returns can furnish information such as whether the proprietor was the head of the household, her marital status and age, whether she had children, servants and live-in employees and the size of her household. This information can also be compared with the household characteristics of female insurers engaged in other trades, in this case the Sun Fire's most popular trades.[32] Of course people moved frequently in this time period and, in addition, addresses in the census were not always entered as a precise house number and street name. This can make locating individuals problematic. Nonetheless, 52 per cent lodging house keepers recorded in the insurance policies were successfully linked in the census (*n* = 13). In the absence of other detailed evidence such as diaries, this small sample provides a vital insight into the homes of London's nineteenth-century female lodging house keepers. In this way, it builds a more detailed and varied picture of the lives and circumstances of these women.

The linkage revealed that like the women engaged in the popular trades, lodging house keepers were likely to be head of their household (77%). The remainder resided with elderly mothers and in one case with a husband. What this indicates is that lodging house keepers will have been heavily involved in the decision to turn their homes into businesses and to open up their private space to paying guests. This need not have been a response to calamity such as widowhood. In contrast to the women in the Sun Fire's popular trades, the lodging house keepers were far more likely to be spinsters than widows at 54 and 39 per cent compared to 27 and 64. (The proportion of married women in either group was small). This paints a different picture than that portrayed in the London Post Office Directory listings, in which married or widowed women made up 80 per cent of female proprietors. Perhaps, spinsters were more likely to run the smaller establishments at a further distance from the major thoroughfares and were therefore less likely to make it into the directory listings.

However, although spinster-proprietors predominated amongst the lodging house keepers of the Sun Fire Office, in the 1850s and 1860s this was seemingly not an occupation into which they stepped on coming of age. Indeed, only one spinster in this study was below 40 years of age. Generally, disregarding marital status, lodging house keepers were between 30 and 50 years of age, with some younger and older exceptions. This is a much narrower range than that found for the women in the popular trades—19 to 84 years old (see Chapter 4). This suggests that lodging house keeping was an activity taken up once a sufficient income had been generated from an alternative source—possibly another trade, or inherited. Alternatively, perhaps this was the best option for women who found themselves unsupported and without specialist training in their middle years.

Perhaps not too surprisingly, in addition to the greater propensity towards spinsterhood, there was a greater tendency towards partnership with other women than in the popular trades. Over 30 per cent operated with a sister or cousin, compared to the 11 per cent of women that did so in the popular trades (most cases of which were in the needle trades). There were additional lodging cases of women working alongside mothers, taking the percentage to 50 per cent. Perhaps many such sisters, cousins and mothers were already sharing domestic space and decided collectively to open it to the public. Alternatively, they could have been roped in from the household support network. Nonetheless, whilst this clearly did happen it did not dominate the experience of the female lodging house keeper.

Hence, although many lodging house keepers were not married, they were not alone in their endeavours. They might also have young female relatives over the age of 14 residing with them. They will almost certainly have assisted in the running of the lodging house. Indeed, one of these daughters was blatantly recorded in the census as 'employed in house'. In addition, perhaps because this familial labour supply was lower than that which benefited those women in the popular trades (42 per cent), 62 per cent of the lodging house keepers also employed residential servants. (This compares to 48 per cent for the women engaged in the most popular trades.) All but one of the 10 lodging-house servants was female and their work was often arduous. In particular when lodgings were supplied on a scale large enough to produce profit, the lot of these servants could be very hard indeed. It has been argued that the lowest form of domestic service was the 'slavery' in a lodging house and this was often the fate of young girls from workhouses or orphanages.[33]

As was suggested in the preceding chapter, making your home into your business was a good means of balancing income and childcare needs. The desire for additional income but the need for flexibility in hours and effort made this particularly attractive to mothers or guardians of young children. In addition, as children grew in size and increased in dexterity they could be incorporated into the enterprise, creating more household revenue and solving childcare problems. In this study, although a third of the linked Sun Fire popular trade proprietors had children under the age of 14 living in their household, it was not so common for the lodging house keepers. This is largely explained by the predominance of spinsters in their ranks. Although, the one married lodging house keeper and two of the five widow-proprietors did have children under the age of 14 living in their household (23 per cent).

Turning from the proprietors themselves to the nature of their lodging enterprises, these varied in size and character considerably. Contemporary, Mayhew commented that there seems to have become tacitly established 'an arrangement as to what character of lodgers shall resort thither; the thieves, the prostitutes, and the better class of street-sellers or traders, usually resorting to the houses where they will meet the same class of persons'.[34]

Table 6.4 Households of 'Popular' Trade Proprietors and Lodging House Keepers (%).

Category	1851/1861	
	Popular Trade	*Lodging House*
Household head	81	77
Married	9	7
Spinster	27	54
Widowed	64	39
Residential servants	39	62
Children < 14 years	33	23
Children > 14 years	42	23

Source: Sun Fire Policy registers, series 11,936, LGL.

Examining their visitors on census night reveals this sample was characterized by this diversity. The number of their guests varied from as little as two people up to nine in one case. Some were devoted to providing accommodation for the spinster fundholders. This was the case with Cesilia Ruedi's establishment on Cambridge Terrace.[35] Others catered for a clientele that was predominantly young and unmarried. For example, Anne White on William Street and Elizabeth Warmsley on Grafton Street.[36] More distinguished guests crossed the threshold of 35-year-old Cassandra Wilby's lodging house, at 44 Watling Street in the City. Her visitors included three married men, two of which were merchants, and one unmarried woman, a 35-year-old annuitant called Margaret Heel. Her insurance policy was for a substantial £1,150.[37] In contrast, 43-year-old Rebecca Darnell, a married proprietor, took out a policy in the same year for £150 on her house located at 4a Angel Alley, Whitechapel. The names of her visitors were not included, only their gender and age. All were under 30 and their occupations went unrecorded.[38]

The Angel Alley lodging house raises the spectre of the 'low' lodging house—the type of establishments that most certainly did not make it into the London Post Office Directory. Not a genteel option but perhaps a profitable one. And while the desire to retain respectability no doubt influenced many women, there will have been some happy to exchange their social standing for a fuller purse. It was estimated that there were at least 200 or so of these low lodging houses in London. The existence of such establishments run by women represented not only their negotiation of public and private space but also challenged the private sphere of home as the respectable, gilded cage of womanhood. These establishments were referred to as 'low' by contemporaries because of the small charge for lodging or because of the character of their frequenters. They catered for a lower class of visitor, the disreputable and the transient. Only a minority of prostitutes ever resided in brothels in the city. Indeed the number of reported brothels declined from 933 in 1841 to 410 in 1857. Around the same time, new licensing laws also resulted in the number of public houses letting out rooms to prostitutes declining significantly. Rather, prostitutes tended to reside in cheap lodging houses, the external respectability of which varied.[39]

Low lodging houses were usually over-crowded due to the increasing population density in London, and the paucity of working class housing. Their over-crowding was argued to encourage immorality. Porter highlights a report written in 1850, which stated that the question was never asked, 'when a man and woman go to a lodging house, whether they are man and wife . . . I have known the bedding to be unchanged for three months . . . They are all infested with vermin, I never met with exception . . . .'[40] Migrants to London fresh from the countryside and with little money had nowhere to go except to these cheap, crowded and sometimes squalid common lodging houses, which in turn proliferated in the most overcrowded districts. Lord Shaftesbury in 1847 commented:

> The astonishment and perplexities of a young person on his arrival here, full of good intentions to live honestly, would be almost ludicrous, were they not the prelude to such mournful results. He alights—and is instantly directed, for the best accommodation, to Duck Lane, St Gile's, Saffron Hill, Spitalfields, or Whitechapel. He reaches the indicated region through tight avenues of glittering fish and rotten vegetables, with doorways or alleys gaping on either side—which, if they be not choked with squalid garments or sickly children, lead the eye through an almost interminable vista of filth and distress . . . The pavement, where there is any, rugged and broken, is bespattered with dirt of every hue, ancient enough to rank with the fossils, but offensive as the most recent deposits. The houses, small, low, and mournful, present no one part, in windows, door-posts, or brickwork, that seems fitted to stand for another week— rags and hurdles stuff up the panes, and defend the passages blackened with use and by the damps arising from the undrained and ill-ventilated recesses. Yet each one affects to smile with promise, and invites the country-bumpkin to the comfort and repose of 'Lodgings for single men'.[41]

Lord Shaftesbury's Act of 1851 placed the registration, inspection, cleansing and limitation of overcrowding in these establishments in the hands of the Metropolitan Police. In a further act of the same year, also sponsored by Shaftesbury, the London local authorities were empowered to buy, lease or build lodging houses. Yet the adoption of this power was extremely limited, leaving the private lodging houses to dominate the housing marketplace until much later in the century.[42]

Starting a low lodging house was not a costly matter and Mayhew estimated that the average takings of lodging house keepers was about 17s 6d a night. Mrs Cummins was the owner of lodging houses in St Giles. Her houses contained over 100 beds for which she charged as much as 18d to 2s per hour. This was high and probably derived from the reputation her establishments possessed for protecting the customers of prostitutes from the risk of robbery. Nevertheless, Henderson argues the keepers of quite ordinary houses were able to demand hugely inflated rents from the prostitutes who lodged with them.[43] Besides taxes, and rent if the lodging house keeper did not own the property, their principal expenditure was on coal and gas. In some of the better houses, blacking, brushes, and razors were supplied, without charge. Newspapers were commonly available and sometimes pen and ink, and soap. In one house in Kent Street, the following ditty adorned the mantel-piece:

To save a journey up the town,
A razor lent here for a brown:
But if you think the price too high,
I beg you won't the razor try.[44]

In some places a charge of a halfpenny was made for hot water but more often it was included in the night's rent, or not available.[45] The majority of the cheap or 'low' lodging houses were unlikely to find their way into the trade directories. Rather, they relied on more localised advertising. Signage on the front of the house or 'Lodgings for Travellers' painted on a shutter. According to Mayhew, a few of the better off houses posted up small billheads, inviting the attention of prospective lodgers 'by laudations of the cleanliness, good beds, abundant water and "gas all night", to be met with'. Others distributed trade cards.[46]

So, having considered the suitability of lodging house keeping, built a picture of the women that operated such enterprises, and considered the differing character of their ventures, we are left to wonder why such enterprises have been marginalised in considerations of women's involvement in the public sphere of business. Schoolkeeping, also frequently using the home for teaching and boarding, has increasingly been regarded as a business activity. The provision of accommodation carried similar domestic advantages and responsibilities but has received far less attention from historians. Yet a lodging house was acknowledged by contemporaries to be a suitable and respectable income generation method for women in the nineteenth century. Some women let only a room, others the whole house. Some engaged in other business activities at the same time, others dedicated all their energies into making the business of accommodation a profitable venture. What they all had in common was the negotiation of public and private space.

It seems to be the overlap between business and domesticity that has encouraged a downplaying of the business elements of accommodation enterprises. Although many women may have cultivated this themselves, for historians it is problematic. The accommodation business has been caught up in an argument for the increasing economic passivity of women. Davidoff and Hall have written of middle-class women's propensity to turn away from active economic activity as the nineteenth century progressed. They argued that widows and spinsters formed the core of those investors requiring a steady income without administrative worries. They pointed to the variety of sources and types of income, including rents from accommodation, which provided a living to those who wished for a genteel competence not requiring active intervention.[47] Whilst there is much in this, it underplays the interaction of many women with their customers. Also, an income earned from rents was not always used as an alternative to other activities, as a move to greater passivity, but rather alongside them. Of the 456 London women who held policies covering business assets with the Sun Fire in 1851 and 1861, 180 were successfully located in the census and nearly 20 per cent of these were also providing lodging in their household. Victuallers and coffee-house keepers, in particular, often provided accommodation of some description and both these trades were popular options for metropolitan women. For example, Esther Goatley, widow-proprietor of the coffee rooms at 37 Bermondsey Street, accommodated five lodgers, in addition to two sons, a son-in-law and a daughter.[48]

Although by the nineteenth century, taking in a houseful or even a solitary lodger could be regarded by some as a sign of the loss of genteel status, this was not an opinion shared by all and this activity did provide women with a means of obtaining an income using her private assets and domestic know-how. Financially, it could help a woman to retain her own residence, whilst socially it could extend her network of acquaintances and business contacts. These benefits she could achieve without compromising her respectability in the eyes of her contemporaries. Nonetheless, it is important to recognise that this activity did take a woman into the public sphere. Although the provision of accommodation has been seen as merely an extension of domestic activity, in reality it was more than this and required many of the skills common to business generally: an establishment suitable to the proprietors, available capital and space had to be set up; it had to be promoted in the right circles; staff needed to be located and managed and additional familial help drafted in; appropriate and satisfactory services needed to be supplied to the lodgers; and payment had to be collected. A head for business was as vital as good housekeeping skills. Women who opened their houses to paying guests did not always get paid and could find their livelihoods pawned along with their furniture and bedding with the guest nowhere to be found.[49] These risks multiplied for the woman who set up an entire 'house of accommodation'. Furthermore, while many women set-up in the accommodation business, what was more difficult was making the establishment pay. As

Walton found of the Blackpool landladies, the transition from keeping a lodging house to being kept by it was difficult and uncertain of attainment.[50] Nonetheless, the number of women who engaged in lodging house keeping in the mid-decades of the century attests that this was a popular avenue for women in London. However, these women should not be relegated in studies of business as victims of circumstance. They took advantage of their varied means and training, the buoyant demand for lodging space and the flexible nature of its supply, to turn their private sphere into a public one and their homes into businesses.

7   Historical Female Entrepreneurship

In 2006 entrepreneur Lucy Martin argued that male business proprietors start by thinking 'in ten years time I want to retire with £20 million' but their female equivalent think 'I want to take control of my life, I want my own money, I want to see my kids'.[1] The expressions may be very modern but their meaning has significant continuity with the businesswomen encountered in this historical study. Independence, limited options and domestic commitments were primary motivators for women setting-up in business in the nineteenth century. Although the goals of business proprietors were not and are not now always gender specific to the extreme, there has continued to be a gender distinction, particularly in terms of self-representation and representation by others. The humble dressmaker of 1850 with whom we started this book was keen to mark out her business practices as different to what she perceived as the normal pursuit of profits.[2] Similarly, when businesswomen of the year competitions today run with the headline: 'Don't try to be like a man', it does not raise an eyebrow.[3]

A further continuity is that the difference in the size, nature and capitalization of men's and women's businesses is often directly correlated with the external constraints on performance of female proprietors. Yet as Chapter 3 has demonstrated, even at a time in British history when such barriers were very evident, many men and women operated in the same sectors and trades and at similar levels of capitalization. Although on a scale of capitalization, men did dominate the higher end, the extent of this is exaggerated by the outliers, for example the merchants and factors whose capitalization values need to be handled with caution. External barriers to entry and access to capital were limiters but so too were differential goals, and cultures of representation also need to be recognized as powerful influencers.

Whilst the twenty-first-century woman can turn easily to guides to working for herself, 'how to' books specifically for women in business in the nineteenth century were thin on the ground. However, guidance was not completely absent. There were establishments set to train younger women in the skills needed for independence in business such as that of the Society for the Promotion of Female Employment and that of the entrepreneurial Matilda Pullan, who clearly spotted a gap in the market.[4] Later, guide books on work choices would offer some direction, for example, Mercy Grogan's *How Women May Earn a Living* or Phillis Brownes' *What Girls Can Do*, albeit their entrepreneurial wisdom was limited.[5] In the meantime, and useful for women of all ages, were the handful of financial guides being published in this period. *A Guide to the Unprotected in Everyday Matters Relating to Property and Income*, went through at least five editions. Authored by 'A banker's daughter', it included keeping accounts, technical terms used in business, house property and money transactions among other things. Although not expressly oriented at how to run a business, it extended women's transferable know-how beyond the already useful experience of household management, accounting and provisioning. It also included useful proforma for those involved in the accommodation business.[6]

In addition, although the domestic ideal was strong in this period, it was never absolute. It is more useful to think of competing ideologies rather than one catch-all dominant ideology to which all sang along. Being virtuous, working hard, being thrifty, keeping respectable company, meeting your debts—all counted. Furthermore, because the nineteenth-century middle-class was so broad, those at the lower end of the income scale had considerably more elbow-room to live respectably than the romanticized ideal first suggests. This is often missed because fictional, working women in the early and mid-Victorian period are largely restricted to either working class labour or middle-class education. These imaginary, economically active women rarely take the explicit guise of a woman engaged in business. However, such engagement is implicit in many depictions of women at the margins, albeit muffled under blankets of acceptable presentation—a reluctant drudgery; an emergency endeavour; the last resort activity of a cast adrift woman; an elder sister-come-mother; the result of a wretched father or a weak, fiscally insufficient husband. A little enterprise was, for a fictional woman, the last chance saloon before at best the death of her respectability or at worst genuine starvation. Even coated in a heavy dripping of pathos, such depictions were not that far from the truth for some real proprietors although this was by no means the case for all.

Different stages in the lifecycle will have influenced motives, often related to changing familial circumstances. Women engaged in business at a young age, others juggled a business alongside family commitments, or set up in business after having children. Some women will have engaged with different businesses at various stages in their life, adapting the enterprise to their changing needs. Self-employment has historically provided women with an advantage specific to the position of their sex within society as a whole, as a form of work that allows greater flexibility to accommodate domestic tasks, especially child-care. Furthermore, it is also important to recognise that self-employment and small business proprietorship is one among a whole range of women's responses to need. Women often utilised a number of different overlapping strategies. Other responses included investment in the business activities of others, re-marriage, paid employment including the provision of domestic services to relatives and neighbours, and the taking in of lodgers and boarders.

Although as Phillips cautioned, treating businesswomen as a homogenous group is a hazardous undertaking because it obscures differences, there are similarities between London and other economies, within and without of the United Kingdom. Phillip's herself found continuities of practice between London and the provinces, most notably Durham.[7] For Glasgow, Gordan and Nair found that not only did the trade directories underestimate the number of women in business but they also erroneously indicated a downward trend after 1871. In contrast, the Valuation Rolls for the years 1861 and 1881 revealed that the numbers of women in business trebled from 600 to over 1,500. Most of these businesses were in retail and concentrated in food, drink and clothing.[8] Similarly, in early nineteenth-century Manchester, Leeds and Sheffield, Barker demonstrated that the unique characteristics of northern 'industrial' towns offered women an unusual level of opportunity in clothing, food and drink, shopkeeping and dealing. Women of the lower middling sort here demonstrated independence, entrepreneurship and a strong sense of occupational identity. Her study concluded that we need to reconceptualize middling women, acknowledging their significance as producers and distributors, as well as consumers—the role to which they are traditionally ascribed.[9]

Looking beyond British shores, in his work on northern Sweden, where the number of women of marriageable age also exceeded the number of men, Ericsson found that single women and widows, especially those supporting children, were encouraged by circumstance to go into trade. This was partly an act of survival, but as found here for women in London, it allowed them to preserve their social status. Retailing was the most likely type of business activity, regarded as a 'suitable' and a 'respectable occupation' and the state took various steps to remove restrictions to it, such as abolishing the guilds.[10] Interestingly he also found that these entrepreneurial women were, like the London women, often responsible for someone else—an aged parent, younger sibling, a legitimate or illegitimate child or fostered child. Their businesses were also small. Single, widowed and married women all participated, although the latter did so in the face of legal restrictions similar to those in England.[11] A very similar story is told for Belgium, where Piette reports that tradeswomen were 'small-scale, independent operators who kept retail stores'. They were especially visible in food and textiles, tavern keeping, street vending and the sale of tobacco and stationary.[12] Seemingly, social and legal boundaries were circumnavigated across Europe, sometimes in a discretionary way and at other times much more ambitiously. For example, the clandestine silk, hat and button manufacturing workshops of women in Lyon discovered by Hafter. These women, excluded by the guilds, secured control of raw materials, labour, and distribution networks within an underground economy.[13]

Beyond retailing, there does appear to be more divergence in experience. In her comparative study of women engaged in the business of schoolkeeping in England and France, de Bellaigue found that it was in the latter that the business nature of their efforts was more recognized. In England the women who ran boarding school businesses tended to be caricatured, discarded as reduced gentlewomen or derided as self-interested profiteers. As a consequence, although they were as much entrepreneurs as they were teachers, in England these women had to distance themselves from the idea that teaching was a business. They can be seen emphasizing the domesticity of their arrangements.[14] Of course there were many domestic activities associated with boarding schools, with the daily organization resembling the management of a sizeable household. The feeding, washing and clothing of pupils aged between 5 and 18 could demand several kitchen and maidservants. However, larger establishments also had to deal with receipts, expenditure and the hiring, training and supervising of teachers; not to mention business promotion. Little surprise then that partnerships were common and those involved often divided up the responsibilities.[15]

So, although London's female proprietors may have shared many similarities with their counterparts in other locations, the practice and perception of their activities still reflected the dominant values of their nation and culture.[16] In particular, this seems to account for the very varied experience of married women in relation to business. Craig found that in northern France retail provided opportunities for women, especially married ones.[17] Although single women were less constrained in doing business as men, married female proprietors were not difficult to find in this location, although their trade tended to be subordinated to their family's needs. Much as elsewhere, Craig also found that women's activities have been hidden by the nature of the available records but that in reality the businesswomen of Lille were not just concentrated in female trades. She argues that gender was only one factor in influencing business and not necessarily the most important one.[18] Indeed, whether in Lille, London or elsewhere in Europe, women's business, whilst exhibiting some clustering, have been found to be less intensely focussed in the female trades as first thought.

American women's ventures, like their European counterparts, were also very varied and it is not difficult to find examples of female proprietors engaged in both home-based and heavy production trades. For example, Polly Bemis and her boarding house on the Western frontier and Rebecca Lukens and her iron manufacturing company.[19] Credit company ledgers are filled with examples of women trying to engage with the market as businesswomen. In addition to dressmaking and millinery, shops selling everything dotted the landscape. Interestingly, many of these women appeared to be married and were supplementing their husband's income.[20] Less legal restriction and an economic culture of greater freedom seems to have made business activity even more accessible for married women than in other countries.[21] It was also seen by some as a logical combination with motherhood.[22] However

American female proprietors, like their sisters elsewhere, were also likely to have been motivated by barriers to entry to other revenue raising activities. Despite their diversity, they still displayed a tendency to opt for the sectors with the lower barriers to entry, for example lodging house keeping and the beauty related trades.[23] And, as Gamber discovered, the garment trades were a popular habitation.[24] Hence, greater legal freedom or not, female proprietors in America seem to have faced other similar constraints to proprietors elsewhere.

In modern studies, an entrepreneur is increasingly recognized as someone who specialises in taking judgemental decisions about the coordination of scare resources. Building on this, Da Silva Lopes and Duguid recently argued that this means that they are not necessarily a capitalist or inventor, but rather someone who 'gets things done' with an economic aim. Borrowing this broad interpretation seems very apt in application to women in business in the nineteenth century. They were very much co-ordinating scare resources—their own personal ones. They used their home, their household, their skills, their savings, their credit and they exploited the niches of respectability and frugality to attract customers. Their economic aim was to survive and retain their standing and this could only happen through the success of their venture. In turn, their enterprise needed to obey certain balance sheet principles for this to happen. Although this may seem a little awkward or obvious to some readers, it is point worth making as whilst there are lots of suggestions there is little consensus in the broad field of business history, as to what entrepreneurial activity actually entails.[25]

Despite obvious similarities discovered between female proprietors in London and elsewhere, it remains reductionist and simplistic to attempt to identify "the" female entrepreneur. Types or typologies are deliberate simplifications and abstractions and can be useful but in any regard in working towards a generalized typology of nineteenth-century historical female entrepreneurship, we meet a number of analytical complexities. Survivalist entrepreneurship for example can be recognized as a 'type', however it is not necessarily specific to women in business. Female entrepreneurship is itself a 'type' and need not be tied to survivalist or domestic contexts. The resource constraint version of the disadvantage theory of entrepreneurship offers a potential helping hand. This holds that members of destitute groups often respond to labour market exclusion by becoming survivalist entrepreneurs - that is persons who start marginal businesses in response to a need to enter self-employment. This is usually applied to ethnic groups but fits here although the labour disadvantage experienced has a very different cultural context. However, conceptually there is a sense in which these historical proprietors appear to have been defined as entrepreneurs at the margins, the core being defined as an innovative or emerging corporate entrepreneurship. Yet, recognizing different types of entrepreneurship in the past is vital. If one type of entrepreneur is dismissed and another held aloft as more important, this conveniently simplifies the concept of what entrepreneurship is but it is a false economy. It creates a misunderstanding of the diverse nature of historical entrepreneurship—why it occurred, changed, ceased or failed.

What these potential types (survivalist-, female-, disadvantaged entrepreneurship) have in common is that they have been relegated as sub-types outside of a main type of entrepreneurship that defines the norm as masculine and large scale. This can too easily become treated as a benchmark against which other types of entrepreneurship become sub-types, failing to make the grade of real business worthiness. Yet this downgrades the real business experience of many in enterprise. This has partly come about because studies of historical entrepreneurship in the British context have been slow to move beyond the 'agent of great change' and it is with some difficulty that female entrepreneurs or entrepreneurs of small businesses regardless of gender are recognised as entrepreneurial at all. This is because, as Mathias described, there are two contrasting entities concealed in the word *entrepreneur*. It can be simply a descriptive term for a person engaged in business. In this sense, historians can look at entrepreneurs simply as creatures of flesh and blood, who did what they did for the motives they had at the time. However, historians have also ascribed conceptual meaning and it is from here that some rigidity has stemmed. Most famously, Schumpeter defined the entrepreneur as the agent for changing an economy from a stable state to being progressive and expanding. That is, he put a type of entrepreneur at the centre of the process of economic growth. Habakkuk's counter-theory reduced the entrepreneur to a product of circumstance. The entrepreneur in his eyes was not the originating cause of change or lack of it but a responder to economic competitive forces within industries. Nonetheless, in both cases the entrepreneur is given conceptual importance.[26] This conceptual importance within models of economic growth and decline has tended to overwhelm the descriptive dimension of the term entrepreneur in business history. The agent of great change, the profit chaser, has been conflated with the creature of flesh and blood when this is in fact only one conceptual usage of the word entrepreneur. Hence, the term *entrepreneur* stands like a monolith on the historical landscape, as if to acknowledge the diverse nature of historical entrepreneurship were to dilute the worth of the term. We are left with a typology based on extreme innovators and industrialists, the natural extension of which being that anything else is not really entrepreneurship. Yet, alongside the findings of this study and those of Barker, Benson, Gordon and Nair, Phillips, Rose, Sanderson and others, UK studies of women's historical economic activity clearly demonstrate that women set-up, inherited and adapted, and ran enterprises. They were not always or indeed often, agents of great change individually but they were entrepreneurial and their economic efforts did have a ripple effect on the broader marketplace.

American scholars have largely led the way in terms of engendering business history and thereby recognizing the validity of women's enterprises and endeavours. Indeed as Honeyman energetically put it: 'In many areas of political, social and economic activity the gap between the US and the UK is wide, but with respect to engendering business history a chasm separates the two.'[27] Walsh suggested that one reason for the lack of gendered insights in British business history is that the discipline's very roots can be located in economic history, itself a discipline preferring a concrete, even quantitative base. From its early days as an independent discipline, the conceptual base of business history was informed by notions of structure, efficiency, rationality and profitability, and as such attention was focused on robust, quantifiable elements to the neglect of socio-cultural forces. Consequently, Europeans have been more reluctant to examine women's entrepreneurial activities and look around the masculine frameworks. Hence, there is a 'taken for granted' masculinity which permeates study of business activity, and a tendency to focus on the efficiency of specific forms of organisation rather than on the human relationships that underpin them'.[28] As a result, women in business and women's businesses have often been judged as exceptions to male indicators of success, rather than as 'part of the gendered history of economic life'.[29]

It is obviously not so simple that we can just add in women, using the same interpretative models and judgements—they need to be assessed in their own right—and not as lesser economic agents, falling below the size, capitalization, longevity and profit benchmarks of 'successful' business and therefore enterprises deemed worthy of recognition. As Craig found in northern France, if business was entered into as a function of family need, then it follows that these women often exited or ended the enterprise when it had exhausted its usefulness, rather than this shorter longevity of women's businesses in comparison to men's being a sign of men being more successful.[30] Yes there are barriers to women's access and success in business—but not in all areas and not as strong as previously thought. A point reinforced by Gardiner who explores the ways in which skills acquired by women within the domestic sphere have value within the wider economy including business. Gardiner's argument is that the experience accumulated by women through organising a home and family, and engaging in a variety of caring and educative roles, rather than limiting them actually equipped them well for the world of business.[31] This can be seen in the lodging housekeepers of this study and De Bellaigue's schoolkeepers, examples of women who used the family home or rent or bought external premises. Hence, they were already equipped with the knowledge and experience that came from financing such property transactions and the legal mechanisms surrounding ownership of property.[32]

The reductionism in the idea of the entrepreneur is not just about a need to engender business history. It can also be traced back to the ideal of separate spheres itself and Victorian understandings of masculinity conveyed through business and the market. Over time these have become embedded in our understanding of business. In the nineteenth century, it is important

to recognize that the discourse of work or business being essentially masculine in nature did exist. Separate spheres may now be a much discussed
and qualified paradigm for viewing the Victorians but they themselves did
make reference to their spheres of duty. These spheres may not have always
been a physical reality but they were a psychological one. Gordon and Nair,
in their study of women, family and the marketplace in Victorian Glasgow,
point out that the 'middle-classness' of women is commonly underestimated
in the ways it influenced their identity formation. The middle-class home
was not the secluded haven often imagined. As arbiters of taste, managers
of display and consumers of culture, women were central to the creation of
middle-class identity and culture. Furthermore, they argue that the defining
concepts of the dominant political philosophy of liberalism were individu-
alism, justice, obligation, rights and freedom. These values could conjoin
with those of Christian duty to provide alternative aspirational models for
middle-class women that were rooted in self-reliance, independence and
self-fulfilment rather than dependence. Coupled with the emphasis on dignity, work and duty, this could legitimize and motivate women to make
their own living. Their desire for employment, of some nature, was rooted
in Victorian values, not running counter to them.[33]

Success for the women in this study was striking the delicate balance
between revenue and respectability, not profit at all social cost. In *Cassandra*
(1852), Florence Nightingale, noted that women who dreamed of activity
were accompanied by a phantom—'the phantom of sympathy guiding and
lighting the way'.[34] Increasingly, as long as the work was imperative, the novelist was on the side of the working woman. However, in most cases, as soon
as there was a suspicion of her getting any satisfaction out of her self-supporting existence, the forces of anti-feminism were rallied.[35] She was not expected
to aspire beyond sufficiency. Hence, cultural prejudice in nineteenth-century
England could cause women in business to underplay their profitable success
even when they did desire or achieve it because this appeared unfeminine
and reinforced negative stereotypes. De Bellaigue found this to be the case
for women who ran boarding schools. Anxious to avoid the label of self-
interested profiteer, their correspondence refers to 'old fashioned ways', less
profit oriented in emphasis. Like the humble dressmaker, these women were
keen to promote the merits and honour of their work, recoiling from the
harsh accusations of commentators such as one in *Fraser's Magazine*, 1845:
'one might be tempted to believe that the end most schoolmistresses pro-
pose themselves in teaching is to get themselves handsome houses, furnish
sumptuous drawing-rooms, keep livery servants'.[36] Hence, even if women did
achieve high profits, they would not necessarily be respected for it.

This highlights the crudity of the profit maximisation model in exploring
business proprietorship in any period. These women might well have been
able to secure a higher rate of return in a different trade or activity. However,
alongside the benefits of independence, flexibility in effort, and respectability, the premium placed on respectability skewed women's opportunities

and choices. As Mary Taylor said of women who maintained themselves: 'Respect is more to them than money'.[37] Similarly, Mrs Elizabeth Hakewell, who ran a millinery and dressmaking shop near Grosvenor Square employing six or seven women, told the 1854 House of Lords Committee that they were: ' . . . very respectable young people [who] would not like to mix with common young people. They were the daughters of clergymen and half-pay officers and of first-rate professionals.'[38] Such concerns to preserve respectability pervaded society across the nineteenth century. As Nenadic also found in her study of the Edinburgh women's garment trades, business activity went beyond profit maximisation and could emphasise 'non-utilitarian satisfactions'.[39] Hence, a catch-all entrepreneurial theology which separates business from the economic culture and societal concerns of the day is a shortsighted one. The nature of enterprise cannot be separated from the social discourse of the period, in particular the virtues, codes and moral aspirations. Rather than being discounted as too feminine, too undercapitalized, too 'little' an entrepreneurial encounter to be called entrepreneurship, the type of enterprise engaged in by nineteenth-century middling women needs to be valued for its common and significant contribution to family, local, national economies and international trading links. Indeed, it would seem that women's involvement in business is far more a story of continuity than departure. Self-employment and entrepreneurship have been central to women's economic agency across the centuries, including the nineteenth. To paraphrase Kwolek-Folland, the specifics of their business involvement may be new but the fact of their involvement is not. A meaningful evaluation of this is often missed because of the problematic business history assumption of firms and entrepreneurship as being socially neutral.[40]

There was a very particular idea of work for the women's movement in Victorian England, which in turn influenced perceptions of women of enterprise. It was an idea of work that was embedded in a culture in which Christian and materialist paradigms were quite readily aligned. An idea that not only blurred the distinction between waged and unwaged work but one that emphasized the integrative potential in relation to separate spheres. It drew heavily on the cult of altruism, which though itself was not gendered could become so in its application. Within this discourse, it was the nature of work, not its setting and remuneration that was crucial. Self-dependence or self-help were good things but conduct and character were central. Hence it was possible to condone self-sufficiency through engaging in a little enterprise, so long as the expressed motivations and manner of conducting that business emphasized public service and played down private gain. Pederson argues that this was partly a reflection of the close contact of the liberal feminist campaigners with the emerging new professionalism, which distanced itself from the distasteful market.[41] Consequently, far from viewing work as a regrettable necessity, many saw it as a desideratum for all individuals regardless of sex and invested work with existential hopes that were both religious and secular in character. The religious aspects were cross denominational and even broadly shared by many doubters. It was the association of work with moral / spiritual agency that was key.[42] Work them, writes Pederson, in its most admirable guise might incidentally promote individual self-interest, but it was not undertaken primarily with an eye to self-advancement.[43] This is where the woman of enterprise had to tread carefully. She could set up a little enterprise with moral / spiritual purpose and conduct that business honourably for the greater good but how could she justify actions that related to the reward of profits? This aspect was consequently downplayed in the self-representation and representation of businesswomen.

Something similar appears to have been taking place elsewhere. For example, in 1870s America there remained 'a marked tension between liberal ideals, which espoused the importance of self-making, and essentialist ideas about what constituted a man and a woman.' Although women were frequently engaged in small business, their ventures were downplayed. This was not just because their enterprises tended towards the lower end of the capitalization scale, or because they were subordinated to domestic responsibilities, but also because the very concept of 'success' in business was gendered. Male proprietors were self-reliant but female proprietors were self-dependent, indicating a clear awkwardness. Consequently American women had problems laying claim to, and owning, money and the wealth and power that came with it. Many worried about appearing too 'mannish' and emphasized the feminine qualities of their businesses or the ways in which their products or services helped people or the domestic environment. In this way, they avoided the risk of social ostracism by openly pursuing profit. Those that did not want to downplay their endeavours and aspired to expansion could utilise the socially acceptable strategy of finding a 'beard', usually a husband or son, to represent their interests in certain forums. However, this should not be confused with the woman having stepped back from business. It was a strategy to promote the best interests of her business in the current social climate.[44] Her exploration of these themes has caused Yohn to argue that the experience of American female entrepreneurs in the nineteenth century suggests that we must consider the impact of essentialist ideas about what constitutes a man and a woman in how a person constructs his or her economic 'self'.[45]

Back in England, the good provider role was one way that even hardy traditionalist could allow for women's involvement in business. In *Sketches from Boz*, Dickens depicts a diligent, dutiful, young woman combing a fancy stationery shop with her responsibility to care for her young siblings. Her mother having died and her father working elsewhere, the shop is a means of providing for an insufficiently supported household. Dickens writes, 'We occasionally caught a glimpse of two or three children, in mourning like herself, as they sat in the little parlour behind the shop; and we never passed at night without seeing the oldest girl at work, either for them, or in making some elegant trifle for sale.'[46] Interestingly the stationary shop is also combined with the letting of lodgings—a common supplementary tactic as revealed in Chapters 5 and 6. The good provider was an incarnation through which the observer or novelist could allow women in business a positive portrayal because by being the good provider they were taking the morality of the family into business.

Beyond this role, female proprietors fitted into a 'needs must' box or they walked a tightrope to social danger. To use another example from Dickens, the account of landlady Mrs Tibbs begins by praising her for possessing the virtues of thrift and cleanliness and making up for her 'faulty' husband. It then descends into a comedy of misunderstandings with ultimately both her and her boarding house ruined by a false accusation of indisgression with a male guest—a danger just waiting to happen.[47] Single women, even in the female trades, were even more worrying to Dickens and rarely occurred in his work, suffering misfortune or responsible for very modest trifles of enterprise if they did. For example, Miss Amelia Martin, about whom he claims 'ill-natured people would call plain, and police reports interesting'. She is acceptable in the sense that she is living 'on her business but not above it' and running her little enterprise in so friendly a manner that shopping with her 'really wasn't like a matter of business' anyway.[48] Although these women are depicted as honourable, dutiful, hardworking and so on, embarrassment and misfortune never seem to be far away. The fancy stationer's shop fails. What becomes of her? 'We believe the girl is past all suffering, and beyond all sorrow. God help her! We hope she is'.[49]

Whatever the 'hedges and thickets' of contemporary fictional or elaborated observational accounts;[50] however much the status of wife was lauded; to whatever extent the 'angel in the house' was held up as an example; in the British context: 'all women knew legions of lone women: all women could reasonably expect to be lone women at some stage.'[51] Such women could in reality enjoy considerable independence without sacrificing their respectability. Indeed, Albermarle argued that the attitude of middle-class writers tended to lag behind actual economic change. In her study of the structure and assumptions of popular American historical fiction she notes the tendency for writers to seek moral continuity within the new economic order, displayed as a defence of female-morality-as-home.[52] If this can be applied to the British context too then there is much insight to be gained from the New Woman novels, especially *The Odd Women* by George Gissing, cluttered with characters trying to organize their economic lives around a moral code so at odds with daily experience. Indeed there is a direct parallel between Mary Barfoot's fictional business school on Great Portland Street with the 1859 founding of the Society for Promoting the Employment of Women, which tried to find new occupational fields for untrained middle-class women.[53]

In addition to later fictional depictions there is also other printed evidence that women could be respected in business. A series of letters to women on the earning of money were carried in *The Alexandra Magazine* in 1864, including one focussed on business. The author was keen to point out that women had as much high moral worth attached to their money-getting character as men. 'Men of business acknowledge that women who are thoroughly schooled into their line of life stand on the same platform with them, in all the affairs that bring them into association', the author proclaimed.[54] Nonetheless, even if gradually accepted and acknowledged in some quarters, there still remains a strong sense that on some level women did approach the practice of business differently to many of their male counterparts—or at least what they perceived to be the masculine defined norm. Women were certainly advised to aspire to do business differently, whether or not in reality they actually did. The message to women was that honour and wealth were combined goals, managed by conscience. To pursue profits for pure gain without any intention of making the money useful was presented as below their moral value.[55] No doubt some will have internalized such rhetoric but for others it will have been recognized as a way of acknowledging women's involvement; a way of making their contact with the business world more acceptable. A discourse of women doing business differently rendered it a 'suitable' means of generating a living.

Conclusion

'My business is one very important sphere of my own duty'.[1]

Even at the height of the domesticity ideal, women engaging in business in London did not have to be widowed, in partnership with sisters, or the stereotypical milliner-dressmaker—although many did opt for this genteel trade. They could be young or old, carry any marital status, work alone or with female or male partners, and engage in a wide-range of trades, although most commonly those closely associated with the domestic. Their ventures might well be short-lived, through choice or misfortune, but the broad age range of these women suggests these entrepreneurs could reinvent themselves several times over their life course—that is, they did not necessarily engage in business just once but whenever 'needs must'. It is this notion of need that probably best defines the nature of Victorian female enterprise, certainly in mid-Victorian London. Many were survivalist entrepreneurs, creating a venture out of little other than their wits, limited savings, the empathy of wholesalers, their own home (complete with its residents) and their domestic skills.[2] This they did in the absence of other suitable avenues—unsuitable in the eyes of their peers or unsuitable because of their own circumstances and responsibilities. For example, many of the women in this study were the head of their household, working to keep their family fed and sheltered as respectably as possible. Work as a residential schoolteacher or governess would have been impractical for them but using their own home as a business was feasible.[3]

These findings support Humphries view that lone women, or those left heading their own households should not be viewed as having constituted a 'parasitic sub-culture'.[4] Their survival strategies placed them at the forefront of industrialisation. They provided articles of clothing (bespoke and ready-to-wear, fancy and everyday), and the laundry services to wash and iron them. They catered to the hungry bellies and bawdy tensions of the metropolis by supplying food, drink and general hospitality, operated printers and engravers and published newspapers to inform the adult masses, and opened schools to teach their children, too. Omnibus proprietors and wheelwrights also numbered among their ranks, as did library keepers and stationers. Provisions, glass and earthenware, candles, toys, sheet music, firewood and jewellery were just a handful of the products they sold from their shops. Not only did they contribute such energies to the benefit of their households and the metropolitan economy, many supplied lodgings often in addition to these other income generating activities, thus facilitating the migration of men and women and the labour supply essential for the economy's growth. In this sense, female business proprietors were of crucial importance to London and to the process of industrialisation.

Business was a recourse before marriage and widowhood because not all women married and of those that did, many were insufficiently supported. Hence, despite the stereotypical image of the widow-proprietor, business was seen as a strategy for widowhood but it was not the preserve of widowhood. Mid-Victorians were able to regard it in a positive light for other women too because a little enterprise offered independence and an opportunity to be diligent and useful, appealing to the notion of duty. Indeed, the lady reformers frequently promoted the merits of self-sufficiency and independence for its impact on a woman's dignity. As *The Woman's Gazette* responded to the question 'What is there I can do?':

> That definite occupation *is* a very present advantage to a girl or woman, whether needed by her in a remunerative sense or not, no one will deny who has seen the miracle which it works upon an aimless or desultory life. It widens a narrow sphere, and substitutes for the harassing anxieties of poverty a sense of self-sufficing dignity and independence.[5]

However the scale and variety of independent enterprise in the nineteenth century has been well hidden by both the frequent location of their labours in the home and by the vociferous rationalizing efforts of traditionalist and vocal contemporaries. It is also important to recognize that for the Victorian middle-class woman it was the very possibility of working from the home, rather than in paid employ for others, that contributed to the attractiveness of enterprise as a survival option. It was precisely the point to remain respectable and to retain identity with the home and the sphere of domesticity. It was not just that their skills and preparation limited them. They were not all trying to challenge their realm but rather to stretch the boundaries of suitable work and so many of their ventures commercialized aspects of their domesticity. This effort to work *within* the dominant ideology has much in common with the Victorian suffragists use, rather than refutation, of many of the traditional values relating to women in order to justify the benefit to all of their being granted citizenship.

Hence, in mid-nineteenth-century London the triumph of the 'useless woman' was not complete. A little enterprise could secure for its proprietor many things: an income that could be woven around domestic commitments; independence and a measure of respectability; the preservation of her home and household; and a retirement strategy. The limited size of many women's ventures also had certain advantages. More contained activities could be carried on more easily from the home; proprietors could maintain close contact with their often much localised market and were able to respond quickly to changes in demand. Such ventures also required moderate, rather than substantial, start up capital and a sympathetic wholesaler could lower this hurdle even further. These features made enterprise an accessible option for lower middle-class women, many of whom would have already hailed from or been connected to a trading family.

So, the businesswoman is neither a relic of a golden age nor the creation of the twentieth century, of newly acquired liberty and freedoms. She has transmuted across periods. At the height of Victorian rhetoric about domesticity, when *The Times* newspaper was advising women to 'Marry-Stitch-Die- or do worse',[6] enterprising women were engaging in business. They turned to enterprise because a livelihood made through trade was a better thing for the respectable middle-class woman, than to be reduced to 'mechanical' labour. As the research presented within these pages has revealed, many businesses could be carried on from within the home and this meant that a little enterprise could retain for a woman not only the respectability of an income obtained without leaving the sanctity of her home but it also helped her to retain it—a home being itself a hallmark of independence and respectability. The home was also seen as an appropriate domain for women and was used by many women to play down the cultural ramifications of their enterprise. They did this to variable degrees. Some created shopping environments that felt very parlour like, others emphasized they were opening up their homes and extending their maternal reach. In such cases they could benefit from distancing themselves from the idea that their type of venture was a business. The connection with the home also had other benefits in terms of resources. Women were able to use the energy, wisdom and contacts of the other people sharing their homes as a support network and buffer against risk.

As strong as the domesticity ideal was, there was also recognition that the demands of daily life superseded this. As one campaigner exclaimed in 1857, 'God only knows what is the sphere of any human being'.[7] London's women, and many other women elsewhere, negotiated the spheres of home and business in the nineteenth century. Many did this to survive not just economically but socially too. The independence of enterprise could be interpreted as self-help, could be imbued with moralistic intentions, and could be carried out relatively discretely. Although they were knowingly detouring from the more dogmatic path of the day, they were rarely alone or isolated in their endeavours, with many women relying on their entrepreneurial skills to support whole households. They were not able to live-out an idealized role for women at this time but it is important to recognize that they were still largely working *within* Victorian values, stretching the boundaries of suitability and carefully managing the representation of their relationship with enterprise, home and household.

Appendices

APPENDIX 1: CLASSIFICATION OF SUN FIRE TRADES BY SECTOR

a) Food, Drink and Hospitality

Bagnio Keeper
Baker
Beer Shop Keeper
Brewer
Butcher
Cake Baker
Cheesemonger
Coffee-House Keeper
Coffee Seller / Woman / man
Confectioner
Corn Chandler
Corn Factor
Cow Keeper
Dairy Keeper
Dealer in Liquor
Dealer in Beer & Cider
Dealer in Offal
Dealer in Wine & Spirits
Distiller
Eating House Keeper
Farmer
Fishmonger / Seller
Fried Fish Dealer
Fruiterer / Fruit Seller
Fruit Merchant
Grainer
Greengrocer

Grocer
Ham Dealer
Hop Factor
Hop Merchant
Hop & Seed Factor
Hop & Seed Merchant
Hotel Keeper
Importer of Jams
Innholder / Keeper
Italian Warehouse Keeper
Luncheon & Refreshment Room Keeper
Methalated Spirit Merchant
Mild Dealer
Milk Man / Woman
Pastry Cook
Pork Butcher
Potato Seller
Provision Dealer
Provision Merchant
Sauce Maker
Slop Seller
Sugar Baker
Tea Broker
Tea Dealer
Victualler
Vintner
Wine & Spirit Merchant

b) Textiles (including sale, manufacture and laundry)

Army Tailor
Bonnet Maker
Brace & Garter Maker
Cap Manufacturer
Child's Coat Maker
Child's Hood Maker
Cloak & Mantle Maker
Clothes Dealer / Clothier
Cloth Maker
Dealer in Baby Linen
Dealer in Bed Linen
Dealer in Berlin Wool
Dealer in Ladies Materials
Dealer in Ladies Second-Hand Apparel
Dealer in Ready-Made Linen

Dealer in Waistcoats
Dealer in Women's Clothes
Draper
Dressmaker
Dyer
Embroideress
Felt Maker
Flax Dresser
Fringe & Lace Warehouseman
Furrier
Glover
Gold & Silver Bone Lace Maker
Haberdasher
Hair Net Manufacturer
Hat & Cap Seller
Hat Maker
Hatter
Hide & Leather Seller
Hosier
Ladies Outfitter
Laundry Keeper / Laundress
Leather Breeches Maker
Leather Cutter
Leather Factor
Leather Gaiter Manufacturer
Leather Seller
Leather Works Owner
Linen Draper
Linen Factor / Agent
Mantle Maker
Mantua Maker
Mercer
Milliner
Muslin Warehouseman
Petticoat Maker
Rag Merchant
Semptress
Silk Mercer
Silk Thrower
Silk Warehouseman
Silk Winder
Staymaker
Stocking Presser
Straw Bonnet Maker
Sudsman

Tailor
Thread Maker
Trimming Manufacturer
Trimming Seller
Waistcoat Maker
Wardrobe Keeper
Weaver
Wholesale Clothier
Wholesale Milliner
Wool Broker
Wool Comber
Wool Stapler
Woollen Draper
Woollen Warehouseman
Worsted & Fringe Manufacturer

c) Other Retailing (not included in a or b)

Artificial Florist
Book Seller
Bottle Merchant
Broker
Broker of Household Goods
Chandler
Chest Warehouseman
Chinaman
Coal Dealer
Coal Merchant
Dealer in Brushes, Baskets and Toys
Dealer in Charcoal
Dealer in China and Glass
Dealer in Curiosities
Dealer in Earthenware
Dealer in Fancy goods
Dealer in Furniture
Dealer in Hardware
Dealer in Horses and Carts
Dealer in Jewellery
Dealer in Mahogany
Dealer in Marine Stores
Dealer in Mathematical Instruments
Dealer in Mounted and Paper Mache Goods
Dealer in Perfume
Dealer in Rags and Bottles
Dealer in Tools

Dealer in Wardrobes
Drug Merchants
Factor
Fancy Stationer
Florist
Foreign Toy Merchant
Furniture Broker
Furniture Dealer
Iron Merchant
Jeweller
Marine Store Dealer
Merchant
Metal Broker
Metal Merchant
Music Dealer
Music, Toy and Stationery Seller
Needle, Fishhook, Eye Warehouseman
Needle Maker
News Vendor
Oil and Colour Warehouseman
Oil Factor
Oil Merchant
Pawnbroker
Print Seller
Rag and Bottle Dealer
Saleswoman
Ship Chandler
Shopkeeper
Stationer
Tallow Chandler
Tobacconist
Toy Dealer
Umbrella Seller
Wardrobe Seller
Wholesale Metal Merchants
Wholesale Stationer
Woodmonger

d) Miscellaneous (including manufacturing trades and those not included in a to c, excluding the professions)

Artificial Flower Maker
Artist
Artists Mount Cutter
Auctioneer

Basket Maker
Bench Maker
Bench Polisher
Blade Maker
Blue Maker
Bone Collector
Bookbinder
Book Maker
Booking Office Keeper
Boot and Shoemaker
Box Maker
Brass Founder and Platter
Brass Pen Maker
Bricklayer
Briddle Fitter
Brushmaker
Builder
Cab Proprietor
Cabinet Maker
Card Box Manufacturer
Carman
Carpenter
Carter
Carver
Carver and Gilder
Chain Maker
Chair Maker
Coach Joiner
Coach Maker
Coach and Racehorse Van Maker
Cock Founder
Colourman
Cooper
Copper Plate Printer
Cork Cutter
Cork Manufacturer
Currier
Drysalter
Engine, Lathe and Tool Maker
Engraver
Fancy Brush Maker
Fancy Bugle Stringer
Fancy Leather Bag Manufacturer
Farrier
Firewood Cutter

Founder
Gas Fitter
General Merchant
Glass Bender
Glazier
Gold Beater
Gold and Silver Plating Mill Owner
Gold and Silver Wire Drawer
Hair Manufacturer
Hardware Man
Horsehair Manufacturer
Horticultural Builders
Ironmonger
Joiner
Lamp Maker
Leather Pipe Manufacturer
Library Keeper
Lighterman
Livery Stable Keeper
Looking Glass Manufacturer
Machinist
Manufacturing Stationer
Market Gardener
Mast and Block Makers
Mathematical Instrument Maker
Matress Maker
Miller
Money Dealer
Musical Instrument Maker
Musical String Coverer
Oarmaker
Omnibus Proprietor
Organ Builder
Painoforte Manufacturer / Maker
Painter
Palm and Belt Hearth Manufacturer
Pastle Board Maker
Perfume Maker
Pewterer
Picture Frame Maker
Printer
Publisher
Publisher of Newspapers
Railway Carrier
Rigger

Rope and Twine Manufacturer
Saddler
Sailmaker
Seedsman
Ship Joiner
Shipwright
Silversmith
Spectacles Maker
Spring Maker
Stable Keeper
Stone Cutter
Taliswoman
Timber Merchant
Tin Plate Worker
Tobacco Manufacturer
Trunk Maker
Turner
Tyersmith
Umbrella Maker
Undertaker
Upholsterer
Warehouseman
Watch, Clock and Chronometer Maker
Watch Motion Maker
Watchmaker
Wheelwright
Whip maker
Whitesmith
Wool and Cotton Card Machine Maker
Work Box Manufacturer
Worker in Hair
Worker in Ivory

APPENDIX 2: CENSUS REGISTRATION DISTRICTS
OF LINKED FEMALE PROPRIETORS

Table A2.1 Popular Trade Proprietors in 1851.

Registration District	Location	n
1. Kensington	West	2
2. Chelsea	West	1
3. St George Hanover Square	West	6
4 / 5 / 6. Westminster	West	7
7. Marylebone	West	6
9. Pancras	North	5
10. Islington	North	1
11. Hackney	North	1
12. St Giles	Central	2
13. Strand	Central	2
14. Holborn	Central	3
19. London City	Central	5
20. Shoreditch	East	5
21. Bethnal Green	East	2
22. Whitechapel	East	4
23. St George in the East	East	2
24. Stepney	East	2
25. Poplar	East	1
26 / 27 / 29. St George Southwark	South	1
28. Bermondsey	South	1
30. Newington	South	1
31. Lambeth	South	3
33. Camberwell	South	1
35. Greenwich	South	1

Source: Sun Fire Policy registers, series 11,936, LGL; Census returns for 1851/1861.

Table A2.2 Popular Trade Proprietors in 1861.

Registration District	Location	n
1. Kensington	West	6
2. Chelsea	West	1
3. St George Hanover Square	West	2
4 / 5 / 6. Westminster	West	8
7. Marylebone	West	4
9. Pancras	North	6
10. Islington	North	3
11. Hackney	North	1
12. St Giles	Central	2
13. Strand	Central	2
15. Clerkenwell	Central	3
16. St Luke	Central	3
19. London City	Central	5
20. Shoreditch	East	3
21. Bethnal Green	East	2
22. Whitechapel	East	1
24. Stepney	East	1
25. Poplar	East	2
26 / 27 / 29. Southwark	South	5
30. Newington	South	1
31. Lambeth	South	1
33. Camberwell	South	1
34. Rotherhithe	South	1

Source: Sun Fire Policy registers, series 11,936, LGL; Census returns for 1851/1861.

Table A2.3 Manufacturing Trade Proprietors in 1851.

Registration District	Location	n
5 / 6. Westminster	West	3
7. Marylebone	West	1
9. Pancras	North	1
12. St Giles	Central	1
13. Strand	Central	1
15. Clerkenwell	Central	2
16. St Luke	Central	3
19. London City	Central	2
20. Shoreditch	East	2
22. Whitechapel	East	1
31. Lambeth	South	1

Source: Sun Fire Policy registers, series 11,936, LGL; Census returns for 1851/1861.

Table A2.4 Manufacturing Trade Proprietors in 1861.

Registration District	Location	n
5 / 6. Westminster	West	1
7. Marylebone	West	1
13. Strand	Central	1
20. Shoreditch	East	1
21. Bethnal Green	East	1
22. Whitechapel	East	1
24. Stepney	East	1
25. Poplar	East	1
27. Southwark	South	1

Source: Sun Fire Policy registers, series 11,936, LGL; Census returns for 1851/1861.

APPENDIX 3: CONTINGENCY TABLES—INFLUENCE OF GENDER ON SECTOR OF BUSINESS: INCLUDING DUPLICATE POLICIES (EXPECTED VALUES IN BRACKETS)

F: Food, drink & hospitality. T: Textiles—manufacture, sale & laundry. OR: Other retailing. M: Miscellaneous. OTH: Other.

Table A3.1 Contingency Table for 1747.

		F	T	OR	M	OTH	Total
Male	*n*	10	4	9	10		37
	%	(12.3)	(5.5)	(9.8)	(6.8)	(2.6)	
Female	*n*	19	9	14	6	2	50
	%	(16.7)	(7.5)	(13.2)	(9.2)	(3.5)	
Total	N	29	13	23	16	6	87

$\chi^2 = 5.6$ C = 0.25

Table A3.2 Contingency Table for 1761.

		F	T	OR	M	OTH	Total
Male	*n*	41	13	7	29	6	96
	%	(35.5)	(20.7)	(16.1)	(20.3)	(3.4)	
Female	*n*	43	36	31	19	2	131
	%	(48.5)	(28.3)	(22.0)	(27.7)	(4.6)	
Total	N	84	49	38	48	8	227

$\chi^2 = 25.18$ C = 0.32

Table A3.3 Contingency Table for 1851.

		F	T	OR	M	OTH	Total
Male	*n*	55	21	27	72	9	184
	%	(47.7)	(44.8)	(34.3)	(52.4)	(4.8)	
Female	*n*	45	73	45	38	1	202
	%	(52.3)	(49.2)	(37.7)	(57.6)	(5.2)	
Total	N	100	94	72	110	10	386

$\chi^2 = 50.33$ C = 0.34

Table A3.4 Contingency Table for 1861.

		F	T	OR	M	OTH	Total
Male	*n*	45	27	40	105	7	224
	%	(49.0)	(57.1)	(46.7)	(65.1)	(6.1)	
Female	*n*	59	94	59	33	6	251
	%	(55.0)	(64.0)	(52.3)	(73.0)	(6.9)	
Total	N	104	121	99	138	13	475

$\chi^2 = 78.99$ C = 0.378

APPENDIX 4: AGE OF PROPRIETORS

Table A4.1 Age Group of Linked Proprietors by Marital Status, 1851.

Age Group	Married n	Married %	Spinsters n	Spinsters %	Widows n	Widows %
Under 20	0	0	1	5	0	0
20 to 29	1	17	6	32	2	5
30 to 39	1	17	8	42	6	15
40 to 49	1	17	2	11	10	25
50 to 59	3	50	1	5	11	28
60 to 69	0	0	1	5	8	20
70 and over	0	0	0	0	2	5
Unknown	0	0	0	0	1	3
Total	6	100	19	100	40	100
Youngest	29		19		24	
Oldest	57		61		84	
Mean age	45.5		33.7		49.8	

Source: Sun Fire Policy registers, series 11,936, LGL; Census returns for 1851/1861.

Table A4.2 Age Group of Linked Proprietors by Marital Status, 1861.

Age Group	Married n	Married %	Spinsters n	Spinsters %	Widows n	Widows %
Under 20	0	0	0	0	0	0
20 to 29	0	0	4	27	1	2
30 to 39	4	67	5	33	7	17
40 to 49	1	17	4	27	11	26
50 to 59	1	17	2	13	16	38
60 to 69	0	0	0	0	7	17
70 and over	0	0	0	0	0	0
Unknown	0	0	0	0	0	0
Total	6	100	15	100	42	100
Youngest	30		25		24	
Oldest	51		54		69	
Mean age	37.7		38.1		49.1	

Source: Sun Fire Policy registers, series 11,936, LGL; Census returns for 1851/1861.

Table A4.3 Age of Linked Proprietors by Trade, 1851.

Trade	< 20	20 to 29	30 to 39	40 to 49	50 to 59	60 to 69	≥ 70	un	Y	O	M
Chandler	0	0	2	1	2	1	1	0	30	70	49.4
Clothier	0	1	0	2	0	0	0	0	27	46	39.3
Coffee-house Keeper	0	1	0	0	2	1	0	0	27	61	47.0
Grocer & Greengrocer	0	0	1	1	1	2	0	1	30	60	50.2
Hosier & Haberdasher	0	2	1	2	2	0	0	0	21	59	40
Linen Draper	0	0	1	1	2	1	0	0	37	68	51.8
Milliner & Dressmaker	0	3	9	2	4	1	1	0	24	84	42.4
Stationer	0	0	0	2	0	0	0	0	42	44	43.0
Tobacconist	0	1	0	1	0	1	0	0	24	61	44.0
Victualler	1	1	1	1	2	2	0	0	19	65	43.5

Source: Sun Fire Policy registers, series 11,936, LGL; Census returns for 1851/1861.
Note: un = unknown age; Y = youngest; O = oldest; M = mean.

Table A4.4 Age of Linked Proprietors by Trade, 1861.

Trade	< 20	20 to 29	30 to 39	40 to 49	50 to 59	60 to 69	≥ 70	un	Y	O	M
Milliners & Dressmakers	0	2	3	5	5	1	0	0	28	60	44.4
Coffee-House Keepers	0	0	4	1	2	0	0	0	37	57	43.7
Laundry Services	0	1	1	1	1	4	0	0	24	69	50.6
Linen Drapers	0	0	0	1	2	0	0	0	48	52	50.0
Grocers & Greengrocers	0	0	2	1	2	1	0	0	30	60	45.3
Chandlers	0	0	2	3	1	1	0	0	30	67	45.9
Victuallers	0	1	1	1	5	0	0	0	25	59	48.3
Stationers	0	1	1	0	0	0	0	0	27	34	30.5
Tobacconist	0	0	0	2	0	0	0	1	40	49	44.5
Haberdashers & Hosiers	0	0	2	1	1	0	0	0	31	50	40.0

Source: Sun Fire Policy registers, series 11,936, LGL; Census returns for 1851/1861.
Note: un = unknown age; Y = youngest; O = oldest; M = mean.

Notes

NOTES TO THE INTRODUCTION

1. B. Raynor Parks, *Essays on Women's Work*, London, 1865, p. 140.
2. Anon, 'Thoughts of a Dressmaker', *The Words of Fashion: Monthly magazine of the courts of London and Paris fashions, literature, music, fine arts, the opera and the theatres*, Issue 323, Friday, Nov. 1850, p. 126.
3. D.R. Green, 'The metropolitan economy: continuity and change 1800–1939', in K. Hoggart and D.R. Green (eds.) *London. A New Metropolitan Geography, London, 1991*. Figure taken from *London County Council, London Statistics*, Vol. 35, 1930–1931, p. 23. E.A. Wrigley, 'A simple model of London's importance in changing English society and economy, 1650–1750', in J. Patten (ed.) *Pre-Industrial England: Geographical Essays*, Folkestone, 1979, pp. 191–192.
4. Green, 'The metropolitan economy', p. 10–11.
5. R. Porter, *London. A Social History*, London, 1994, p. 99.
6. L.D. Schwarz, *London in the Age of Industrialization*, Cambridge, 1992, p. 8.
7. Green, 'The metropolitan economy', pp. 15–16.
8. F. Sheppard, *London 1808–1870: The Infernal Wen*, London, 1971; Porter, *London. A Social History*.
9. S.R. Gorsky, 'Old maids and new women. Alternatives to marriage in English women's novels, 1847–1915', *Journal of Popular Culture*, Summer, 1973, p. 69.
10. W.F. Neff, *Victorian Working Women. An Historical and Literary Study of Women in British Industries and Professions 1832–1850*, London, 1929, p. 186.
11. P. Earle, *The Making of the English Middle Class. Business, Society and Family Life in London 1660–1730*, London, 1989; 'The female labour market in London in the late seventeenth and early eighteenth centuries', in P. Sharpe (ed.) *Women's Work. The English Experience 1650–1914*, London, 1998.
12. Schwarz, *London in the Age of Industrialization*.
13. D. Barnet, *London, Hub of the Industrial Revolution. A Revisionary History 1775–1825*, London, 1998.
14. A.C. Kay, 'Reaction not retreat: Small business proprietorship and the redundant woman', *The Economic History Society New Researchers' Papers*, 2002; 'A little enterprise of her own: Lodging-house keeping and the accommodation business in nineteenth-century London', *The London Journal*, 28, 2, 2003; 'Small business, self-employment and women's work-life choices in nineteenth century London', in D. Mitch, J. Brown and M.H.D. Van Leeuwen (eds.) *Origins of the Modern Career*, Aldershot, 2004; 'Revealing her

assets: Liberating the Victorian businesswoman from the sources', *Business Archives: Sources and History*, 92, 2006.

15. N. Phillips, *Women in Business 1700–1850*, Woodbridge, 2006.

16. H. Barker, *The Business of Women. Female Enterprise and Urban Development in Northern England 1760–1830*, Oxford, 2006; C. Wiskin, 'Urban businesswomen in eighteenth-century England', in R. Sweet and P. Lane (eds.) *Women and Urban Life in Eighteenth-Century England*, Aldershot, 2003; 'Businesswomen and financial management: Three eighteenth century case studies', *Accounting, Business and Financial History*, 16, 2006; E. Gordon and G. Nair, 'The economic role of middle class women in Victorian Glasgow', *Women's History Review*, 9, 2000; *Public Lives: Women, Family and Society in Victorian Britain*, New Haven, 2006.

17. C. de Bellaigue, 'The business of schoolkeeping' in C. de Bellaigue, *Schooling and Identity in England and in France, 1800–1867*, Oxford, 2007; see also S. Skedd, 'Women teachers and the expansion of girls' schooling in England, c.1760–1820', in H. Barker and E. Chalus (eds.) *Gender in Eighteenth-Century England*, London and New York, 1997.

18. M. Hunt, *The Middling Sort: Commerce, Gender and the Family in England, 1680–1780*, London, 1996; M. Prior, *Women in English Society, 1500–1800*, London, 1985; E.C. Sanderson, *Women and Work in Eighteenth-Century Edinburgh*, Basingstoke, 1996.

19. A. Owens, 'Inheritance and the lifecycle of firms in the early industrial revolution, *Business History*, 44, 2002; D. Green and A. Owens, 'Gentlewomanly capitalism? Spinsters, widows and wealthholding in England and Wales, c.1800–1860, *Economic History Review*, 56, 3, 2003; M. Freeman, R. Pearson and J. Taylor, 'A doe in the city: Women shareholders in eighteenth and early nineteenth century Britain', *Accounting, Business and Financial History*, 16, 2006; J. Rutterford and J. Maltby, 'The widow, the clergyman and the reckless: Women investors in England, 1830–1914', *Feminist Economics*, 12, 2006; J. Maltby and J. Rutterford, 'She possessed her own fortune: Women investors from the late nineteenth century to the early twentieth century', *Business History* 48, 2006; R.J. Morris, *Men, Women and Property in England, 1780–1870*, Cambridge, 2005.

20. D. van den Heuval, 'Book Reviews', *International Review of Social History*, 52, 2008, p. 315.

21. Wiskin, 'Urban businesswomen', pp. 87, 104.

NOTES TO CHAPTER 1

1. P. Wakefield, *Reflections on the Present Condition of the Female Sex*, London, 1798, pp. 9–10.

2. L. Kerber, 'Separate spheres, female worlds, woman's place: the rhetoric of women's history', *Journal of American History*, 75, 1, 1998, p. 17.

3. A. Clark, *Working Life of Women, in the Seventeenth Century*, London, 1919 (reprinted London, 1982). I. Pinchbeck, *Women Workers and the Industrial Revolution, 1750–1850*, London, 1930 (reprinted London, 1969).

4. A. Vickery, 'The neglected century: writing the history of eighteenth century women', *Gender & History*, 3, 2, 1991.

5. N.F.R. Crafts, *British Economic Growth during the Industrial Revolution*, Oxford, 1986; J. Mokyr, 'Has the Industrial Revolution been crowded out? Some reflections on Crafts and Williamson', *Explorations in Economic*

History, 24, 1987; E.A. Wrigley, *Continuity, Chance and Change. The Character of the Industrial Revolution in England*, Cambridge, 1988.

6. B. Hill, *Women. Work and Sexual Politics in Eighteenth-Century England*, London, 1989 (see Chapter 1, 'Pinchbeck and after' and Chapter 2, 'The social context').

7. Clark, *Working Life of Women*, p. 308.

8. Clark, *Working Life of Women*, pp. 6, 296.

9. J. Thirsk, 'Foreward', in M. Prior (ed.) *Women in English Society 1500–1800*, London, 1985, p. 11.

10. C. Middleton, 'Women's labour and the transition to pre-industrial capitalism', in L. Charles and L. Duffin (ed.) *Women and Work in Pre-Industrial England*, London, 1985.

11. D. Simonton, *A History of European Women's Work 1700 to the Present*, London, 1998, p. 167.

12. P. Hudson and W.R. Lee, *Women's Work and the Family Economy in Historical Perspective*, Manchester, 1990 (see introductory commentary).

13. Pinchbeck, *Women Workers*, Chapter 12.

14. Pinchbeck, *Women Workers*, pp. 287, 293, 315.

15. Pinchbeck, *Women Workers*, p. 316.

16. Pinchbeck, *Women Workers*, pp. 148–149.

17. P. Earle, *A City Full of People. Men and Women of London 1650–1750*, London, 1994, pp. 113–120. See also: P. Earle, 'The female labour market in London in the late seventeenth and early eighteenth centuries', in P. Sharpe (ed.) *Women's Work. The English Experience 1650–1914*, London, 1998.

18. S. Wright, 'Holding up half the sky: Women and their occupations in eighteenth-century Ludlow', *Midland History*, 14, 1989, pp. 56, 59.

19. E.C. Sanderson, *Women and Work in Eighteenth-Century Edinburgh*, Basingstoke, 1996, pp. 2, 170, 168, 105. See also: M. Hunt, *The Middling Sort. Commerce, Gender and the Family in England 1680–1780*, London, 1996; M. Prior, 'Women and the urban economy: Oxford 1500–1800', in M. Prior, (ed.) *Women in English Society 1500–1800*, London, 1985.

20. A. Briggs, 'The language of class in early nineteenth-century England', in A. Briggs and J. Saville (eds.) *Essays in Labour History* Vol. 1, London, 1967, p. 52.

21. E. Royle, *Modern Britain. A Social History. 1750–1985*, London, 1990, p. 102.

22. S. Nenadic, 'The rise of the urban middle-class', in T.M. Devine and R. Mitchison (eds.) *People and Society in Scotland Vol. 1, 1760–1830*, Edinburgh, 1988, p. 111.

23. Nenadic, 'The rise of the urban middle-class', p. 121.

24. L. Davidoff and C. Hall, *Family Fortunes. Men and Women of the English Middle Class 1780–1850*, London, 1987, pp. 20–22, 30.

25. C. Hall, 'Private persons versus public someones: Class, gender and politics in England, 1780–1850', in C. Hall (ed.) *White, Male and Middle Class*, Cambridge, 1992, pp. 153–155.

26. C. Hall, 'The early formation of Victorian domestic ideology', in Hall, *White, Male and Middle Class*, pp. 78–80.

27. S. Alexander, 'Women's work in nineteenth century London; A study of the years 1820–1850', in J. Mitchell and A. Oakley (eds.) *The Rights and Wrongs of Women*, London, 1977, p. 61.

28. For a literary analysis of Patmore's poem see: C. Church, 'Victorian masculinity and the Angel in the House', in M. Vicinus (ed.) *A Widening Sphere. Changing Roles of Victorian Women*, London, 1990.

29. For a selection of broad commentaries see: E. Richards, 'Women in the British economy since about 1700', *History*, 59, 1974; M. Berg, 'What difference

did women's work make to the industrial revolution?', *History Workshop*, 35, 1993 (Berg argues the labour of women and children dominated the expanding industries of the Industrial Revolution. Hence, their exclusion from the narrative has radically distorted our understanding of economic trends.); S. Horrell and J. Humphries, 'Women's labour force participation and the transition to the male-breadwinner family, 1790–1865', in P. Sharpe (ed.) *Women's Work. The English Experience 1650–1914*, London, 1998 (reprinted from *The Economic History Review*, 48, 1995); P. Hudson and W.R. Lee (eds.), *Women's Work and the Family Economy in Historical Perspective.*

30. E. Avdela, 'Work, gender and history in the 1990's and beyond', *Gender and History*, 11, 3, 1999, p. 530.

31. E. Gordon and G. Nair, *Public Lives. Women, Family and Society in Victorian Britain*, New Haven, 2003, p. 232.

32. Gordon and Nair, *Public Lives*, p. 234.

33. M. Anderson, 'The social position of spinsters in mid-Victorian Britain', *Journal of Family History*, Winter, 1984, p. 378.

34. Parliamentary Papers. Session 4, November 1852—20 August 1853. Volume LXXXVIII, Part 1. 1852–1853 Accounts and Papers. 32nd Volume, Part 1, p. xxvii.

35. W.R. Greg, *Why are Women Redundant?*, London, 1869, p. 5.

36. J. Humphries, 'Female headed households in early industrial Britain: the vanguard of the proletariat?' *Labour History Review*, 63, 1, 1998, p. 31.

37. E.C. Wolstenholme, 'The education of girls, its present and its future', in J.E. Butler (ed.) *Women's Work and Women's Culture. A Series of Essays*, London, 1869, p. 319.

38. Wolstenholme, 'The education of girls', p. 330.

39. H. Taylor, 'Enfranchisement of women', in J.S. Mill (ed.) *Dissertations and Discussions. Political Philosophical and Historical* Vol. 2, London, 1859, p. 419.

40. Taylor, 'Enfranchisement of women', p. 427.

41. Taylor, 'Enfranchisement of women', p. 423.

42. A. Houston, *The Emancipation of Women from Existing Industrial Disabilities: Considered in its Economic Aspect*, London, 1862, p. 28.

43. J.D. Milne, *Industrial and Social Position of Women in the Middle and Lower Ranks*, London, 1857, p. 129.

44. M.A. Ashford, *Life of a Licensed Victualler's Daughter. Written by Herself*, London, 1844, pp. 20, 51.

45. Ashford, *Life of a Licensed Victualler's Daughter*, p. 20.

46. Ashford, *Life of a Licensed Victualler's Daughter*, p. 20.

47. Ashford, *Life of a Licensed Victualler's Daughter*, p. 21.

48. C. Townsend, 'I am a woman for spirit: A working woman's gender transgression in Victorian London', *Victorian Studies*, 36, 3, 1993, p. 295.

49. R.M. Dekker and L.C. van de Pol, *The Tradition of Female Transvestism in Early Modern Europe*, London, 1989, p. 1.

50. Townsend, 'I am a woman for spirit', pp. 293–296.

51. Townsend, 'I am a woman for spirit', pp. 296–298.

52. Townsend, 'I am a woman for spirit', pp. 299, 307.

53. Townsend, 'I am a woman for spirit', p. 307.

54. Townsend, 'I am a woman for spirit', p. 295.

55. R. Trumbach, 'London's Sapphists: From three sexes to four genders in the making of modern culture', in J. Epstein and K. Straub (eds.) *Body Guards. The Cultural Politics of Gender Ambiguity*, London, 1991, p. 125.

56. Trumbach, 'London's Sapphists', p. 123.

57. J. Wheelwright, *Amazons and Military Maids*, London, 1989, p. 19.
58. P. Parley, *The Book of Trades, Arts, & Professions Relative to Food, Clothing, Shelter and Ornament; for the Use of the Young*, London, 1855.
59. M. Grogan, *How Women May Earn a Living*, London, 1880, pp. 9–10.
60. Grogan, *How Women May Earn a Living*, p. 114.
61. P. Browne (pseud. Sarah Sharp Hamer), *What Girls Can Do: A Book for Mothers and Daughters*, London, 1880 (reprinted London, 1885), pp. 308–368, 360.
62. Browne, *What Girls Can Do*, p. 6.
63. B. Rayner Parkes, *Essays on Woman's Work*, London, 1865, p. 159.
64. Parkes, *Essays on Woman's Work*, p. 163.
65. Parkes, *Essays on Woman's Work*, p. 157.
66. Parkes, *Essays on Woman's Work*, p. 55.
67. P.A. Nester, 'A new departure in women's publishing: The English Woman's Journal and The Victoria Magazine', *Victorian Periodicals Review*, 15, 3, 1982, p. 96.
68. *English Woman's Journal* Vol. 4, September 1859, p. 57.
69. *English Woman's Journal* Vol. 4, September 1859, p. 59.
70. Parkes, *Essays on Woman's Work*, pp. 65–66.
71. Parkes, *Essays on Woman's Work*, p. 62.
72. Nester, 'A new departure in women's publishing', p. 97.
73. *English Woman's Journal* Vol. 4, September 1859, p. 59.
74. Miscellanea, *The Lady's Newspaper*, Issue 404, London, Saturday, September 23, 1854, p. 188.
75. L.D. Schwarz, 'Income distribution and social structure in London in the late eighteenth century', *Economic History Review*, 32, 1979, p. 254.
76. Browne, *What Girls Can Do*, p. 308.
77. Milne, *Industrial and Social Position of Women*, p. 135.
78. A. M. Froide, 'Old maids: the lifecycle of single women in early modern England', in L. Botelho and P. Thane (eds.) *Women and Ageing in British Society Since 1500*, Essex, 2001, pp. 90, 94, 96–97, 99.
79. Alexander, 'Women's work', p. 63.

NOTES TO CHAPTER 2

1. 'Struggle for existence', *John Bull*, Issue 2, London, Saturday, May 27, 1865, p. 330.
2. J.D. Milne, *Industrial and Social Position of Women in the Middle and Lower Ranks*, London, 1857, p. 177.
3. E. Gordon and G. Nair, *Public Lives: Women, Family and Society in Victorian Britain*, New Haven, 2003, p. 188.
4. Davidoff and Hall, 'The hidden investment: Women and the enterprise', in P. Sharpe (ed.) *Women's Work. The English Experience 1650-1914*, London, 1998, p. 252.
5. Quoted in B. Hill, *Women, Work and Sexual Politics in Eighteenth-Century England*, London, 1989, p. 196.
6. N. Phillips, *Women in Business 1700–1850*, Woodbridge, 2006, p. 24.
7. Phillips, *Women in Business*, p. 41.
8. L. Holcombe, 'Victorian wives and property. Reform of the married women's property law, 1857–1882', in M. Vicinus (ed.) *A Widening Sphere. Changing Roles of Victorian Women*, London, 1990, p. 7.
9. A.L. Erickson, *Women and Property in Early Modern England*, London, 1993, pp. 150, 225–227.

10. P. Earle, *The Making of the English Middle Class. Business, Society and Family Life in London 1660–1730*, London, 1989, pp. 159–160.
11. C.Wiskin, 'Urban businesswomen in eighteenth-century England' in R.Sweet and P.Lane, *Women and urban life in eighteenth-century England*, Aldershot, 2003, p.89.
12. M. Prior, 'Women and the urban economy: Oxford 1500–1800', in M. Prior (ed.) *Women in English Society 1500–1800*, London, 1985, p. 103.
13. Phillips, *Women in Business*, p. 42.
14. M. Hunt, *The Middling Sort. Commerce, Gender and Family in England 1680–1780*, London, 1996, pp. 140–141.
15. Quoted in Hunt, *The Middling Sort*, p. 125.
16. Hunt, *The Middling Sort*, p. 141.
17. Hunt, *The Middling Sort*, p. 139.
18. W. Hart, *The Autobiography of William Hart, Cooper, 1776–1857. A Respectable Artisan in the Industrial Revolution*, in P. Hudson and L. Hunter (eds.) *The London Journal*, 7, 2, Winter, 1981, pp. 144–145.
19. Hart, *Autobiography*, p. 73.
20. Hart, *Autobiography*, p. 73.
21. E.C. Sanderson, *Women and Work in Eighteenth-Century Edinburgh*, Basingstoke, 1996, p. 75.
22. D.V. Glass, 'Socio-economic status and occupations in the City of London at the end of the seventeenth century', in A.E.J. Hollaender and W. Kellaway (eds.) *Studies in London History*, London, 1969, p. 385, Table 9.
23. D. Simonton, 'Apprenticeship: Training and gender in eighteenth-century England' in M. Berg (ed.) *Markets and Manufacture in Early Industrial Europe*, London, 1991, pp. 230, 233.
24. Simonton, 'Apprenticeship', p. 233.
25. J.R. Kellett, 'The breakdown of gild and corporation control over the handicraft and retail trade in London', *The Economic History Review*, 10, 3, 1958, p. 385.
26. Prior, 'Women and the urban economy', pp. 111–113.
27. Kellett, 'The breakdown', p. 387.
28. Kellett, 'The breakdown', pp. 389–390.
29. Kellett, 'The breakdown', p. 390.
30. Kellett, 'The breakdown', p. 394.
31. Hunt, *The Middling Sort*, p. 145.
32. Quoted in J.R. Walkowitz, *Prostitution and Victorian Society. Women, Class and the State*, Cambridge, 1980, p. 24.
33. L. Davidoff and C. Hall, *Family Fortunes. Men and Women of the English Middle Class 1780–1850*, London, 1987, pp. 211, 279.
34. W. Gamber, *The Female Economy. The Millinery and Dressmaking Trades 1860–1930*, Bloomington, 1997, p. 160.
35. Gamber, *The Female Economy*, p. 165.
36. Anon, *Reminiscences of an Old Draper*, London, 1876, pp. 145–146.
37. Wiskin, 'Urban businesswomen', pp. 96–97.
38. Davidoff and Hall, *Family Fortunes*, p. 278.
39. L. Newton, 'Trust and virtue in English banking: The assessment of borrowers by bank managements at the turn of the nineteenth century', *Financial History Review*, 7, 2, 2000, pp. 177–181.
40. Newton, 'Trust and virtue', p. 181.
41. Newton, 'Trust and virtue', p. 189.
42. M.A. Ashford, *Life of a Licensed Victualler's Daughter. Written by Herself*, London, 1844, pp. 8–9.
43. Wiskin, 'Urban businesswomen', p. 101.

44. B. Lemire, 'Petty pawns and informal lending: Gender and the transformation of small-scale credit in England, c.1600–1800', in K. Bruland and P. O'Brien (eds.) *From Family Firms to Corporate Capitalism*, Oxford, 1998, p. 134.
45. Lemire, 'Petty pawns', pp. 127–130.
46. M.J. Winstanley, *The Shopkeeper's World 1830–1914*, Manchester, 1983, p. 183.
47. Hunt, *The Middling Sort,* p. 144.
48. D.R. Green, 'Charity begins at home: Women, wealth and inheritance among the London middle-class 1800–1860', draft paper for the European Social Science History Conference (The Hague, Netherlands, 27 February—2 March 2002), pp. 14–16 (Copy courtesy of D.R. Green).
49. Hunt, *The Middling Sort,* p. 127.
50. Hunt, *The Middling Sort,* p. 131.
51. Hunt, *The Middling Sort,* p. 131.
52. Hunt, *The Middling Sort,* p. 131.
53. Hunt, *The Middling Sort,* p. 132.
54. Wiskin, 'Urban businesswomen', p. 94.
55. B. Taylor, *Eve and the New Jerusalem. Socialism and Feminism in the Nineteenth Century*, London, 1983, p. 88.
56. Taylor, *Eve and the New Jerusalem,* p. 231.
57. Taylor, *Eve and the New Jerusalem,* pp. 235–236.
58. W. Cobbett, *Advice to Young Men and (Incidentally) to Young Women, in the Middle and Higher Ranks of Life*, London, 1829 (reprinted 1863), p. 181.
59. Cobbett, *Advice to Young Men,* p. 180.
60. H. Barker, *The Business of Women. Female Enterprise and Urban Development in Northern England 1760–1830*, Oxford, 2006, pp. 2, 104.
61. Wiskin, 'Urban businesswomen', p. 93.
62. Davidoff and Hall, *Family Fortunes,* pp. 277, 212.
63. Hart, *Autobiography,* p. 56.
64. R.J. Morris, 'The middle-class and the property cycle during the industrial revolution', in T.C. Smout (ed.) *The Search for Wealth and Stability*, London, 1979, p. 110.
65. A.C. Kay, 'A little enterprise of her own: Lodging-house keeping and the accommodation business in nineteenth-century London', *The London Journal*, 28, 2, 2003, pp. 41–53.
66. Barker, *The Business of Women,* pp. 2, 10.

NOTES TO CHAPTER 3

1. H.A.L. Cockerell and E. Green, *The British Insurance Business*, Sheffield, 1994, p. xi.
2. C. Trebilcock, *Phoenix Assurance and the Development of British Insurance. Vol.1: 1782–1870*, London, 1994, p. 3.
3. Trebilcock, *Phoenix,* p. 388.
4. Cockerell and Green, *The British Insurance Business*, pp. 26–28. B. Henham, *Hand in Hand. The Story of the Hand in Hand Fire and Life Insurance Society 1696–1996*, London, 1996, pp. 9–19.
5. Anon, *Sun Insurance Office Ltd of London,* London, 1932, p. 8.
6. E.A. Davies, *An Account of the Formation and Early Years of the Westminster Fire Office*, Glasgow, 1952, p. 14.
7. Cockerell and Green, *The British Insurance Business*, p. 29. P.G.M. Dickson, *The Sun Insurance Office 1710–1960,* London, 1960, p. 70.

8. D.T. Jenkins, 'The practice of insurance against fire, 1750–1840, and historical research', in O.M. Westall (ed.) *The Historian and the Business of Insurance*, Manchester, 1984, p. 24.
9. Cockerell, and Green, *The British Insurance Business*, p. 43–44.
10. According to Beresford, simple renewals rarely involved the issue of a new policy, annual renewals were automatic and information was only scrutinised by the company after 7 years. M.V. Beresford, 'Building history from fire insurance records', *Urban History Yearbook*, 1976, p. 11.
11. Jenkins, 'The practice', p. 12.
12. Dickson, *The Sun Insurance*, p. 73.
13. Jenkins, 'The practice', p. 13.
14. Jenkins, 'The practice', p. 14.
15. Sun Fire Office policy registers, series 11,936, LGL.
16. It was not in the interests of women who used private assets to support business activity to declare their enterprise to the insurance company in case this led to higher premiums.
17. D. Barnet, *London, Hub of the Industrial Revolution. A Revisionary History 1775–1825*, London, 1998, pp. 6–7
18. Cockerell and Green, *The British Insurance Business*, p. 50.
19. Barnet, *London*, p. 209
20. Barnet, *London*, p. 7.
21. Sun Fire 721/1968401 (Adkin, 31 Aldgate, tobacco manufacturer) and 649/1662366 (Charles Curtis, 6 Assembly Row, distiller).
22. Barnet, *London*, pp. 208–209.
23. Barnet, *London*, pp. 33–34.
24. Sun Fire 639/1649686.
25. Sun Fire 721/1953165.
26. A breakdown of trades by sector, along with a listing of trades by sample year, is included in the appendices.
27. W. Gamber, *The Female Economy. The Millinery and Dressmaking Trades 1860–1930*, Bloomington, 1997, p. 5.
28. J. Treuherz, *Victorian Painting*, London, 1993, p. 38. NB. Redgrave pained a series of pictures of unhappy women including a governess, a country girl forced into domestic service and an out-of-wedlock mother thrown out of home.
29. H. Rogers, 'The good are not always powerful, nor the powerful always good. The politics of women's needlework in mid-Victorian London', *Victorian Studies*, 40, 4, 1997, pp. 591, 592, 597, 606.
30. This is a criticism likely to hold more truth after the Married Women's Property Act of 1870, which granted married women the right to own and control personal property. Until the passage of the Act the doctrine of coverture gave the husband legal ownership over a wife's personal property (such as stocks, jewellery, money and clothing) and managerial rights over her real property (immovables such as housing and land).
31. Sun Fire 722/1968746.
32. Sun Fire 720/1958334.
33. Sun Fire 720/723/1966307.
34. Sun Fire 646/1651108.
35. Parliamentary Papers. Session 4, 1852–53. Vol. LXXXVIII—Part 1.1852–1853. Census of Great Britain 1851. Population Tables, II Ages, Civil Conditions and Birth Place of the People. See Occupations of the People, Division 1—London.
36. Barnet, *London*, p. 208.

NOTES TO CHAPTER 4

1. 'Myra's Dress and Pattern Depot', *Myra's Journal of Dress and Fashion*, Issue 1, Jan. 1878, London, p. viii. NB. This is a self-promotional journal.
2. 'Madame Valery's Neolin Hair Wash', *The Lady's Newspaper*, Issue 837, Saturday, Jan. 10, 1863, London, multiple classified advertising.
3. Anon, 'Thoughts of a dressmaker', *The World of Fashion: Monthly Magazine of the Courts of London and Paris Fashions, Literature, Music, Fine Arts, the Opera and the Theatres*, Issue 323, Friday Nov. 1, London 1850, p. 125.
4. C. Walsh, 'The advertising and marketing of consumer goods in eighteenth-century London', in C. Wischermann and E. Shore (eds.) *Advertising and the European City. Historical Perspectives*, Aldershot, 2000, pp. 79, 89, 91.
5. Maxine Berg and Helen Clifford, 'Selling consumption in the eighteenth century: Advertising and the trade card in Britain and France', *Cultural and Social History* 4, 2, 2007, pp. 146–147, 150–151.
6. Berg and Clifford, 'Selling consumption', p. 159.
7. M. Rickards, *Encyclopaedia of Ephemera: A Guide to the Fragmentary Documents of Everyday Life for the Collector, Curator, and Historian*, London, 2000, p. 334.
8. Rickards, *Encyclopaedia*, p. 334.
9. P. Parley, *The Book of Trades, Arts & Professions*, London, 1855, p. 115.
10. London Guildhall Library Trade Card Collection, Box 1 Aar-Bar. c.1830, LGL.
11. H. Sampson, *A History of Advertising*, London, 1874, p. 9.
12. Sampson, *A History of Advertising*, pp. 10–11.
13. W. Gamber, *The Female Economy. The Millinery and Dressmaking Trades 1860–1930*, Bloomington, 1997, p. 5.
14. Anon, *The Young Tradesman; or, Book of English Trades: Being a Library of the Useful Arts, for Commercial Education*, London, 1839, p. 222.
15. Anon, *The Young Tradesman*, p. 224.
16. Anon, *The Young Tradesman*, p. 222.
17. Cartoon 4, London Guildhall Library Collection, LGL.
18. Anon, *The Young Tradesman*, p. 222.
19. I. Pinchbeck, *Women Workers and the Industrial Revolution, 1750–1850*, London, 1930, (reprinted London 1969, 1981), p.287–288; R. Campbell, *The London Tradesman*, London, 1747, pp.207–208.
20. Anon, *Reminiscences of an Old Draper*, London, 1876, p. 30.
21. Anon, *The Young Tradesman*, p. 227.
22. N. Cox, *The Complete Tradesman. A Study of Retailing 1550–1820*, Aldershot, 2000, pp. 114, 96–99.
23. R. Porter, *London. A Social History*, London, 1994, p. 145.
24. Anon, *The Young Tradesman*, pp. 227–229.
25. Anon, *The Young Tradesman*, pp. 230–231.
26. Anon, *Reminiscences of an Old Draper*, pp. 146–147.
27. Pinchbeck, I., *Women Workers and the Industrial Revolution, 1750-1850*, London, 1930 (reprinted London 1969, 1981), p. 294.
28. D. Alexander, *Retailing in England during the Industrial Revolution*, London, 1970, pp. 143–144.
29. Banks Collection, 72.61 and 72.190, dated 1805 and 1807, respectively, BM.
30. Heal Collection, 86.24 and 86.25, dated 1800 and 1804, respectively, BM.
31. Banks Collection, 40.16, BM.

32. D. Simonton, *A History of European Women's Work 1700 to the Present*, London, 1998, p. 158.
33. Pinchbeck, *Women Workers*, p. 295.
34. London Guildhall Library Trade Card Collection, Box 7, Cra-Der, LGL.
35. J. Blackman, 'The corner shop: The development of the grocery and general provisions trade' in D. Oddy and D. Miller (eds.) *The Making of the Modern British Diet*, London, 1976, p. 149.
36. Blackman, 'The corner shop', pp. 149, 150–151.
37. Blackman, 'The corner shop', p. 153.
38. Banks Collection, 38.7, dated 1812, BM.
39. Pinchbeck, *Women Workers*, p. 295.
40. Blackman, 'The corner shop', p. 151. Alexander, *Retailing in England*, p. 115, 123–124.
41. London Guildhall Library Trade Card Collection, Box 10, LGL.
42. Cox, *The Complete Tradesman*, pp. 90, 78, 79, 96.
43. J. O'Neill, 'Fifty years' experience of an Irish shoemaker in London', St Crispin, 1–2. Quoted in L. Schwarz, *London in the Age of Industrialisation*, Cambridge, 1992, p. 43.
44. Cox, *The Complete Tradesman*, p. 146.
45. M.J. Winstanley, *The Shopkeeper's World 1830–1914*, Manchester, 1978, pp. 55–56.
46. P.E. Malcolmson, *English Laundresses. A Social History, 1850–1930*, Chicago, 1986, p. 7.
47. Malcolmson, *English Laundresses*, pp. 7–8.
48. Simonton, *A History of European Women's Work*, p. 198.
49. As late as 1901, 72.8 per cent of the laundries on the factory inspectorate's register for the London district were hand laundries. See Malcolmson, *English Laundresses*, pp. xiii, 8.
50. Laundries and laundresses were so numerous in these areas that Kensal New Town became known as 'Soap Suds Island', and 'Laundry Land' replaced 'Piggeries and Potteries' as the nickname for Notting Dale. See Porter, *London*, p. 199.
51. Malcolmson, *English Laundresses*, p. 11.
52. Malcolmson, *English Laundresses*, p. 19.
53. Malcolmson, *English Laundresses*, p. 41.
54. Malcolmson, *English Laundresses*, p. 20.
55. Malcolmson, *English Laundresses*, p. 33.
56. Malcolmson, *English Laundresses*, pp. 32–33.
57. S. Christopher, *Cleaning and Scouring. A Manual for Dyers and Laundresses, and for Domestic Use*, London, 1817.
58. Malcolmson, *English Laundresses*, p. 13–14, 22.
59. Pinchbeck, *Women Workers*, p.24.
60. Recounted in Malcolmson, *English Laundresses*, p. 23.
61. Malcolmson, *English Laundresses*, pp. 25–26.
62. M.A. Ashford, *Life of a Licensed Victualler's Daughter. Written by Herself*, London, 1844, p. 10
63. Banks Collection, I.14, dated 1795, BM.
64. Pinchbeck, *Women Workers*, p. 296.
65. Simonton, *A History of European Women's Work*, p. 158.
66. Simonton, *A History of European Women's Work*, p. 158.
67. Davidoff, L. and Hall, C., *Family Fortunes. Men and Women of the English Middle Class 1780-1850*, London, 1987, p. 300.
68. Girouard, *Victorian Pubs*, London, 1975, p. 18.
69. Davidoff and Hall, *Family Fortunes*, p. 300.
70. Davidoff and Hall, *Family Fortunes*, p. 301.

71. B. Lillywhite, *London Coffee Houses. A Reference Book of Coffee Houses of the Seventeenth, Eighteenth and Nineteenth Centuries*, London, 1963, for examples see, pp. 647, 746, 647.
72. Lillywhite, *London Coffee Houses,* pp. 719, 275.
73. Heal Collection, I.104, BM.
74. Heal Collection, I.108, BM.
75. H. Mayhew, *London Labour and the London Poor*, London, Penguin, 1985, p. 83.
76. Mayhew, *London Labour,* p. 89.
77. Mayhew, *London Labour,* p. 89.
78. Lillywhite, *London Coffee Houses,* pp. 95–96.
79. Heal Collection, 9.2, BM.
80. Minna Wood: FRO, RD 13 HO 107 / 1511 180 (back). Sun Fire 651 / 1658774.
81. John Johnson Collection, JJ Bill Headings 21 (1) and 32 (152), dated 1817 and 1812, BOD.
82. John Johnson Collection, JJ Trade cards 28 (105), dated 1800, Bodleian Library.
83. John Johnson Collection, JJ Trade cards 21(13), dated 1830, Bodleian Library.
84. London Guildhall Library Trade Card Collection, Box 3 Bir-Bre, dated 1824, LGL.
85. Banks Collection, 59.46, dated 1801, BM.
86. London Guildhall Library Trade Card Collection, Box 7 Cra-Der, dated 1830, LGL.
87. Anne Ingram: Sun Fire 720 / 1948481 and 720 / 1948482.
88. London Guildhall Trade Card Collection, Box 6 Cla-Cox, LGL.
89. Pinchbeck, *Women Workers*, p. 295.
90. Heal Collection, 111.47, BM.
91. Sophia Sewell: Sun Fire 639 / 1653468.
92. Mary Parkes: Sun Fire 646 / 1651139 and 651 / 1662173.
93. Sophia Bain: Sun Fire 646 / 1645615.
94. Pinchbeck, *Women Workers*, pp. 294–295.
95. D.R. Green, 'The metropolitan economy: Continuity and change 1800–1939', in K. Hoggart and D.R. Green (eds.) *London. A New Metropolitan Geography*, London, 1991, p. 18.
96. Green, 'The metropolitan economy', p. 19.
97. Alexander, *Retailing in England,* pp. 199–201.
98. Alexander, *Retailing in England,* pp. 203–204.
99. Alexander, *Retailing in England,* pp. 199–201.
100. W. Hart, *The Autobiography of Willam Hart, Cooper, 1776–1857. A Respectable Artisan in the Industrial Revolution*, in P. Hudson and L. Hunter (eds.) *The London Journal*, 7, 2, 1981, p. 73.
101. Heal Collection, No. 104, BM.
102. Banks Collection, No. 104, BM.
103. Anon, 'An enquiry into the state of girls' fashionable schools', *Fraser's Magazine*, 31, 1856, p. 703. Quoted in C. de Bellaigue, 'The business of schoolkeeping' in C. de Bellaigue (ed.) *Schooling and Identity in England and in France, 1800–1867*, Oxford, 2007, p. 76.
104. S. Skedd, 'Women teachers and the expansion of girls' schooling in England, c.1760–1820' in H. Barker and E. Chalus (eds.) *Gender in Eighteenth-Century England*, London and New York, 1997, pp. 101–107.
105. London Guildhall Library Trade Card Collection, Box 22 Pri-Rob, LGL.
106. Skedd, 'Women teachers', p. 117.
107. Skedd, 'Women teachers', p. 112.

108. H. Barker, *The Business of Women. Female Enterprise and Urban Development in Northern England 1760–1830*, Oxford, 2006, p. 74.
109. Barker, *The Business of Women*, pp. 80–87.
110. Barker, *The Business of Women*, p. 74.
111. Banks Collection, 86.16, dated 1804, BM.
112. Heal Collection, 86.5, dated 1819, BM.
113. Heal Collection, 86.69, BM.
114. Banks Collection, 86.44, dated 1816, BM.
115. L.A. Loeb, *Consuming Angels: Advertising and Victorian Women*, Oxford, 1994, p. 21.
116. Heal Collection, 86.26, BM.
117. Berg and Clifford, 'Selling consumption', p. 159.
118. E. Rappaport, *Shopping for Pleasure: Women in the Making of London's West End*, Princeton, 2000. L. Walker, 'Vistas of pleasure: Women consumers and urban space in the West End of London, 1850–1900', in C. C. Orr (ed.) *Women in the Victorian Art World*, Manchester, 1995, pp. 70–85.

NOTES TO CHAPTER 5

1. E. Higgs, 'Women, occupations and work in nineteenth-century censuses', *History Workshop*, 23–24, 1987, p. 61. S. Lumas, *Making Use of the Census*, Kew, Surrey, 1997, p. 5.
2. Lumas, *Making Use of the Census*, p. 6.
3. E. Gordon and G. Nair, *Public Lives: Women, Family and Society in Victorian Britain*, New Haven, 2003, pp. 65, 171.
4. Gordon and Nair, *Public Lives*, p. 38.
5. Elizabeth Booth: FRO, RD 12, RG 9/170 53 (back), Sun Fire 717 / 195 87141. Susan Richards: FRO, RD 4/5, RG 9/51 42 (front), Sun Fire 721 / 1948541. Mary Ann Harrison: FRO, RD 16, RG 9/209 5 (front), Sun Fire 723 / 1968824.
6. Parliamentary Papers. Session 4, November 1852—20 August 1853. Volume LXXXVIII—Part 1. 1852–1853 Accounts and Papers. 32nd Volume—Part 1, p. xxvii.
7. Abriah Reynolds: FRO, RD 9 HO 107/1493 794(back), Sun Fire 649/1651659.
8. Elizabeth Baldwin: FRO, RD 4 RG 9/50 57(front), Sun Fire 720 / 1955671.
9. There are a number of surviving trade cards of sisters in trade in the Banks, Heal and Guildhall Collections, BM and LGL, respectively.
10. Bank Collection, 86.61, dated 1807, BM.
11. Lucy Walter: FRO, RD 9, HO 107 / 1496 108 (front), Sun Fire 641 / 1647417.
12. Margery Hall: Sun Fire 647 / 1656453 and 650 / 1656909.
13. D. Simonton, *A History of European Women's Work 1700 to the Present*, London, 1998, p. 103.
14. Simonton, *A History of European Women's Work*, p. 102.
15. Simonton, *A History of European Women's Work*, p. 99.
16. Dorothy Genge: FRO, RD 22 HO 107 / 1524 156 (front and back), Sun Fire 648 / 1647922.
17. E. Higgs, 'Domestic service and household production' in A.V. John (ed.) *Unequal Opportunities. Women's Employment in England 1800–1918*, Oxford, 1986, p. 135.
18. Higgs, 'Domestic service', p. 135.

19. Simonton, *A History of European Women's Work,* p. 104.
20. *The Economist and General Adviser,* No. 36, 22 January 1825. Quoted in J. Burnett (ed.) *Useful Toil,* London, 1994, pp. 148–149.
21. Quoted in Burdett, *Useful Toil,* p. 149.
22. Burdett, *Useful Toil,* p. 155.
23. D. Baxter, *The National Income of the United Kingdom,* London, 1868, appendix IV, p. 88. Quoted in Burdett, *Useful Toil,* p. 264.
24. Selina Martin employed 13-year-old Eliza Armar: FRO, RD 4 HO 107 / 1480 325 (front), Sun Fire 651 / 1656202. Mary Lambert employed 12-year-old Ann Murey: FRO, RD 19 HO 107 / 1530 300 (back), Sun Fire 649 / 1649738. Dorothy Genge employed 71-year-old Maria Hart: FRO, RD 22 HO 107 / 1524 156 (front and back), Sun Fire 648 / 1647922.
25. Julia Town: FRO, RD 4 HO 107 / 1483 5 (front), Sun Fire 646 / 1647277.
26. Ellen Gracefield: FRO, RD 19 RG 9/229 85 (front), Sun Fire 723 / 1947929.
27. M.A. Ashford, *Life of a Licensed Victualler's Daughter. Written by Herself,* London, 1844, p. 35.
28. L. Eldersveld Murphy, 'Business ladies: Midwestern women and enterprise, 1850–1880' in M.A, Yeager (ed.) *Women in Business* Vol. II, Cheltenham, 1999, p. 71.
29. J. Humphries, 'Female headed households in early industrial Britain: the vanguard of the proletariat?', *Labour History Review,* 63, 1, 1998, p. 33.
30. Martha Phillips and Julia Phillips: FRO, RD 19 HO 107 / 1525 457 (back) and 458 (front), Sun Fire 650 / 1664110.
31. The others were mainly located in the households of proprietors in the coffee-house keeping and victualling trades. No employees were listed on the night of the census for the linked proprietors in four trade areas: the chandlers, hosiers and haberdashers, tobacconists and stationers.
32. Jane Feamont: FRO, RD 25 HO 107 / 1556 709 (back), Sun Fire 640 / 1635545.
33. Elizabeth Wise: FRO, RD 3 HO 107 / 1475 452 (back), Sun Fire 646 / 1647815.
34. Susannah Armstrong: FRO, RD 5, HO 107 / 1481 247 (back), Sun Fire 651 / 1653346.
35. Elizabeth Sinpson: FRO, RD 19, HO 107 / 1526 260 (front), Sun Fire 649 / 1651629.
36. Hannah Fairburn: FRO, RD 15, HO 107 / 1516 173 (back), Sun Fire 647 / 1658870.
37. Anne Longfoot: FRO, RD 4/5 RG 9/51 42(front), Sun Fire 721 / 1948541.
38. Ann Jane Dowsell: FRO, RD 31 RG 9/349 22(back), Sun Fire 724 / 195963.
39. Hannah Cune and family: FRO, RD 7 RG 9/74 132(back), Sun Fire 724 / 1964015.
40. Maria Lawrance: FRO, RD 31 HO 107 / 1572 434 (back), Sun Fire 650 / 1664135.
41. Catherine Rebbeck: FRO, RD 14 HO 107 / 1515 244 (back), Sun Fire 650 / 1658620.
42. Maria Kaye: FRO, RD 12 HO 107 / 1494 18 (back), Sun Fire 648 / 1651593.
43. Walter Lock: FRO, RD 20 RG 9/238 8(back), Sun Fire 719 / 196368.
44. John, son of Agnes: FRO, RD 15, HO 107/1516 92(back), Sun Fire 649/1649799.
45. Thomas son of Elizabeth Huntley: FRO, RD 6, HO 107/1475 11(back), Sun Fire 641 / 1649375.

46. James Dean, nephew of Susannah Armstrong: FRO, RD 5, HO 107/1481 247(back), Sun Fire 651 / 1653346.
47. Joseph Peter, son of Mary Draper: FRO, RD 7, RG 9/68 3(back), Sun Fire 725 / 1966021.
48. George, son of Mary Ann Tubbs: FRO, RD 24, RG 9/284 185(back), Sun Fire 719 / 1955916.
49. Abriah Reynolds: FRO, RD 9 HO 107 / 1493 794 (back), Sun Fire 649 / 1651659.
50. Harriet Bradshaw: FRO, RD 2 HO 107 / 1472 114 (front), Sun Fire 646 / 1647245.
51. Ann Arrowsmith: FRO, RD 21 HO 107 / 1541 325 (front), Sun Fire 649 / 1658567.
52. A.M. Froide, 'Old maids: The lifecycle of single women in early modern England' in L. Botelhoe and P. Thane (eds.) *Women and Ageing in British Society Since 1500*, Essex, 2001, p. 94.
53. Ann Boxall: FRO, RD 13 Ho 107 / 1510 526 (front), Sun Fire 651 / 1656511. Jane and Ann Giddings: FRO, RD 7 HO 107 / 1488 593 (front), Sun Fire 651 / 1658768.
54. Elizabeth Wise: FRO, RD 3 RG 9/44 56(back), Sun Fire, 720 / 1953531.
55. William Woolcott, apprentice to Elizabeth Simpson: FRO, RD 19, HO 107 / 1526 260 (front), Sun Fire 649 / 1651629.
56. Elizabeth Simpson: FRO, RD 19, HO 107 / 1526, Sun Fire 649 / 1651629.
57. Maria Stockdale: FRO, RD 25, RG 9/306 140(back), Sun Fire 719 / 1948102.
58. Charlotte Walton: FRO, RD 4–6, RG 9/59 75(back), Sun Fire 725 / 1971911.
59. Esther Goatley: FRO, RD 26, 27, 29 RG 9/323 41(back), Sun Fire 724 / 1953426.
60. Elizabeth Jones: FRO, RD 9 HO 107 / 1497 588 (back), Sun Fire 651 / 1653362 Ann Vaughan: FRO, RD 3 HO 107 / 1475 650 (front), Sun Fire 646 / 1647206. Harriet Stiffs: FRO, RD 11 HO 107 / 1505 37 (back), Sun Fire 649 / 1662342.
61. Mary Ann Corrie: FRO, RD 9 RG 9/123 96(front and back), Sun Fire 719/1963887.
62. Gordon and Nair, *Public Lives*, p. 46.
63. Gordon and Nair, *Public Lives*, pp. 171, 197–198.

NOTES TO CHAPTER 6

1. J.K. Walton, *The Blackpool Landlady. A Social History*, Manchester, 1978. L. Davidoff, 'The separation of home and work? Landladies and lodgers in nineteenth and twentieth century England', in S. Burman (ed.) *Fit Work for Women*, London, 1979.
2. Rebecca Gordon: Sun Fire 647 / 1651009.
3. Nine policies insured rent only.
4. Elizabeth Trotter: Sun Fire 723 / 1968853.
5. Emma Atkins: Sun Fire 720 / 1958386.
6. Maria Hardy: Sun Fire 1861 720/1947524.
7. Eliza Ann Johnson: Sun Fire 1861 722/1973479.
8. Margaret Wilson: Sun Fire 1861 722/196617.
9. Quoted in R. Porter, *London. A Social History*, London, 1994, p. 268.

10. R.J. Morris, 'The middle-class and the property cycle during the industrial revolution', in T.C. Smout (ed.) *The Search for Wealth and Stability*, London, 1979, p. 110.
11. N. Phillips, *Women in Business 1700–1850*, Woodbridge, 2006, pp. 160–162.
12. P. Wakefield, *Reflections on the Present Condition of the Female Sex*, 1798, p. 170.
13. F. Sheppard, *London 1808–1870: The Infernal Wen*, London, 1971.
14. E. Kingsbury, *Work for Women*, London, 1884, pp. 72–73.
15. Kingsbury, *Work for Women*, p. 115.
16. Kingsbury, *Work for Women*, p. 73.
17. Kingsbury, *Work for Women*, pp. 185–186.
18. Wakefield, *Reflections*, p. 170.
19. Wakefield, *Reflections*, p. 72.
20. B. Taylor, *Eve and the New Jerusalem. Socialism and Feminism in the Nineteenth Century*, 1983, pp. 30–31.
21. Kingsbury, *Work for Women*, p. 85.
22. Kingsbury, *Work for Women*, p. 74.
23. Davidoff, 'The separation of home and work?', pp. 70, 82, 90.
24. Davidoff, 'The separation of home and work', p. 86.
25. London Guildhall Trade Card Collection, Box 15, Hub-Jon, dated 1853, LGL.
26. C. Dickens, 'The boarding house', in *Sketches by Boz*, London, 1839 (reprinted Penguin Classics, 1995), pp. 321–361.
27. Mrs Wilby: 648/1658377; Mrs Peters Brotherson: 650/1664891; Miss Johnstone: 651/1662138; Mrs Sheppard: 651/1651463.
28. Five streets accounting for 14 proprietors (3.5 per cent) could not be located. The following was used to locate addresses: *The A to Z of Victorian London*, London Topographical Society, 1987, index of place names. It is based on Bacon's Atlas of 1888.
29. One street could not be located.
30. Assets include dwelling house and/or household goods and fixtures. Only two policies, both from 1861, had more than one policyholder. In both cases, the additional persons were female and shared the same surname as the main policyholder: Christiana Edwards and Henrietta Edwards, Sun Fire 720 / 1955596 and Caroline Ward and Maria Ward, Sun Fire 722 / 1950662.
31. London Guildhall Trade Card Collecton, Box 16, Jor-Lav, dated 1859, LGL.
32. Census linkage on the proprietors active in the ten most common trades for 1851 / 1861 had a 57.6 per cent combined success rate.
33. Davidoff, 'The separation of home and work', p. 89.
34. H. Mayhew, *London Labour and the London Poor*, 1851. Selections made by V. Neuburg, London, 1985, p. 111.
35. Cesilia Ruedi: FRO, RD 1 RG 9/9 79 (front) and Sun Fire 726/1971258.
36. Anne White: FRO, RD 9 RG 9/95 93 (front) and Sun Fire 718/1958894. Elizabeth Warmsley: FRO, RD 9 RG 9 / 103 12 (back) and 13 (front) and Sun Fire 717/1955030.
37. Cassandra Wilby: FRO, RD 19 HO 107 / 1530 211 (back) and Sun Fire 648 / 1658377.
38. Rebecca Darnell: FRO, RD 22 HO 107 / 1545 202(back) and Sun Fire 646 / 1658584.
39. J.R. Walkowitz, *Prostitution and Victorian Society. Women, Class and the State*, Cambridge, 1980, p. 24.
40. Porter, *London. A Social History*, p.268.

41. Taken from the *Quarterly Review*, vol. 82, 1847, pp. 142–152. Quoted in Sheppard, *London*, pp.4–5.
42. Sheppard, *London*, p. 289.
43. T. Henderson, *Disorderly Women in Eighteenth Century London. Prostitution and Control in the Metropolis 1730–1830*, Essex, 1999, p. 34.
44. Mayhew, *London Labour*, p. 113.
45. Mayhew, *London Labour*, p. 112–113.
46. Mayhew, *London Labour*, p. 112.
47. L. Davidoff and C. Hall, *Family Fortunes. Men and Women of the English Middle Class 1780–1850*, London, 1987, pp. 277–278.
48. Esther Goatley: FRO, RD 26,27,29 RG 9/323 41(back), Sun Fire 724 / 19531426.
49. Rees provides various examples of this kind of theft in the late eighteenth century, see S. Rees, *The Floating Brothel*, St Ives, 2001, pp. 12–13.
50. Walton, *The Blackpool Landlady*, pp. 85, 114.

NOTES TO CHAPTER 7

1. Lucy Martin (author of *Make it Your Business: A Woman's Guide to Working for Herself*, 2006) interviewed in *The Times*, London, 30 March 2006, *Times2*, p. 9.
2. Anon., 'Thoughts of a dressmaker', *The World of Fashion: Monthly Magazine of the Courts of London and Paris Fashions, Literature, Music, Fine Arts, the Opera, and the Theatres*, Issue 323, Friday 1 November 1850, London, p. 126.
3. Anon., Harper's Bazaar Chanel Businesswoman of the Year Competition 2006, *The Times*, 30 March 2006, *Times2*, p. 9.
4. *English Woman's Journal* Vol. 4, September 1859, p. 57 / Miscellanea. *The Lady's Newspaper*, Issue 404, Saturday, 23 September 1854, London, p. 188.
5. M. Grogan, *How Women May Earn a Living*, London, 1880. P. Browne, (pseud. Sarah Sharp Hamer), *What Girls Can Do: A Book for Mothers and Daughters*, London, 1880 (reprinted 1885).
6. Anon, *Guide to the Unprotected in Every-Day Matters Relating to Property and Income by A Banker's Daughter*, London, 1864 (fifth edition, revised in 1881).
7. N. Phillips, *Women in Business 1700–1850*, Woodbridge, 2006, p. 258.
8. E. Gordon and G. Nair, *Public Lives. Women, Family and Society in Victorian Britain*, New Haven, 2003, p. 186.
9. H. Barker, *The Business of Women. Female Enterprise and Urban Development in Northern England 1760–1830*, Oxford, 2006, pp. 66, 79, 167–171.
10. T. Ericsson, 'Limited opportunities? Female retailing in nineteenth-century Sweden', in R. Beachy et al (eds.) *Women, Business and Finance in Nineteenth-Century Europe*, Oxford: Berg, 2006, pp. 139, 150.
11. Ericsson, 'Limited opportunities', p. 146.
12. V. Piette, 'Belgium's tradeswomen' in R. Beachy et al (eds.) *Women, Business and Finance in Nineteenth-Century Europe*, Oxford: Berg, 2006, pp. 127, 131, 136.
13. D.M. Hafter, 'Women in the underground business of eighteenth-century Lyon, *Enterprise & Society*, 2, March 2001, pp. 11–40.

14. C. de Bellaigue, 'The business of schoolkeeping', in C. de Bellaigue (ed.) *Schooling and Identity in England and in France, 1800–1867*, Oxford, 2007, pp. 74, 76, 82, 98.
15. S. Skedd, 'Women teachers and the expansion of girls' schooling in England, c.1760–1820' in H. Barker and E. Chalus (eds.) *Gender in Eighteenth-Century England*, London and New York, 1997, p. 119.
16. For a further discussion of these themes see, A.S. Thomas and S.L. Mueller, 'A case for comparative entrepreneurship: Assessing the relevance of culture' *Journal of International Business Studies*, 31, 2.
17. B. Craig, 'Petites Bourgeoises and Petty Capitalists: Women in retail in the Lille area during the nineteenth century', *Enterprise and Society*, 2, June 2001, pp. 198–224.
18. Craig, 'Petite bourgeoises and petty capitalists', pp. 202, 208.
19. V.G. Drachman, *Enterprising Women. 250 Years of American Business*, Cambridge, MA, 2002, pp. 31, 36.
20. S.A. Yohn, 'Crippled capitalists: The inscription of economic dependence and the challenge of female entrepreneurship in nineteenth-century America', *Feminist Economics*, 12, Issues 1 and 2, 2006, p. 92.
21. B.Z. Khan 'Married women's property laws and female commercial activity: Evidence from United States Patent Records, 1790–1895', *The Journal of Economic History*, 56, 2, 1996.
22. L. Eldersveld Murphy, 'Business ladies: Midwestern women and enterprise 1850–1880', *Journal of Women's History*, 3, Spring, 1991.
23. R. L. Boyd 'Race, labour market disadvantage, and survivalist entrepreneurship: Black women in the urban north during the great depression', *Sociological Forum*, 15:4, 2000.
24. W. Gamber, *The Female Economy. The Millinery and Dressmaking Trades 1860–1930*, Illinois, 1997.
25. T. da Silva Lopes and P. Duguid, 'Entrepreneurship, brands and the development of global business', *XIV International Economic History Congress*, Helsinki 2006, Session 40, p. 1–2.
26. P. Mathias, 'Entrepreneurs, managers and business men in eighteenth-century Britain, in P. Mathias and J.A. Davies (eds.) *Enterprise and Labour*, Oxford: Blackwell, 1996, pp. 12–15.
27. K. Honeyman, 'Doing business with gender: The case of business history in the UK', *European Business History Association Conference*, Barcelona 16–18 September 2004.
28. M. Walsh, *Business History News,* 28, October 2004, pp. 2, 5.
29. W. Gamber, 'A gendered enterprise: Placing nineteenth-century businesswomen in history', *Business History Review,* 72, Summer, 1998, p.191.
30. Craig, 'Petites bourgeoises and penny capitalists', p. 218.
31. Jean Gardiner, *Gender, Care and Economics,* Basingstoke, 1997; 'Rethinking self-sufficiency: employment, families and welfare' *Cambridge Journal of Economics*, 24, 2000, pp. 671–689.
32. Bellaigue, 'The business of schoolkeeping', pp. 76–78.
33. Gordon and Nair, *Public Lives*, pp. 5, 179.
34. F. Nightingale, *Cassandra*, London, 1852. Reprinted in full in R. Strachey, *The Cause. A Short History of the Women's Movement in Great Britain*, London, 1929 (reprinted 1979), p. 407.
35. P. Thomson, *The Victorian Heroine: A Changing Ideal 1837–1873*, London, 1956, p. 71.
36. Anon, 'An enquiry into the state of girls' fashionable schools', *Fraser's Magazine*, 31, 1856, p. 703. Quoted in Bellaigue, 'The business of schoolkeeping', p. 76.

37. M. Vicinus, *Independent Women. Work and community for single women 1850–1920*, London, 1985, p. 25.
38. House of Lords Sessional Papers, 1854–1855, Vol.5, p. 27. Quoted in S. Alexander, 'Women's work in nineteenth century London; A study of the years 1820–50', in J. Mitchell and A. Oakley (eds.) *The Rights and Wrongs of Women*, London, 1977, p. 85.
39. S. Nenadic 'The social shaping of business behaviour in the nineteenth century women's garment trades' *Journal of Social History, 31,* 1998.
40. A. Kwolek-Folland, *Incorporating Women: A History of Women and Business in the United States*, New York, 1998, pp. 2, 212–213.
41. J.S. Pederson, 'Victorian liberal feminism and the idea of work', in K. Cowman and L.A. Jackson (eds.) *Women and Work Culture. Britain c.1850–1950*, Aldershot, 2005, pp. 36, 43.
42. Pederson, 'Victorian liberal feminism', pp. 28–29.
43. Pederson, 'Victorian liberal feminism', pp. 32.
44. Yohn, 'Crippled capitalists', pp. 88, 93, 96, 102.
45. Yohn, 'Crippled capitalists', p. 103.
46. Charles Dickens, *Sketches by Boz*, London, 1839, (reprinted Penguin Classic, London, 1995), p. 82.
47. Dickens, *Sketches by Boz*, p. 321.
48. Dickens, *Sketches by Boz*, p. 290.
49. Dickens, *Sketches by Boz*, p. 83.
50. E. Copeland, *Women Writing about Money*, Cambridge, 1995, p. 190.
51. Gordon and Nair, *Public Lives*, p. 198.
52. S. Albermarle, 'Breaking the silent partnership: Businesswomen in popular fiction', *American Literature*, 62, 2, June 1990, pp. 238–261.
53. E. Showalter, 'Introduction' to G. Gissing's *The Odd Women*, reprinted Penguin Classic, London, 1993, p. ix.
54. Anon, 'Letters to women on money earning, No.11-Business', *The Alexandra Magazine*, Wed. 1 June, 1864, London, p. 123.
55. Anon, 'Letters to women on money earning', pp. 122, 124.

NOTES TO THE CONCLUSION

1. Anon, 'Thoughts of a Dressmaker', *The Words of Fashion: Monthly magazine of the courts of London and Paris fashions, literature, music, fine arts, the opera and the theatres*, Issue 323, November 1865, p. 126.
2. The latter were of course far more valuable than have commonly been recognised, especially household accounting and management. See B. Lemire, *The Business of Everday Life*, Manchester, 2006.
3. 'Miscellanea', *The Lady's Newspaper*, Issue 404, 23, 1854, London p. 188.
4. J. Humphries, 'Female headed households in early industrial Briaitian: The vanguard of the proletariat?' *Labour History Review*, 63, 1, 1998, pp. 31–32.
5. Anon, 'What is there I can do?', *The Woman's Gazette or News about Work*, 1, 12, September, 1876, p. 180.
6. Quoted by B.L. Smith, *Women and Work*, London, 1857, p. 16.
7. Smith, *Women and Work*, p. 5.

Bibliography

(1) Manuscript and Archival Sources

Banks Collection, The British Museum.
Heal Collection, The British Museum.
John Johnson Collection, Bodleian Library, Oxford (Online access).
London Guildhall Library Trade Card Collection, London Guildhall Library (Prints and Maps).
London Post Office Directory, The British Library, London.
Sun Fire Office policy registers, series 11'936, London Guildhall Library (Manuscripts).

(2) Newspapers and Periodicals

The Alexandra Magazine.
English Woman's Journal.
Fraser's Magazine.
John Bull.
Lady's Newspaper.
Myra's Journal of Dress and Fashion.
The Times.
The Woman's Gazette or News about Work.
The World of Fashion.

(3) Printed Primary Material

Anon., *The Book of Trades*, London, 1862.
Anon., *The Book of Trades or Circle of the Useful Arts*, Glasgow, 1837 (5th edition).
Anon., *The Book of Trades or Library of the Useful Arts. Parts 1, 2 and 3 combined*, London, 1806 (3rd edition).
Anon., *Business Life. The experiences of a London tradesman with practical advice and directions for avoiding many of the evils connected with our present commercial system and state of society*, London, 1861.
Anon., 'An enquiry into the state of girls' fashionable schools', *Fraser's Magazine* 31, 1856.
Anon., *Female Restoration by a Moral and Physical Vindication of Female Talents: in opposition to all dogmatical assertions relative to disparity in the sexes*, London, 1780.

Anon., *Guide to the Unprotected in Every-day Matters Relating to Property and Income by A Banker's Daughter*, London, 1864 (5th edition. Revised in 1881).

Anon., 'Letters to women on money earning, No.11—Business', *The Alexandra Magazine*, 1 June, 1864.

Anon., 'Miscellenea', *The Lady's Newspaper*, Issue 404, No. 23, 1854.

Anon., *Reminiscences of an Old Draper*, London, 1876.

Anon., 'Struggle for existence', *John Bull*, Issue 2, 1865.

Anon., *Sun Insurance Office Ltd of London*, London, 1932.

Anon., 'Thoughts of a dressmaker', *The Words of Fashion: Monthly magazine of the courts of London and Paris fashions, literature, music, fine arts, the opera and the theatres*, Issue 323, 1850.

Anon., *The Young Tradesman; or, book of English Trades: Being a library of the useful arts, for commercial education*, London, 1839 (12th edition).

Anon., 'What is there I can do?', *The Woman's Gazette or News about Work*, 1, 12, September, 1876.

Ashford, M.A., *Life of a Licensed Victualler's Daughter. Written by Herself*, London, 1844.

Baxter, D., *The National Income of the United Kingdom*, London, 1868.

Boyd-Kinnear, J., 'The Social Position of Women in the Present Age', in J.E. Butler (ed.) *Women's Work and Women's Culture. A Series of Essays*, London, 1869.

Browne, P., *What Girls Can Do: A Book for Mothers and Daughters*, London, 1880.

Butler, J.E., *The Education and Employment of Women*, Liverpool, 1868.

Butler, J.E., 'Introduction', in J.E. Butler (ed.) *Woman's Work and Woman's Culture. A Series of Essays*, London, 1869.

Campbell, *A General Description of All Trades*, London, 1747.

Campbell, R., *The London Tradesman*, London, 1747.

Christopher, S., *Cleaning and Scouring. A Manual for Dyers and Laundresses, and for Domestic Use*, London, 1817.

Cobbett, W., *Advice to Young Men and (Incidentally) to Young Women, in the Middle and Higher Ranks of Life*, London, 1829 (reprinted 1863).

Dickens, C., *Sketches by Boz*, London, 1839.

Engels, F., *The Origin of the Family, Private Property and the State*, Hottingen-Zurich, 1884.

Gisborne, T., *Duties of the Female Sex*, London, 1801.

Gissing, G., *The Odd Women*, London, 1893.

Greg, W.R., *Why are Women Redundant?* London, 1869.

Grogan, M., *How Women May Earn a Living*, London, 1880.

Hart, W., *The Autobiography of William Hart, Cooper, 1776–1857. A Respectable Artisan in the Industrial Revolution*, reprinted by P. Hudson and L. Hunter (eds.) *The London Journal*, 7, 2, 1981.

Houston, A., *The Emancipation of Women from Existing Industrial Disabilities: Considered in its Economic Aspect*, London, 1862.

Kingsbury, E., *Work for Women*, London, 1884.

Mayhew, H., *London Labour and the London Poor*, London, 1851 (Edition used here: selections by V. Neuburg, London: Penguin, 1985).

Milne, J.D., *Industrial and Social Position of Women in the Middle and Lower Ranks*, London, 1857.

Moore, H., *Essays Principally Designed for Young Ladies*, London, 1777.

Moore, H., *Thoughts on the Importance of the Manners of the Great to General Society*, London, 1788.

Nicholson, W., *Practical Fire Insurance*, London, 1893.

Nightingale, F., *Cassandra*, London, 1852. Reprinted in full in R. Strachey, R., *The Cause. A Short History of the Women's Movement in Great Britain*, London, 1929 (reprinted 1979).

Parkes, B.R., *Essays on Woman's Work*, London, 1865.

Parley, P., *The Book of Trades, Arts, & Professions Relative to Food, Clothing, Shelter and Ornament; for the Use of the Young*, London, 1855.

Penny, A.J., *The Afternoon of Unmarried Life*, London, 1858.

Ruskin, J., *Sesames and Lilies*, Kent, 1887.

Sampson, H., *A History of Advertising*, London, 1874.

Smith, B.L., *Women and Work*, London, 1857.

Taylor, H., 'Enfranchisement of Women', in J.S. Mill *Dissertations and Discussions. Political Philosophical and Historical*, London, 1859.

Trollope, A., *London Tradesmen*, London, 1880.

Wakefield, P., *Reflections on the Present Condition of the Female Sex*, London, 1798.

Wollstonecraft, M., *A Vindication of the Rights of Woman*, London, 1992.

Wolstenholme, E.C., 'The Education of Girls, its Present and its Future', in J.E. Butler (ed.) *Women's Work and Women's Culture. A Series of Essays*, London, 1869.

1854   Printed Secondary Works

The A to Z of Victorian London, London, 1987.

Adams, C.L., *Insurance Points Worth Knowing*, London, 1922.

Albermarle, S., 'Breaking the silent partnership: Businesswomen in popular fiction', *American Literature*, 62, 2, 1990.

Alexander, D., *Retailing in England During the Industrial Revolution*, London, 1970.

Alexander, S., 'Women's work in nineteenth century London; A study of the years 1820–1850', in J. Mitchell and A. Oakley (eds.) *The Rights and Wrongs of Women*, London, 1977.

———, 'Women, class and sexual differences in the 1830's and 1840's: Some reflections on the writing of a feminist history', *History Workshop*, 17, 1984.

Alexander, S. et al., 'Labouring women: A reply to Eric Hobsbawm', *History Workshop*, 8, 1979.

Anderson, M., 'The social position of spinsters in mid-Victorian Britain', *Journal of Family History*, winter, 1984).

Avdela, E., 'Work, gender and history in the 1990's and beyond', *Gender and History*, 11, 3, 1999.

Barker, H., 'Women, work and the industrial revolution: Female involvement in the English printing trades c.1700–1840', in H. Barker and E. Chalus (eds.) *Gender in Eighteenth Century England*, London, 1997.

———, *The Business of Women. Female enterprise and urban development in northern England 1760–1830*, Oxford, 2006.

Barnet, D., *London, Hub of the Industrial Revolution. A Revisionary History 1775–1825*, London and New York, 1998.

Beresford, M.V., 'Building history from fire insurance records', *Urban History Yearbook*, 1976.

———, 'Prometheus insured: The Sun Fire Agency in Leeds during urbanisation, 1716–1826', *Economic History Review*, 35, 1982.

Berg, M., 'What difference did women's work make to the industrial revolution?', *History Workshop*, 35, 1993.

Berg, M., and Clifford, H., 'Selling consumption in the eighteenth century: Advertising and the trade card in Britain and France', *Cultural and Social History* 4, 2, 2007.

Birley, S., 'Female entrepreneurs: Are they really any different? ', *Journal of Small Business Management*, January, 1989.

Blackman, J., 'The corner shop: The development of the grocery and general provisions trade', in D. Oddy and D. Miller (eds.) *The Making of the Modern British Diet*, London, 1976.

Bock, G., 'Challenging dichotomies in women's history', in M.B. Norton and R.M. Alexander (eds.) *Major Problems in American Women's History*, Lexington, MA, 1996.

Briggs, A., 'The language of class in early nineteenth-century England', in A. Briggs and J. Saville (eds.) *Essays in Labour History* Vol. 1, London, 1967.

Burdett, J. (ed.), *Useful Toil*, London, 1994.

Carr, E.H., *What is History?*, London, 1961 (reprinted 1987).

Chaytor, M., and Lewis, J., 'Introduction', in A. Clark (ed.) *Working Life of Women in Seventeenth Century*, London, 1982.

Church, C., 'Victorian masculinity and the Angel in the House', in M.Vicinus (ed.) *A Widening Sphere. Changing Roles of Victorian Women*, London, 1990.

Clark, A., *Working Life of Women in the Seventeenth Century*, London, 1919 (reprinted 1968, 1982, 1992).

Cocherell, H.A.L., and Green, E., *The British Insurance Business*, Sheffield, 1994.

Copeland, E., *Women Writing About Money*, Cambridge, 1995.

Cox, N., *The Complete Tradesman. A Study of Retailing 1550–1820*, Hants, 2000.

Crafts, N.F.R., *British Economic Growth during the Industrial Revolution*, Oxford, 1986.

Craig, B., 'Petites bourgeoises and penny capitalists: Women in retail in the Lille area during the nineteenth century', *Enterprise & Society*, 2, June, 2001.

Crom, T.R., *Trade Catalogues 1542 to 1842*, Florida, 1989.

Cromie, S., and Hayes, J., 'Towards a Typology of Female Entrepreneurs', *The Sociological Review*, 36, 1988.

Curran, J., *Bolton Fifteen Years On: A Review and Analysis of Small Business Research in Britain 1971–1986*, London, 1986.

Curran, J., Burrows, R., and Evandrou, M., *Small Business Owners and the Self-Employed in Britain. An Analysis of General Household Survey Data*, London, 1987.

Davidoff, L., 'The separation of home and work? Landladies and lodgers in ninetenth and twentieth century England', in S. Burman (ed.) *Fit Work for Women*, London, 1979.

Davidoff, L., and Hall, C., *Family Fortunes. Men and Women of the English Middle Class 1780–1850*, London, 1987.

———, 'The hidden investment: Women and the enterprise', in P. Sharpe (ed.) *Women's Work. The English Experience 1650–1914*, London, 1998.

Davies, E.A., *An Account of the Formation and Early Years of the Westminster Fire Office*, Glasgow, 1952.

Davin, A., 'Women and history', in M. Wandor (ed.) *The Body Politic. Writings from the Women's Liberation Movement in Britain, 1969–1972*, London, 1972.

———'The London Feminist History Group', *History Workshop*, 9, 1980.

———, 'Feminism and labour history', in R. Samuel (ed.) *People's History and Socialist Theory*, London, 1981.

————, 'Redressing the balance or transforming the art? The British experience', in S.J. Kleinberg (ed.) *Retrieving Women's History*, Oxford, 1988.

Davis, N.Z., 'Women's history in transition: The European case', in J.W.W. Scott (ed.) *Feminism and History*, Oxford, 1996.

Deane, P., and Cole, W.A., *British Economic Growth, 1688–1959*, Cambridge, 1962.

de Bellaigue, C. 'The business of schoolkeeping' in *Schooling and Identity in England and in France, 1800–1867*, Oxford, 2007.

Dekker, R.M., and van de Pol, L.C., *The Tradition of Female Transvestism in Early Modern Europe*, London, 1989.

de Vries, L., *History as Hot News. The World of the Early Victorians Through the Eyes of the Illustrated London News 1842–1865*, London, 1995.

Dickson, P.G.M., *The Sun Insurance Office 1710–1960*, London, 1960.

Drachman, V.G., *Enterprising Women. 250 years of American business*, Cambridge, MA, 2002.

Earle, P., *A City Full of People. Men and Women of London 1650–1750*, London, 1994.

Earle, P., 'The female labour market in London in the late seventeenth and early eighteenth centuries', in P. Sharpe (ed.) *Women's Work. The English Experience 1650–1914*, London, 1998.

Earle, P., *The Making of the English Middle Class. Business, Society and Family Life in London 1660–1730*, London, 1989.

Ericcson, T., 'Limited opportunities? Female retailing in nineteenth-century Sweden', in R. Beachy et al (eds.) *Women, Business and Finance in Nineteenth-Century Europe*, Oxford: Berg, 2006.

Erickson, A.L., *Women and Property in Early Modern England*, London, 1993.

Evans, R.J., *In Defense of History*, London, 1997.

Fox-Genovese, E., 'Placing women's history in history', *New Left Review*, 133, 1982.

Freeman, M., Pearson, R., and Taylor, J., 'A doe in the city: Women shareholders in eighteenth and early nineteenth century Britain', *Accounting, Business & Financial History*, 16, 2006.

Froide, A.M., 'Old maids: the lifecycle of single women in early modern England', in L. Botelhoe and P. Thane (eds.) *Women and Ageing in British Society Since 1500*, Essex, 2001.

Gamber, W., *The Female Economy. The Millinery and Dressmaking Trades 1860–1930*, Illinois, 1997.

————, 'A gendered enterprise: Placing nineteenth-century businesswomen in history', *Business History Review*, 72, summer, 1998.

Garber, M., *Vested Interests. Cross-Dressing and Cultural Anxiety*, London, 1992.

Gardiner, J., *Gender, Care and Economics*, Basingstoke, 1997.

————, 'Rethinking self-sufficiency: employment, families and welfare', *Cambridge Journal of Economics*, 24, 2000.

George, M.D., *London Life in the Eighteenth Century*, London, 1951 (reprinted, 1966).

Gibb, A.A., and Ritchie, J., 'Understanding the process of starting small business', *International Small Business Journal*, 1, 1982.

Girouard, M., *Victorian Pubs*, London, 1975.

Glass, D.V., 'Socio-economic status and occupations in the City of London at the end of the seventeenth century', in A.E.J. Hollaender and W. Kellaway (eds.) *Studies in London History*, London, 1969.

Goffee, R., and Scase, R., 'Business ownership and women's subordination: A preliminary study of female proprietors', *The Sociological Review*, 31, 1983.

Goffee, R., Scase, R., and Pollack, M., 'Why some women decide to become their own boss', *New Society*, 9, 1982.

Goodman, D., 'Public sphere and private life: toward a synthesis of current historiographical approaches to the old regime', *History and Theory*, 31, 1992.

Gordon E. and Nair G., 'The economic role of middle class women in Victorian Glasgow', *Women's History Review*, 9, 2000.

———, 'The myth of the Victorian patriarchal family', *The History of the Family*, 7, 1, 2002.

———, *Public Lives: Women, Family and Society in Victorian Britain*, New Haven, 2003.

Gordon, L., 'Women's history', in Gardiner, J. (ed.) *What is History Today?* London, 1988, (reprinted 1992).

Gorsky, S.R., 'Old maids and new women. Alternatives to marriage in English women's novels, 1847–1915', *Journal of Popular Culture*, summer, 1973.

Green, D.R., 'The metropolitan economy: Continuity and change 1800–1939', in K. Hoggart and D.R. Green (eds.) *London. A New Metropolitan Geography*, London, 1991.

Green, D., and Owens A., 'Gentlewomanly capitalism? Spinsters, widows and wealth holding in England and Wales c.1800–1860', *Economic History Review*, LVI, 3, 2003.

Hafter, D.M., 'Women in the underground business of eighteenth-century Lyon, *Enterprise & Society*, 2, March, 2001.

Hagen, E., *The Economics of Development*, Homewood, 1975.

Hakim, C., 'The sexual division of labour and women's heterogeneity', *British Journal of Sociology*, 47, 1, 1996.

Hall, C., 'The early formation of Victorian domestic ideology', in C. Hall (ed.) *White, Male and Middle Class*, Cambridge, 1992.

———, 'Private persons versus public someones: Class, gender and politics in England, 1780–1850', in C. Hall (ed.) *White, Male and Middle Class*, Cambridge, 1992.

———, 'Strains in the firm of wife, children and friends: middle class women and employment in early nineteenth-century England', in C. Hall (ed.) *White, Male and Middle Class*, Cambridge, 1992.

Hammerton, A.J., *Emigrant Gentlewomen*, London, 1979.

Harvey, C., Green, E., and Corefield, P.J., 'Continuity, change, and specialization within metropolitan London: The economy of Westminster, 1750–1820', *Economic History Review*, 52, 3, 1999.

Heal, A., *The Sign Boards of Old London Shops*, London, 1945.

Henderson, T., *Disorderly Women in Eighteenth Century London. Prostitution and Control in the Metropolis 1730–1830*, Essex, 1999.

Henham, B., *Hand in Hand. The Story of the Hand in Hand Fire and Life Insurance Society 1696–1996*, London, 1996.

Higgs, E., 'Domestic service and household production', in A.V. John (ed.) *Unequal Opportunities. Women's Employment in England 1800–1918*, Oxford, 1986.

———, 'Women, occupations and work in nineteenth-century censuses', *History Workshop*, 23–24, 1987.

Hill, B., *Women, Work and Sexual Politics in Eighteenth-Century England*, London, 1989.

Hobsbawm, E., 'Labour history and ideology', *Journal of Social History*, 7, 4, 1973.

———, 'Man and woman in Socialist iconography', *History Workshop*, 6, 1978.

Holcombe, L., *Victorian Ladies at Work*, Conneticut, 1973.

———, 'Victorian wives and property. Reform of the married women's property law, 1857–1882', in M. Vicinus (ed.) *A Widening Sphere. Changing Roles of Victorian Women*, London, 1990.

Horrell, S., and Humphries, J., 'Women's labour force participation and the transition to the male-breadwinner family, 1790–1865', in P. Sharpe (ed.) *Women's Work. The English Experience 1650–1914*, London, 1998.

Hosgood, C.P., 'The knights of the road. Commercial travellers and the culture of the commercial room in late-Victorian and Edwardian England', *Victorian Studies*, 37, 4, 1994.

Hudson, P., and Lee, W.R. (eds.), *Women's Work and the Family Economy in Historical Perspective*, Manchester, 1990.

Hufton, O., 'Women in history I: Early modern Europe', *Past and Present*, 101, 1983.

Humphries, J., 'Female headed households in early industrial Britain: the vanguard of the proletariat?' *Labour History Review*, 63, 1, 1998.

Humphries, S., 'Women's history', in J. Gardiner (ed.) *What is History Today?* London, 1988 (reprinted 1992).

Hunt, M., *The Middling Sort. Commerce, Gender and Family in England 1680–1780*, London, 1996.

Jenkins, D.T., 'The practice of insurance against fire, 1750–1840, and historical research', in O.M. Westall (ed.) *The Historian and the Business of Insurance*, Manchester, 1984.

Kay, A.C., 'Reaction not retreat: small business proprietorship and the redundant woman', *The Economic History Society New Researchers' Papers*, 2002.

——, 'A little enterprise of her own: Lodging-house keeping and the accommodation business in nineteenth-century London', *The London Journal*, 28, 2, 2003.

——, 'Small business, self-employment and women's work-life choices in nineteenth century London', in D. Mitch, J. Brown, and M.H.D. Van Leeuwen (eds.) *Origins of the Modern Career*, Aldershot, 2004.

——, 'Retailing, respectability and the independent woman in nineteenth-century London', in R. Beachy, B. Craig, and A. Owens (eds.) *Women, Business and Finance in Nineteenth-Century Europe. Rethinking Separate Spheres*, Oxford: Berg, 2006.

——, 'Revealing her assets: liberating the Victorian businesswoman from the sources', *Business Archives: Sources and History*, 92, 2006.

Kellett, J.R., 'The breakdown of gild and corporation control over the handicraft and retail trade in London', *The Economic History Review*, 10, 3, 1958.

Kelly-Gadol, J., 'The social relation of the sexes: Methodological implications of women's history', *Signs*, 1, 4, 1976.

Kenyon, O., *Women's Voices. Their Lives and Loves Through Two Thousand Years of Letters*, London, 1995.

Kerber, L., 'Separate spheres, female worlds, woman's place: The rhetoric of women's history', *Journal of American History*, 75, 1, 1988.

Khan, B.Z. 'Married women's property laws and female commercial activity: Evidence from United States Patent Records, 1790–1895', *The Journal of Economic History*, 56, 2, 1996.

Kwolek-Folland, A., *Incorporating Women: A History of Women and Business in the United States*, New York, 1998.

Lees, L.H., *Exiles of Erin. Irish Migrants in Victorian London*, Manchester, 1979.

Lemire, B., 'Petty pawns and informal lending: Gender and the transformation of small-scale credit in England, c.1600–1800', in K. Bruland and P. O'Brien (eds.) *From Family Firms to Corporate Capitalism*, Oxford, 1998.

——, *The Business of Everyday Life*, Manchester, 2006.

Lerner, G., 'Placing women in history', in M.B. Norton and R.M. Alexander (eds.) *Major Problems in American Women's History*, Lexington, MA, 1996.

Leydesdorff, S., 'Politics, identification and the writing of women's history', in A. Angerman et al. (eds.) *Current Issues in Women's History*, London, 1989.

Lillywhite, B., *London Coffee Houses. A Reference Book of Coffee Houses of the Seventeenth, Eighteenth and Nineteenth Centuries*, London, 1963.

———, *London Signs*, London, 1972.

Lindert, P.H., 'English occupations, 1670–1811', *Journal of Economic History*, 14, 1980.

Lindert, P.H., and Williamson, J.G., 'English Workers living standards during the industrial revolution: A new look', *Economic History Review*, 36, 1983.

Lumas, S., *Making Use of the Census*, Kew, Surrey, 1997.

Malcolmson, P.E., *English Laundresses. A Social History, 1850–1930*, Chicago, 1986.

Maltby J., and Rutterford J., 'She possessed her own fortune: Women investors from the late nineteenth century to the early twentieth century', *Business History*, 48, 2006.

Marlow, S., and Strange, A., *The Effect of Labour Market Discrimination on Women's Expectations of Self Employment*, Warwick Business School: Working Paper No 10, 1992.

Mathias, P., 'Entrepreneurs, Managers and Business Men', in P. Mathias and J.A. Davis (eds.) *Enterprise & Labour: From the Eighteenth Century to the Present*, Oxford, 1996.

Middleton, C., 'Women's labour and the transition to pre-industrial capitalism', in L. Charles and L. Duffin (eds.) *Women and Work in Pre-Industrial England*, London, 1985.

Mokyr, J., *The Economics of the Industrial Revolution*, London, 1985.

———, 'Has the Industrial Revolution been crowded out? Some reflections on Crafts and Williamson', *Explorations in Economic History*, 24, 1987.

Morris, R.J., 'The middle-class and the property cycle during the industrial revolution', in T.C. Smout (ed.) *The Search for Wealth and Stability*, London, 1979.

———, *Men, Women and Property in England, 1780–1870*, Cambridge, 2005.

Murphy, L.E., 'Business ladies: Midwestern women and enterprise, 1850–1880', in M.A. Yeager (ed.) *Women in Business* Vol. II, Cheltenham, 1999.

Neff, W.F., *Victorian Working Women. An Historical and Literary Study of Women in British Industries and Professions 1832–1850*, London, 1929.

Nenadic, S.,'The rise of the urban middle-class', in T.M. Devine and R. Mitchison (eds.) *People and Society in Scotland Vol. 1, 1760–1830*, Edinburgh, 1988.

———, 'The social shaping of business behaviour in the nineteenth century women's garment trades', *Journal of Social History*, 31, 1998.

Nester, P.A., 'A new departure in women's publishing: The English Woman's Journal and The Victoria Magazine', *Victorian Periodicals Review*, 15, 3, 1982.

Newton, L., 'Trust and virtue in English banking: The assessment of borrowers by bank managements at the turn of the nineteenth century', *Financial History Review*, 7, 2, 2000.

Oakley, A., *Housewife*, London, 1974.

———, *The Rights and Wrongs of Women*, London, 1977.

Ortner, S.B., 'Is female to male as nature is to culture?', in R. Zimbalist and L. Lamphere (eds.) *Women, Culture and Society*, California, 1974.

Ottaway, S., 'The old woman's home in eighteenth century England', in L. Botelho and P. Thane (eds.) *Women and Ageing in British Society since 1500*, Essex, 2001.

Owens A., 'Inheritance and the lifecycle of firms in the early industrial revolution', *Business History*, 44, 2002.

Peterson, M.J., 'No angels in the house: The Victorian myth and the Paget woman', *American Historical Review*, 89, 3, 1984.

Phillips, N., *Women in Business 1700–1850*, Woodbridge, 2006.

Piette V., 'Belgium's tradeswomen' in R. Beachy et al (eds.) *Women, Business and Finance in Nineteenth-Century Europe*, Oxford: Berg, 2006.

Pinchbeck, I., *Women Workers and the Industrial Revolution, 1750–1850*, London, 1930 (reprinted London 1969, 1981).

Porter, R., *London. A Social History*, London, 1994.

Prior, M., 'Women and the urban economy: Oxford 1500–1800,' in M. Prior (ed.) *Women in English Society 1500–1800*, London, 1985.

Rappaport, E., *Shopping for Pleasure: Women in the Making of London's West End*, Princeton, 2000.

Ravel, J., 'Masculine and feminine: The historiographical use of sexual roles', in M. Perrot (ed.) *Writing Women's History*, London, 1992 (English translation).

Rees, S., *The Floating Brothel*, St Ives, 2001.

Rendall, J., *Women in an Industrialising Society: England 1750–1880*, Oxford, 1990.

Richards, E., 'Women in the British economy since about 1700', *History*, 59, 1974.

Rickards, M., *Encyclopaedia of Ephemera: A Guide to the Fragmentary Documents of Everyday Life for the Collector, Curator, and Historian*, London, 2000.

Roberts, M., 'Words they are women, and deeds they are men. Images of work and gender in early modern England', in L. Charles and L. Duffin (eds.) *Women and Work in Pre-Industrial England*, London, 1985.

Rogers, H., 'The good are not always powerful, nor the powerful always good. The politics of women's needlework in mid-Victorian London', *Victorian Studies*, 40, 4, 1997.

Rose, H., 'Women's work: Women's knowledge', in J. Mitchell and A. Oakley (eds.) *What is Feminism?* Oxford, 1986.

Royle, E., *Modern Britain. A Social History 1750–1985*, London, 1990.

Rowbotham, S., 'Interview', in MAHRO, *Visions of History*, Manchester, 1983.

———, 'The trouble with patriarchy', S. Rowbotham (ed.) *Dreams and Dilemmas*, London, 1968, (reprinted 1983).

Rutterford, J., and Maltby, J., 'The widow, the clergyman and the reckless: Women investors in England, 1830–1914', *Feminist Economics,* 12, 2006.

Samuel, R., 'History and theory,' in R. Samuel (ed.) *People's History and Socialist Theory*, London, 1981.

———, 'History Workshop, 1966–80', in R. Samuel (ed.) *People's History and Socialist Theory,* London, 1981.

Sanderson, E.C., *Women and Work in Eighteenth-Century Edinburgh*, Basingstoke, 1996.

Scase, R., and Goffee, R., *The Entrepreneurial Middle Class*, London, 1982.

Schwarz, L.D., 'Income distribution and social structure in London in the late eighteenth century', *Economic History Review,* 32, 1979.

———, *London in the Age of Industrialization*, Cambridge, 1992.

Schwartz, L.D., and Jones, L.J., 'Wealth, occupations, and insurance in the late 18th century', *Economic History Review*, 36, 1983.

Shapiro, A., 'Introduction: History and feminist theory, or talking back to the Beadle', *History and Theory. Beiheft*, 31, 1992.

Sharpe, P., 'Introduction', in P. Sharpe (ed.) *Women's Work. The English Experience 1650–1914*, London, 1998.

Shaw, M., *Man Does, Woman Is. An Anthology of Work and Gender,* London, 1995.

Sheppard, F., *London 1808–1870: The Infernal Wen*, London, 1971.

Simonton, D., 'Apprenticeship: Training and gender in eighteenth-century England', in M. Berg (ed.) *Markets and Manufacture in Early Industrial Europe*, London, 1991.

———, *A History of European Women's Work 1700 to the Present*, London, 1998.

Skedd S., 'Women teachers and the expansion of girls' schooling in England c.1760–1820' in H. Barker and E. Chalus (eds.) *Gender in Eighteenth-Century England*, London, 1997.

Taylor, B., *Eve and the New Jerusalem. Socialism and Feminism in the Nineteenth Century*, London, 1983.

Taylor, M., 'What should we do with the Victorians?', *BBC History Magazine*, 2, 1, January 2001.

Thirsk, J., 'Forward', in M. Prior (ed.) *Women in English Society 1500–1800*, London, 1985.

Thomson, P., *The Victorian Heroine: A Changing Ideal 1837–1873*, London, 1956.

Townsend, C., 'I am a woman for spirit: A working woman's gender transgression in Victorian London', *Victorian Studies*, 36, 3, 1993.

Trebilcock, C., *Phoenix Assurance and the Development of British Insurance. Vol.1: 1782–1870*, London, 1994.

Treuherz, J., *Victorian Painting*, London, 1993.

Trumbach, R., 'London's Sapphists: From three sexes to four genders in the making of modern culture', in J. Epstein and K. Straub (eds.) *Body Guards. The Cultural Politics of Gender Ambiguity*, London, 1991.

van den Heuval, D., in 'Book Reviews', *International Review of Social History*, 52, 2008.

Vicinus, M., *Independent Women. Work and Community for Single Women 1850–1920*, London, 1985.

Vickery, A., 'The neglected century: Writing the history of eighteenth century women', *Gender & History*, 3, 2, 1991.

———, *The Gentleman's Daughter. Women's Lives in Georgian England*, London, 1998.

———, 'Golden age to separate spheres? A review of the categories and chronology of English women's history', in P. Sharpe (ed.) *Women's Work. The English Experience 1650–1914*, London, 1998.

Walker L., 'Vistas of pleasure: Women consumers and urban space in the West End of London, 1850–1900' in C.C. Orr (ed.) *Women in the Victorian Art World*, Manchester, 1995).

Walkowitz, J.R., *Prostitution and Victorian Society. Women, Class and the State*, Cambridge, 1980.

Walsh C., 'The advertising and marketing of consumer goods in eighteenth-century London' in C. Wischerman and E. Shore (eds.) *Advertising and the European City. Historical Perspectives*, Ashgate, Hants, 2000.

Walsh, M., 'Untitled', *Business History News*, 28, 2004.

Walton, J.K., *The Blackpool Landlady. A Social History*, Manchester, 1978.

Watkins, J., and Watkins, J., 'The female entrepreneur: Background and determinants of business choice—Some British data', *International Small Business Journal*, 4, 1984.

Weinreb, B., and Hibbert, C., *The London Encyclopaedia*, London, 1993.

Wheelwright, J., *Amazons and Military Maids*, London, 1989.

Winstanley, M.J., *The Shopkeeper's World 1830–1914*, Manchester, 1983.

Wiskin C., 'Urban businesswomen in eighteenth-century England' in R. Sweet and P. Lane (eds.) *Women and Urban Life in Eighteenth-century England*, Aldershot, 2003.

————, 'Businesswomen and financial management: Three eighteenth century case studies', *Accounting, Business and Financial History,* 16, 2006.

Wrigley, E.A., *Continuity, Chance and Change. The Character of the Industrial Revolution in England*, Cambridge, 1988.

Wright, S., 'Holding up half the sky: Women and their occupations in eighteenth-century Ludlow', *Midland History*, 14, 1989.

Wrigley, E.A., 'A simple model of London's importance in changing English society and economy, 1650–1750', in J. Patten (ed.) *Pre-Industrial England: Geographical Essays*, Folkestone, 1979.

Yohn, S.A., 'Crippled capitalists: The inscription of economic dependence and the challenge of female entrepreneurship in nineteenth-century America', *Feminist Economics*, 12, Issues 1 and 2, 2006.

(4) Unpublished Papers and Theses

Chaplin, D., 'The structure of London households in 1851', unpublished paper, Western Michigan University, 1975. Quoted in Lees, L.H., *Exiles of Erin. Irish Migrants in Victorian London*, Manchester, 1979.

Clarke, M.A., *Household and Family in Bethnal Green, 1851–71. The Effects of Social and Economic Change*, PhD thesis: University of Cambridge, 1986.

Fraser, C.G., *The Household and Family Structure of Mid-Nineteenth Century Cardiff in Comparative Perspective*, PhD thesis: University of Wales, Cardiff, 1988.

Index

needlework trades, distinctions
  between, 14, 23, 48-59, 92, 100,
  114
Nenadic, Stana, 8, 128
networks, business, 19, 26-27, 102,
  118, 122; civic, 29-30; consumption, 55, 81; credit, 4, 26-27;
  family and household, 27, 29,
  83, 97-98, 101, 114; local, 29,
  83, 134; support, 29, 83, 104,
  114, 118
newspapers, 29, 36, 54, 57, 75, 79,
  117, 132; advertising in, 16, 33,
  54-57, 62, 76-77
Newton, Lucy, 26
nieces, 28, 93, 100
Nightingale, Florence, 127
North America, 25, 97, 123-126, 129,
  130

O
Old age, 16-19, 31, 91-92, 96, 100,
  113, 132
Owens, Alastair, 41

P
Pamphlet shops, 75
Paris, France, 59
partnerships, business, 21, 36, 50, 52,
  71, 76, 79, 93, 10-114, 123,
  132
Pearson, Robin, 4
pensions, insufficient or lack of, 23, 91,
  111
philanthropy, 1
Phillips, Nicola, 4, 20, 107, 122, 125
Piette, Valérie, 122
Pinchbeck, Ivy, 6-7, 62, 64-65, 70, 72,
  76
printing, 14, 16, 56, 74
Prior, Margaret, 4, 24
private sphere. *See* separate spheres
profit and gender, 1, 5, 13, 19-22,
  25, 28, 37, 40, 45, 53, 66, 69,
  75, 77, 114-117, 120, 123-
  131
property (real estate), 4, 50, 104-109,
  110, 121, 126. *See also* fire
  insurance and law
prostitution, 25, 48, 73, 114-117. *See
  also* brothel keeping
public houses. See coffee house keepers,
  innkeepers, and victuallers
public sphere. *See* private spheres

R
Rent, paying it, 10, 24, 31, 39, 45, 48,
  62, 72, 76; receiving it, 104-106,
  110, 117-118
reputation, business, 55, 66, 73-74,
  77, 79, 111; personal 26-27, 72,
  73-74, 77, 79, 111
respectability, 11-17, 45, 54-82,
  98-103, 110-111, 115-118, 121,
  124, 127, 130, 133-134
retailing, 45, 54-82. *See also* display
  of goods, glazing and window
  dressing
risk, 22, 26-27, 31, 34-36, 39, 83, 104-
  107, 117, 118, 129, 134
Rose, Mary, 125
Rutterford, Janette, 4

S
Sanderson, Elizabeth, 8, 23, 125
school keeping, complications with
  insurance, 38; examples of,
  22-23, 77-81; partnership,
  50-51; using the home for business, 126-127. *See also* boarding
  school, De Bellaigue and Skedd,
  Susan
Schumpeter, Joseph, 125
Schwarz, Leonard, 4, 66
separate spheres, background, 3, 6-9;
  challenging, 103-104, 115-119,
  126-128, 132-134
servants. *See* domestic servants
shareholding. *See* investment
shop fronts, 25, 55, 60, 62, 76-77. *See
  also* window dressing
shopping, 56, 77, 81, 96, 134. *See also*
  retailing and tradecards
siblings, 28, 83, 85, 92, 96, 122, 129
Simonton, Deborah, 7, 68, 93
single women. *See* spinsters
sisters, 10, 14, 28, 51, 92-93, 114, 124,
  132, 96, 121
Skedd, Susan, 79
sons, 19, 28, 66-67, 73-74, 85, 98-101,
  118, 129
spinsters, 9, 17, 23, 28, 69, 73, 79,
  88-92, 96-98, 101-107, 113-
  115, 118, 148
start-up costs, 31, 79, 117, 134. See
  also borrowing and credit
stationers, 45-49, 74-76, 86, 88, 90, 99,
  100, 129, 132
stores. *See* retailing; shop fronts

4